CADOGAN

Guatemala

Cadogan Books plc
27–29 Berwick Street, London W1V 3RF, UK
e-mail: guides@cadogan.demon.co.uk
Distributed in North America by
The Globe Pequot Press
6 Business Park Road, PO Box 833, Old Saybrook,
Connecticut 06475–0833

Black and white illustrations © Antonia Phillips and Pauline Pears 1997
Cover photographs and material © Natascha Norton
Cover design by Animage
Maps © Cadogan Guides, drawn by Map Creation Ltd

Series Editor: Rachel Fielding
Editor: Katrina Burroughs
Editorial assistant: Kamin Mohammadi
Copy-editing and additional information: Joanna West
Proofreading: Simon Adams
Indexing: Dorothy Frame
Production: Book Production Services
Printed and bound in Great Britain by Redwood Books Ltd.
A catalogue record for this book is available from the British Library
ISBN 1-86011-082-7

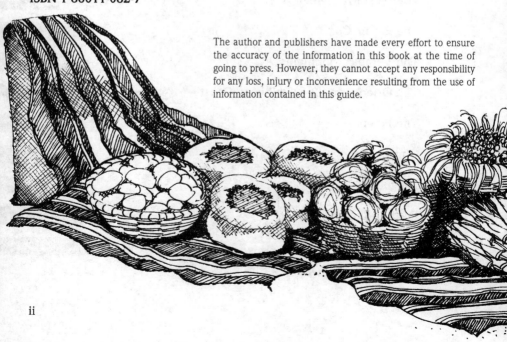

About the Author

Getting soaked by freezing rain halfway up a volcano, hitching lifts in bullet-riddled buses or drinking *cuba libres* in gringo bars was all in the line of research for Natascha Norton, who spent over a year based in Central America. A seasoned Latin American traveller, she thought she knew what to expect—everything, that is, except meeting her future husband in Guatemala.

Researching and updating this second edition, the author travelled to all corners of Guatemala, carrying not only her backpack, but also her unborn son, who has since arrived safely into the world.

Acknowledgements

First and foremost I must thank the staff of the National Tourist Office in Guatemala (INGUAT), who contributed immeasurably to the research process. In particular I thank Marco Tulio Ordóñez, Carolina Gonzalez and Sandra Morales. Lissa Hanckel provided excellent introductions and great company, and my path was further smoothed by the excellent help of Mike Shawcross, Alfredo Toriello of Izabal Adventure Tours, Carlo Roesch of Hotel Camino Real, Ana Lucia Asensio, Julio Alvarado and Francisco Florian of Panamundo Tours, John Heaton of the Quinta Maconda, Richard Bronson, Claudio Angeletti, Jungle Flying, Tikal Jet, Séan N. Acuña of Epiphyte Adventures, Leslie Fairhurst, Evelyn Búcaro de Altamiro, Hotel Cayos del Diablo, Hotel Tucan Dugú, Hotel Marimonte, Hotel La Posada, and Johnny's Place. In England I would like to thank my editor Katrina Burroughs and everyone else at Cadogan who contributed to the production of this guide.

Please help us to keep this guide up to date

We have done our best to ensure that the information in this guide is correct at the time of going to press. But telephone numbers, places and facilities are constantly changing, and standards and prices in hotels and restaurants fluctuate. We would be delighted to receive any comments concerning existing entries or omissions. Authors of the best letters will receive a copy of the Cadogan Guide of their choice.

Contents

People and Culture 43–58

Guatemala City 59–80

The Western Highlands 81–146

The Pacific Coast 147–58

Guatemala is a small country, known for volcanoes and cruelty.
When I crossed the frontier from Mexico I alternately lifted up my
eyes to the hills, and scanned the roadside for corpses. There
weren't any, and I felt slightly cheated by the books about Guatemala
I had read.

Anthony Daniels, *Sweet Waist of America*

Guatemala is like that. You know that terrible things have happened
here, still happen here, but you rarely see any evidence. Human rights
violations usually occur behind closed doors, or in remote areas of the
country, and are rarely reported in the local press. What you do see is a

Introduction

country whose beauty is unmatched in Central America: volcanoes
rumble and rise above golden highland valleys, where mysterious cloud
forests reach through the mists for the sky, and dense tropical jungle
envelops ancient pyramids of the lost Maya civilization.

Guatemala is the size of Ireland or the state of Connecticut; the distance
from the Pacific to the Atlantic coast by road is just 403km, while from
the Mexican to Salvadorean border is no more than 299km, so it only
takes a few hours to travel within this tiny country from temperate highlands to steamy jungle. The slim Pacific plain in the west soon rises into
the Western Highlands punctuated by a string of volcanoes that tower
above a fertile landscape of maize and bean fields, and dotted with countless Indian hamlets and villages. This is the heartland of the modern
Maya. Just over half the population are pure
descendants of the Maya tribes who have
inhabited the region for
millennia, speaking their own
languages, weaving and wearing
their finely embroidered textiles, and
stubbornly holding on to their traditions. Many of their ancient customs
have become mixed with Catholic
rituals, and the result is an annual
calendar peppered with riotous
festivals, at which pagan dances
accompany huge processions for
Christian saints, and acts of
worship can include smoking

cigars and sacrificing chickens. Weekly markets are the cornerstone of Maya social life; every town and village has its own market day, when the Indians come to sell their produce (predominantly maize, beans, cereals and other vegetables), exchange the latest gossip or discuss possible marriages.

Eastern Guatemala is clearly divided into two parts: the southeast is cut in two by the desert valley of the Motagua river, the main corridor from the Western Highlands to the Atlantic coast, with dry hills leading up towards the borders with Honduras and El Salvador on one side, and the moist Verapaz highlands rising towards the north. In these regions you will find mainly *ladino* culture, with its strong Spanish influence. Fiercely Catholic, the people are mestizos, representing all shades of colour from European to Indian, and a few black descendants of West Indian migrants, most of whom live in the Atlantic settlement of Lívingston. *Ladino* is not a racial term, however. Even a pure Indian is a *ladino* if he has abandoned his traditional dress and language in favour of the Spanish inherited culture, and it is a sad fact that many do so to avoid discrimination and abuse.

Beyond the Motagua valley and the Verapaz, the landscape descends to the Petén plain and the dense jungle that eventually melts into the Mexican Yucatán peninsula. This is the least populated area of Guatemala; once home to the civilization that built the giant pyramids of Tikal, now inhabited by toucans and scarlet macaws, and troops of howler monkeys whose loud grunts fill the air at dusk.

Travelling by bus is the best way to explore this little country. Services are frequent and extremely cheap, making it possible to get from one end of the country to the other in no more than a day, for less than US$10. To reach the Maya pyramids is also easy, since at least three flights daily connect the capital with the jungle town of Flores, near the ruins of Tikal.

Itineraries

The Western Highlands

Most visitors head for the Western Highlands, where the scenery of volcanoes, lakes and pine-clad highlands is at its most captivating and where the majority of the country's Indian population lives. The standard circuit first takes you west from **Guatemala City** to the small town of **Antigua**, with its fine colonial architecture. From here the Pan-American Highway leads you northwards to beautiful **Lake Atitlán**. Next the road continues to **Quezaltenango**, the country's second city and an excellent base for hiking or exploring the more inaccessible villages and markets. Beyond here, the northwestern town of **Huehuetenango** has little to offer except its remote and rough landscape; if you want to visit the Indian village of **Todos Santos**, you will have to pass this way. Heading south again, there are two routes you could take: either return via the paved Pan-American Highway, or continue on the slower more scenic route, along dirt roads via Sacapulas (east of Huehuetenango) and Santa Cruz del Quiché, meeting the paved highway again beyond **Chichicastenango**. Either way, make sure you visit Chichi.

Pacific and Atlantic Beaches

Do not bother coming to Guatemala for the beaches. On the Pacific side is a 60km belt of flat plantation country, with few decent access roads to the sea itself. Where there are roads to the beach you will find a grey strip of sand, often separated from the mainland by mangrove swamps and a canal. On the Atlantic side, there is only one place worth going to, and that is **Lívingston**, inhabited by a Caribbean community descended from African slaves, Carib Indians, and the odd shipwrecked sailor. It's at the mouth of the Río Dulce and, while the beach may not be memorable, the river is—with jungle vegetation and plenty of wildlife to see during boat trips, which can take you all the way to **Lake Izabal**, and waterside **El Relleno**, dotted with some of the country's most exclusive hotels and private holiday villas.

The Jungle

The ruined Maya centre of **Tikal** is the most awe-inspiring place in the country. You can go on spectacular jungle tours, or book a guide to remote archaeological sites in the jungle, only accessible on foot, horseback or via the rivers. If you have the time, a visit to either **Ceibal** or **Yaxhá** is highly recommended.

The Verapaz Mountains

This large region is the least visited area of Guatemala, though its departmental capital of Cobán is establishing itself as a popular base from which to make adventurous journeys to remote ecosystems, such as the **Laguna Lachuá** and the cloud forests of the **Sierra de las Minas**. Roads are good for the most part, yet you are off the beaten track here. The mountains hide two particularly rewarding spots: the **Quetzal Reserve**, where you might see the country's extremely rare national bird; and the gorgeous forest pools of **Semuc Champey**, a place you can now get to on an organized day trip if you don't have the time to make your own arrangements.

The back road connecting **Cobán** in the north-east with **Huehuetenango** in the north-west, unrivalled for its spectacular setting, snakes its way along the edges of a terrifyingly steep river valley and into the **Cuchumatanes Mountains**. The last time a bus actually fell off the road was in the mid-seventies.

The Best of Guatemala

Artesanía: Maya textiles and masks

Beach: Monterrico

Birdwatching: Quetzal Sanctuary and any Petén jungle river trip

Books: *Sweet Waist of America* by Anthony Daniels

Colonial Architecture: Antigua

Cup of Coffee: Café Tirol in Cobán or Café Bavaria in Quezaltenango

Diving: sailing tours departing Río Dulce for the Belizean Cayes

Fiestas: Santo Tomás Festival in Chichicastenango in December; Easter Week in Antigua

Hiking: around Todos Santos or around Nebaj

Hot Springs: Fuentes Georginas

Jungle: the jungle around Ceibal ruins

Lakes: Lake Atitlán, unrivalled for beauty and tourist facilities

Markets: Chichicastenango is the easily accessible star, but markets at remoter San Francisco el Alto or Nebaj are more authentic

Month of the Year: November is a magnificent time, when the end of the rains brings azure skies and sunshine

Mountain Road: the dirt road connecting San Cristóbal Verapaz with Huehuetenango or the climb from San Marcos to Tacaná

Museum: Ixchel Museum in Guatemala City

National Park: National Park around Tikal in the Petén jungle

Pre-Columbian Ruins: Tikal and Mixco Viejo

Rafting: River Cahabón

Volcanoes: Agua volcano

Travel

The Pan-American Highway

Getting There

By Air

The main airlines with regular connections to **Guatemala City** (La Aurora Airport) from Europe are British Airways, ✆ (0345) 222111, KLM, ✆ (0990) 750900, Iberia, ✆ (0171) 830 0011, American Airlines, ✆ (0181) 572 5555, and Continental Airlines, ✆ (01293) 776464. There are two direct flight routes, one from Amsterdam with KLM and one from Madrid with Iberia, otherwise you normally change in Houston or Miami. The price of a low-season return ticket will probably be between £500 and £600. Fixed date tickets are cheaper than open ones, and travelling during the week also sometimes lowers the price.

There are flights between Guatemala City and San Francisco, Los Angeles, New York, Washington DC, Houston, New Orleans, Orlando and Miami. Return fares from Miami and Los Angeles are priced at around US$400, but expect to pay twice that if coming from New York, and close to US$1000 if coming from Canada. Do shop around as special deals are often available, especially during the North American winter. The best-value flights leave from or stop off at Miami, Houston or Nerw Orleans. Airlines that fly to Guatemala City from the US include American Airlines, ✆ (1-800) 433 7300, Aviateca, Continental, Copa, Lacsa, Nica and Taca. For information call the Central America Corporation on ✆ (01293) 553330.

For the main airlines serving Guatemala City, *see* p.62.

By Road

Good highways cover the main routes between the **US and Guatemala**, although they do demand a degree of stamina. From Texas the most direct route cuts down the side of the Gulf of Mexico, bypassing the horrors of Mexico City. From California the drive is almost twice as long. By car you should expect to take at least a week to get through Mexico.

By bus you'll almost certainly have to travel via Mexico City and change buses. If you're sleeping on the bus it's just possible to make it through Mexico in four or five days, but don't expect to arrive in a fit state to enjoy yourself.

There is one road connecting **Guatemala and Belize**, running from the Petén jungle town of Flores to Belize City, via the Maya Mountains. The road is unpaved at the Guatemalan end and very rough during the rainy season, but otherwise this route is straightforward, with frequent buses (*see* p.206 for more details).

By Sea

There is no public transport by sea between the US and Guatemala; only private yachts make the journey. The only yacht marinas in Guatemala are up the Río Dulce, near El Remate bridge, so any boats leaving the States for Guatemala would leave from ports on the eastern seaboard. The most likely marinas to check, if you have more time than money, would be those around Fort Lauderdale in Florida.

From Belize, there is a ferry departing from **Punta Gorda** on Tues and Fri, at noon. Journey takes about 2½ hours.

Entry Formalities

Passports and Visas

UK, American and Canadian citizens do not need visas or a tourist card (sold by the airlines for US$5). Irish nationals, New Zealanders and Australians will not be allowed in without one, however. If you do need a visa then try to get hold of one before you go. Contact the relevant embassy or consulate for the latest regulations, which do tend to change every now and then.

The official time limit for tourist visits to Guatemala is 90 days, though the time stamped in your passport can be as little as 14 days. It is always worth saying how long you wish to visit when you get to passport control, and if you fail to get the necessary time, you can get an extension from the immigration office in Guatemala City without too much trouble (*see* pp.66). Extensions are available for a total of six months. A popular alternative is simply to leave the country for 72 hours—either by crossing into Mexico or Honduras—especially if you are staying in Guatemala long-term.

Do remember that you must keep your passport or a photocopy with you at all times; failure to produce it for police involves a great deal of inconvenience and possible arrest. Passport control and border crossings are usually very straightforward, however, and you're through in a matter of minutes, queues permitting. Note that officially you must be in possession of a return flight ticket in order to enter Guatemala; the airlines will not normally allow you to fly without one.

Customs

Leaving Guatemala by air there is an exit fee of US$10, payable in local or US currency. Leaving by land the exit fee is usually about US$1. There are no restrictions about what you can take in or out of Guatemala, although huge sums of cash would undoubtedly attract much attention if discovered.

Getting Around

By Air

Flying is easy and always the most convenient option, though certainly not the cheapest or most interesting, but if time is short you can quickly reach the remotest jungle ruins by plane, saving days of bus travel. Prices for return flights tend to be double the single fare, so there is rarely money to be saved by buying return tickets. You will also find that foreigners often pay a different, more expensive, fare than local nationals. Don't worry, this is standard; but make sure you compare prices between airlines offering the same routes.

The route you are most likely to be interested in is the one between the capital and Flores (for Maya ruins), operated by local airlines such as **Aviateca**, **Aerovías**, **Tapsa** and **Tikal Jet** (*see* pp.62). There are three or four flights daily in either direction, and tickets are available at most travel agencies or at the two airports in Guatemala City. Competition is keen so prices should be the same whoever you fly with, but Tikal Jet usually has the best offers. A return flight costs around US$112 and the journey time is about one hour. You should try to make reservations at least a few days ahead, as flights can be heavily booked, especially during Easter Week or Christmas and New Year. These same companies also offer connections to Belize City.

For a quick visit to Copán in Honduras, if time is short and money no object, you could use the services of **Jungle Flying** (*see* p.62), who can also take you to many other Maya sites.

By Bus

Getting around Guatemala by bus is one of the great pleasures of travel in this country, and is undoubtedly the fastest, cheapest and easiest way to explore. The country's towns and many villages are linked by good paved or passable dirt roads everywhere except in the Petén, where appalling mud roads regularly disintegrate completely during the rainy season. Bus connections are regular and extremely cheap, though you should always try to travel in the morning, since public transport generally stops by late afternoon. It is also much safer to travel during daylight hours, and less daunting to arrive in a new place before nightfall. Tickets are bought on the bus; to avoid 'gringo prices', it is always a good idea to ask a local passenger what the fare is, before the ticket man gets to you. On some routes it is possible to travel by pullman buses, which are more comfortable than the local 'chicken buses' (old Blue Bird buses or retired US school buses, crammed to bursting point with people and often small livestock too). Pullmans are a bit more expensive, but you get a reserved seat to yourself, and the bus makes fewer stops. Increasingly, private, air-conditioned minibuses ply the popular tourist routes, charging about ten times the price of a Pullman but offering genuine comfort, speed and convenience. (You should be aware that these 'tourist buses' are occasionally the target of highway robbers.) For the major bus routes from Guatemala City, *see* pp.63–4.

By Car or Motorbike

Driving around in a hired car or your own vehicle gives you the advantage of complete freedom of movement. However, when weighing the obvious advantages against possible disadvantages, it is worth remembering that the police earn very little and often supplement their income by corruption. Foreigners are easy prey and it is essential that your papers are in perfect order and available for inspection at all times. Usually everything runs smoothly and your way.

The roads in Guatemala, except in the Petén, are generally good, and normal passenger cars have no trouble here. Off the beaten track, you will find mostly dirt and gravel roads, where high-clearance vehicles are recommended. For the drive to Tikal in the Petén, nothing less than a tough four-wheel-drive vehicle will do, and even then it is not advisable to attempt the journey during the rainy season, from May to December. (The section between Río Dulce and Poptún is in the process of being paved; this will leave just one third of the route unpaved and should make a big difference to the time needed for travelling this way.) Be sure to take a spare wheel and other essential spare parts that may be unavailable here; a large canister of petrol would be a good idea as well, as petrol stations are few and far between. The Guatemalan Tourist Office (Inguat) sells a useful road map, which has all the petrol stations marked on it, as well as a mileage chart. Use secure parking facilities wherever possible, since theft and vandalism are commmon hazards—especially in towns and cities or near tourist attractions.

Traffic outside the cities is very sparse, so driving is relatively relaxed, bar the odd example of hazardous local driving and the occasional military checkpoint. These checkpoints are nothing to worry about, however, and you will often simply be waved on. Hassle is more likely to come from the police and Guardia de Hacienda (rural police), who like to stop cars with foreign licence plates. There will always be the occasional corrupt official looking for a bribe, but that is a risk you take driving anywhere in Latin America.

Car hire is available in the capital and most major towns, though expensive, at US$70 per day for the smaller cars, and often you have to pay the first US$800 of any damage, or there is no insurance at all. Read the small print! This is especially important as foreigners have to pay all damages, whether the accident was their fault or not. To hire any vehicle, you will need a current driving licence and a credit card, regardless of how you intend to pay the final bill. Current legislation prohibits driving hire cars from Guatemala into either Mexico or Belize. However, with an authorization letter from the car hire company (US$15), you can cross into Honduras and El Salvador.

Recommended car hire companies in Guatemala City are:

Avis, 12 Calle 2-73, Zona 9, ✆ 3312734, ✉ 3321263
Ahorrent, Bvd Liberacíon 4-83, Zona 9, ✆ 3320544, ✉ 3320548
Budget, Avenida Reforma 15-00, Zona 9, ✆ 3322591, ✉ 3312807
Dollar, Avenida Reforma 6-14, Zona 9, ✆ 3348285, ✉ 3326745
Hertz, 7 Avenida 14-76, Zona 9, ✆ 3322242, ✉ 3317924
Tabarini, 2 Calle 'A' 7-30, Zona 10, ✆ 3319814, ✉ 3341925.

See p.89 for car hire offices in Antigua.

Motorbikes can be hired in Guatemala City, Antigua and Panajachel, for around US$30 per day.

Guatemalan rules of the road. There are no unusual regulations for driving in Guatemala. The basic convention is very much 'each for his own', so never take anything for granted. If you see a pile of branches in the road, it usually means an accident or break-down is immediately ahead.

By Bicycle

Cycling is becoming ever more popular in Guatemala. The roads are often rough and unsurfaced, the terrain can be anything from sand to mud to rocks and pebbles but few other modes of travel allow such close contact with the land and its people. Bicycles are common throughout the region, so basic repairs are no problem, but it is worth carrying essential spares. If you wish, you can take your own (sturdy) machine—for advice, contact the **Cyclist's Touring Club**, 69 Meadow, Godalming, Surrey, ✆ (0483) 417217—but there are bike rental shops in most large towns. The best kind of bike is clearly a mountain or hybrid bike, with tough wheels and plenty of gears. Insurance against theft is vital. Should you get tired of cycling, you can always travel on the local buses, which will transport your bike on the roof, normally at no extra charge.

Travel Agents and Specialist Tour Operators

UK Travel Agents and Tour Operators

Bales Tours, Bales House, Junction Road, Dorking, Surrey RH4 3HB, ✆ (01306) 885991, ✉ (01306) 740048, organize 9-day escorted tours.

Cox and Kings Travel, Fourth Floor, Gordon House, 10 Green Coat Place, London SW1P 1PH, ✆ (0171) 873 5000, ✉ (0171) 630 6038, offers group tours for the over 50s, as well as tailor-made itineraries for individuals.

Dragoman, Camp Green, Kenton Road, Debenham, Suffolk 1P14 6LA, ✆ (01728) 861133, ✉ (01728) 861127, specializes in adventure tours aimed at 18-35year-olds.

Exodus Expeditions, 9 Weir Road, London SW12 0LT, ✆ (0181) 675 5550, ✉ (0181) 673 0779, offers small-group tours following La Ruta Maya.

Explore Worldwide, 1 Frederick Street, Aldershot, Hants GU11 1LQ, ✆ (01252) 344 161, ✉ (01252) 343 170, specializes in small-group exploratory holidays often using local transport, with the emphasis on discovering local cultures and wildlife.

Frontiers International, 18 Albermarle Street, London, W1X 3HA, ✆ (0171) 4930798, ✉ (0171) 4919177, is a fishing holiday specialist.

Journey Latin America, 16 Devonshire Road, Chiswick, London W4 2HD, ✆ (0181) 747 8315, ✉ (0181) 742 1312, organizes a wide range of bespoke and package tours including environmental expeditions and economy journeys.

Steamond Latin American Travel, 23 Eccleston Street, London, SW1 W9LX, ✆ (0171) 730 8646, ✉ (0171) 730 3024, provides tailor-made special-interest tours and itineraries including bird-watching, scuba-diving, etc.

South American Experience, 47 Causton Street, London SW1P 4AT, ✆ (0171) 976 5511, ✉ (0171) 976 6908, offers tailor-made packages.

Trailfinders, 194–196 Kensington High Street, London, W8 7RG, ✆ (0171) 938 3232, ✉ (0171) 938 3305, Birmingham, Bristol, Glasgow and Manchester offices.

Trips Worldwide, 9 Byron Place, Clifton, Bristol, BS8 1JT, ✆ (0117) 987 2626, ✉ (0117) 987 2627, organizes tailor-made tours.

US Travel Agents and Tour Operators

Clark Tours, 310 Lynnway, Suite 304, MA 01901, ✆ (800) 223 6764.

Council Travel, 35 West 8th Street, New York 10011, ✆ (212) 254 2525, 2846 Channing Way, Berkeley, CA 92093, ✆ (510) 415 848, 1314 Northeast 43rd Street, Suite 210, Seattle, WA 98105 ✆ (206) 632 2448.

Guatemala Travel Representatives, 5 Grogaus Park, Suite 102, Woodlands, TX 77380–2190, ✆ (800) 451 8017.

Sobek Expeditions, P.O. Box 1089 60, Angel's Camp, CA 95222, ✆ (800) 777 7939, arranges river-rafting, sea-kayaking, and wildlife tours.

Wildland Adventures Inc., 3516 NE 155th, STE WT, Seattle, WA 98155, ✆ (800) 345 4453, specializes in ecotravel.

Practical A–Z

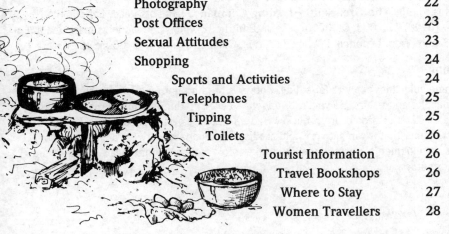

Hygiene and Health

Rule number one is if you really need it bring it with you. As hygiene cannot be guaranteed, bring a suitable container (1 litre) and sterilizing tablets for your bottles and feeding equipment. A bottle and teat cleaning brush is useful. Bring sticking tape in case nappy tabs fail, nappy rash cream and medicated talc for heat rash. If only travelling for a short period, bring nappies and wipes with you, as they will be much cheaper at home.

Your first-aid box should include either a rehydration spoon or rehydration sachets, antiseptic disinfectant, your preferred teething relief, a fever and pain relief medication, thermometer, tweezers, a variety of plasters, nail clippers, insect sting relief, adhesive wound dressing and first-aid skin closures for minor cuts.

Finally, make sure you have purified drinking water with you at all times and encourage your child to drink as much as possible.

Equipment

Note that sleepsuits are fine in the highlands but too sweaty in the tropical heat of the lowlands: use a cotton sleeping bag instead. Baby backpacks are ideal for very young babies, but otherwise too exhausting for walking around all day. (Remember that a sun hat and/or umbrella is essential and you can buy both cheaply in Guatemala.)

Strollers are not very practical as they cannot easily be pushed on cobbled streets, dirt tracks and beaches. The only useful alternative is a specially adapted three-wheeled **multi-terrain stroller** with high clearance wheels. It will make all the difference to your trip. They are usually lightweight and collapsible and can double up as a highchair at feeding times. In the UK they are sold by **PCD Limited**, PO Box 28, Tavistock, Devon PL19 9YT, ✆ (01822) 618 077. Expensive at around £275, but worth every penny. Sun canopy and rain cover are also available.

Another extremely useful item at feeding times is a 'Safe Seat', which is a cleverly designed cotton and velcro gadget that secures your baby or infant to any type of chair; it is lightweight and folds into the smallest bag. In the UK Boots sell a version but the best design is sold by **The Great Little Trading Company**, 134 Lots Road, London SW10 0RJ, ✆ (0990) 673 008, ✆ (0990) 673 010. In the US, the same model is marketed as 'Sit'n Secure' from **Leachco**, PO Box 717, Ada, Oklahoma 74820, ✆ (800) 525 1050.

Clothing

The same guidelines apply as for adults. Cotton is best in the tropics, and babies can just wear nappies and t-shirt. However, bring long-sleeved clothing against sun and evening cold, as well as to protect from bugs. Wind and rain gear is needed in the Highlands and remember that it can get very cold at night. Appropriate footwear depends on your child's developmental stage, but should take into account daytime heat, evening cold and mosquitoes.

Children

Travelling with children here is very easy; you're never excluded from a hotel, bar or restaurant because you have children in tow, and you will not normally be charged extra for their accommodation. Transport on the buses is free for any child not using a seat.

Your main worry is disease and gastric problems, so do consult your doctor regarding immunizations and never give your child anything other than bottled water. Nappies and most other infant equipment, including formula milk, are available in any town or city, but not in the villages or remote areas. Sun screen and insect repellent suitable for children is best brought from home.

In the UK specialist advice on vaccinations for tropical countries is available from **The Hospital for Tropical Diseases Healthline** ✆ (0839) 337733, or the **Medical Advisory Service for Travellers Abroad** (MASTA) ✆ (0891) 224100. Calls cost around 40 pence per minute (50 pence at peak rate). Note that anti-malaria medication for babies is available in the shape of Chloroquin syrup.

Climate and When to Go

The seasons are very simple indeed: it's either raining or it isn't. The rains start around May and end anywhere between November and December. The rains can be very heavy, particularly towards the end of the rainy season, but they need not stop you travelling as they tend to be in the form of afternoon downpours; you'll just get less of a tan. At any time of year the lowland areas are stiflingly hot; during the rainy season high humidity makes it particularly sticky. Up in the highlands it is always pleasantly cool in the shade, although the sun is even sharper.

Average Temperature and Rainfall

Jan	Feb	Mar	Apr	May	June	July	Aug	Sep	Oct	Nov	Dec
23	25	27	28	29	27	26	26	24	23	23	22
11	12	14	14	16	16	16	16	16	15	14	13
2	2	2	5	8	20	17	16	17	13	6	2

The first line is the average maximum temperature per month in degrees Celsius, the second the average minimum; and the last line the average number of rainy days.

Crime and Police Business

Perhaps the best way to ensure your safety is to avoid carrying unnecessary valuables and accept the fact that the ones you do bring may be stolen. Most visitors have no real trouble at all, although petty theft and pickpocketing are widespread and irritating. There is little you can do to prevent this except keep your wits about you and avoid putting your money in easily accessible pockets.

Far more serious and a lot less likely is violent crime. If you are careful to avoid the worst spots—most notably the Pacaya volcano—then you're very unlikely to fall victim to violent crime. Nevertheless women should avoid going out alone at night wherever possible, particularly in the big cities and on beaches. Here the danger of theft and assault, while small during the day, is very real at night.

One last danger is that of getting caught up in political conflict. Although peace is officially established all over the isthmus now, Guatemala's most popular tourist areas, such as Antigua, Lake Atitlán and surrounding places are prone to tourist crime. Care should be taken to find out the latest security information from the local tourist offices, as well as to consult with other travellers. As a general rule, you should never go hiking or walking in the countryside alone, and certainly not camp alone.

Police and Military

In spite of Guatemala's appalling human rights record, it is extremely unlikely that you will be affected. As a foreigner you are not a target for terror. It is the Indians and street children who are in danger.

In fact, Guatemala is one of the safest Latin American countries to travel in, as long as you take the normal care and attention necessary anywhere in this part of the world. Watch out for pickpockets at markets and bus terminals. Although you should guard your baggage while travelling, do not worry too much if your pack is on the roof during bus journeys. Unless it falls off, it will most likely still be there when you arrive at your destination (you have to be much more careful in South America).

You will see guards armed with machine guns in all government offices, banks and many commercial stores, and although intimidating at first, they are quite harmless as far as you are concerned. Most uniformed officials will be very courteous and only too pleased to help you if they can. Should you get stopped, for example at one of the standard military road blocks, or need to report a theft, always remain calm and polite, no matter what. Bribes should never be more than a last resort, and best avoided by unpractised players.

The police wear uniforms of dark blue trousers and light blue shirts. The military are in familiar khaki, with high-ranking members in olive or dark green uniforms. The chaps in grass-green, with strange hats, like Canadian mounties gone wrong, are members of the Guardia de Hacienda, and responsible for policing the countryside.

Disabled Travellers

Travel in Guatemala can be quite rough, and no specific concessions or provisions are made to smooth the way for those with a physical handicap. Poverty and malnutrition mean that many more people suffer from disabilities here than in the West. If you or your travelling companion have special needs, you can make life much easier if you can afford to book organized tours and travel, where all aspects of transport are arranged for you, and provided in comfortable vehicles.

There are quite a few organizations which advise and encourage international travel for disabled people. Two in particular are recommended: **DIVE** (Disabled International Visits and Exchanges), c/o The Central Bureau for Educational Visits and Exchanges, Seymour Mews House, Seymour Mews, London WIH 9PE; **SATH** (Society for the Advancement of

Travel for the Handicapped), International Head Office, Suite 1110, 26 Court Street, Brooklyn, NY 11242, USA.

Specialist guide books or publications include: *Access to the World*, Louise Rice, Facts of File, London (1985); *Disabled Traveller's International Phrasebook*, Ian McNeil, Disability Press, 60 Greenhayes Avenue, Banstead, Surrey; *A List of Guidebooks for Handicapped Travelers*, The President's Committee on Employment of the Handicapped, 1111 20th Street, NW, Washington, DC 20036, USA.

Drugs

Drugs of all varieties, quantities and qualities are widely available and their use often appears to be unofficially tolerated. As a foreigner, you should be very wary of having anything to do with drugs or those who deal in them, as peddlers generally regard tourists as easy money and official penalties are steep, particularly when applied to outsiders.

Earthquakes and Volcanoes

Earthquakes regularly claim lives and from time to time destroy cities and villages. There's absolutely nothing you can do to avoid the danger; your chances of getting caught up in a really dangerous earthquake are extremely scarce and certainly no worse than in Los Angeles. Smaller tremors are very common indeed and you are fairly likely to feel one or two, but there is really nothing to worry about. There are a number of active volcanoes in Guatemala, but again the risk of coming to any harm is very remote. If you happen to be close to an erupting cone, particularly at night, with sensible precautions it's an exhilarating experience.

Ecotourism

In Guatemala the political instability of recent decades, as well as the economic poverty, has meant that environmental concerns have had little chance of being addressed effectively. Efforts are now underway to protect several important biospheres and ecosystems, most notably in the fast disappearing Petén jungles of the north-east. The main threat to the forest comes from the large number of settlers that are coming to the area—many of them refugees from political violence or land disputes elsewhere—and engaging in destructive agricultural practices such as 'slash and burn' and cattle farming.

The American initiative Conservation International is backing a programme called **ProPetén**, Flores, Petén, ✆ 9261370, working towards developing a sustainable economy for the forest, which includes tourism projects, such as the 'Scarlet Macaw Trail' in the Maya Biosphere Reserve, founded in 1990, and covering approximately 16,000 square kilometres (*see* p.194). **Epiphyte Adventures**, Aptd. 94 A Cobán, Alta Verapaz, Guatemala, ✆/✆ 952 2213, is a private company, committed to developing low-impact tourism in support of sustainable living for local communities, offering some highly informative tours to remote areas of pristine forest (*see* p.166).

Electricity

The current runs at 110 volts. This means North Americans can use all their electrical equipment without any problems. Europeans, however, will need adaptors for everything electrical bought in their own countries. Adaptors are not always cheap or easy to find, so do bring your own if you really need one.

Embassies and Consulates

All embassies and consulates are in Guatemala City, and are normally only open on week-days, in the mornings. Onward travellers to other Central American countries may need visas, so the relevant offices are listed, where they exist.

UK: Edificio Centro Financiero, 7 Avenida 5-10 (7th floor), Zona 4, ✆ 3321601, 🖷 3341904

US: Avenida Reforma 7-01, Zona 10, ✆/🖷 3311541–4

Canada: Edificio Edyma Plaza, 13 Calle 8-44 (8th floor), Zona 10, ✆ 3336102

Costa Rica: Edificio Galerías Reforma (office no. 702), Avenida La Reforma 8-60, Zona 9, ✆/🖷 3319604

El Salvador: 12 Calle 5-43, Zona 9, ✆ 3343942, 🖷 3601312

Honduras: 13 Calle 12-33, Zona 10, ✆ 3374337

Mexico: 13 Calle 7-30, Zona 9, ✆ 3318165

Nicaragua: 10 Avenida 14-72, Zona 10, ✆ 3680785

Panamá: Edificio Centro Empresarial, 5 Avenida 15-45, Zona 10, ✆ 3337182, 🖷 3337183

Festivals

Guatemala is rightly famous for its traditional Indian festivals, times when the air is thick with incense and resounds to the constant blast of ear-piercing fire-crackers. You will see the Maya heritage at its most vibrant, with people decked out in their best native costumes, outrageously drunk, yet with energy for another dance or song or candle-lit procession. These festivals are normally in honour of a Christian saint, but contain elements of earlier Indian celebrations that the colonial church was incapable of suppressing. What we see today is a remarkable mixture of two very different heritages.

The festivals of the *ladino* population are no less riotous, with plenty of colour and noise, and a bullfight or two. Both kinds of festival usually have attendant fairs and markets, and normally go on for a week, the last two days being the most important and interesting for visitors.

The most famous Indian festival in the country is the December one in Chichicastenango, while Easter Week in Antigua is celebrated with an extravagance you are unlikely to find anywhere else in Central America. There are many others worth making an effort to see as well, such as the horse races in Todos Santos, or the kite-flying in Santiago Sacatepéquez, both on 1 November. Every town and village has at least one special day for a festival, which is listed in the gazetteer. For the two most famous events, you will need to book accommodation well in advance or get there at least a day early.

Best of the Festivals

January

1–5	**Santa María de Jesús**, a small Indian village near Antigua.
15	Annual pilgrimage to **Esquipulas**, a *ladino* town near the Honduran border and home to the famous Black Christ.
19–25	Traditional dances at **Rabinal**, a small Indian village in the department of Baja Verapaz.
22–26	**San Pablo la Laguna**, a normally quiet Indian village on Lake Atitlán.

February

First Fri of Lent in **Antigua**, former colonial capital near Guatemala City, is celebrated with a small fiesta characterised by much exploding of fire crackers, and church services..

March–April

Semana Santa (Easter Week) is one of the most interesting times to be anywhere in Guatemala, when the whole country is celebrating, and nowhere more so than in **Antigua**, where the streets are carpeted with coloured sawdust and the Crucifixion is re-enacted.

Easter Sat	Indians from all around Lake Atitlán come to be baptized in its waters at **Panajachel**.
Whitsun	**Aguacatán**, a small place near Huehuetenango, celebrates Whitsun with a festival and market.

May

1	Labour Day is celebrated with marches by the unions, labour organizations and left-wingers.
2–3	**Amatitlán**, near the lake of the same name, has its annual pilgrimage across the waters.
8–10	**Santa Cruz la Laguna**, a small Indian village on Lake Atitlán.

June

12–14	**San Antonio Palopó**, an Indian village on Lake Atitlán.
24–29	**San Pedro Carchá**, outside Cobán, a mainly *ladino* festival with plenty of traditional dancing.
27–30	**San Pedro la Laguna**, an Indian village on Lake Atitlán.
28–30	**Almolonga**, a bustling Indian village near Quezaltenango, with nearby hot springs in which to recover.

July

1–4	**Santa María Visitación**, a village near Sololá, above Lake Atitlán.
16–22	**Puerto Barrios**, port city on the Atlantic coast, holds a *ladino* festival, very loud and with plenty of sleaze.
20–25	**Cubulco**, a remote *ladino* farming community in the Baja Verapaz, whose festival still includes many traditional Indian dances.
21 July –4 Aug	**Momostenango**, a remote Indian town in the mountains near Quezaltenango, holds a traditional festival and a market with beautiful woven blankets.
23–27	**Santiago Atitlán**, the country's most visited Indian village, on the shores of the lake, with a very popular festival.
31 July –6 Aug	**Cobán**, coffee capital of Guatemala, has its annual festival at this time, and also hosts the National Festival of Folklore, where representatives come from all over the country to show their native costumes and participate in many traditional dances. An agricultural fair is also held.

August

6–15	**Joyabaj**, an out-of-the-way town east of Santa Cruz del Quiché, where you will see traditional dances rarely performed elsewhere.
11–17	**Sololá**, perched above Lake Atitlán, springs to life for its annual festival, with a good market attached.
12–15	**Nebaj**, northeast of Huehuetenango, where the Indians wear one of the most beautiful costumes in the country.
1–18	**Cantel**, an Indian village outside Quezaltenango, in a gorgeous valley.
22–28	**Lanquín**, a remote town east of Cobán.

September

12–18	**Quezaltenango**, the country's second city.
15	Independence Day is celebrated with military parades throughout the isthmus.
24–30	**Totonicapán**, near Quezaltenango, a traditional town with one of the largest markets.

October

1–6	**San Francisco el Alto**, a hillside settlement near Quezaltenango, with an interesting animal fair.
12	Dia de la Raza (Columbus Day) is big on the Caribbean coast, where the drunken revelling lasts for days.
2–6	**Panajachel**, a favourite gringo spot on Lake Atitlán.

20–26	**Iztapa**, a small town on the Pacific coast, and one of the few places worth visiting there.
29 Oct –1 Nov	**Todos Santos**, a remote Indian village northwest of Huehuetenango, with chaotic horse races.

November

1 Nov	**Santiago de Sacatepéquez**, near the highway between the capital and Chimaltenango, where giant kites are flown in the cemetery as part of the Day of the Dead celebration.
22–26	**Zunil** is a small village outside Quezaltenango, where the local costume is all shocking pinks and purple.
23–25	**Nahualá**, a rarely visited Indian settlement, half-way between Los Encuentros and Quezaltenango, has a very drunken and colourful festival, where men sport their traditional skirts.
25	**Santa Catarina Palopó**, a small village on Lake Atitlán.
27 Nov –1 Dec	**San Andrés Itzapa**, a small town near Antigua, interesting for its shrine to Maximón, the notorious Indian saint.

December

5–8	**Huehuetenango**, the largest town to the northwest of Guatemala City.
7	The Burning of the Devil takes place symbolically, as bonfires of rubbish are lit throughout the country, but mainly around **Quezaltenango** and in **Guatemala City** (very smelly). **Antigua** also has a ceremonial burning, usually attended by a street party and fireworks.
13–21	**Chichicastenango**, a staunch Indian town, where Catholic and Maya traditions have merged into a unique festival of worshipping, dancing, processions, and live music, accompanied by the richest handicraft market you will find in Guatemala. Of the dances, the most famous is the Palo Volador, which is not so much dancing as dicing with death: pairs of men swing from the top of a 20-metre pole on the end of an unravelling rope.
24–31	**Lívingston**, the only black community in Guatemala, on the Atlantic coast, celebrates Christmas with live singing of African songs on the streets, and a couple of good reggae discos at night.
31	New Year's Eve resounds to the deafening noise of dynamite fire-crackers, with the best parties happening in **Antigua**, **Panajachel** and **Lívingston**.

Food and Drink

The classic Guatemalan dish is eggs and black beans (*huevos y frijoles*), usually fried and greasy, served with fried chicken (*pollo frito*) or beef (*lomito*) and warm tortillas or tasteless bread. The other two most common dishes are pasta and pizza.

There are a few tasty local snacks to try, such as the *tamal*, an envelope of banana-leaf (not edible) with steamed maize paste inside, often mixed with other vegetables or bits of meat. *Tamales negros* are sweet, made with prunes. *Chiles rellenos* are peppers stuffed with bits of meat and vegetables, served with hot sauce—as is everything here, unless you request otherwise. *Antojito* is a small tortilla 'sandwich', usually filled with a thin piece of fried beef, onion and tomato. *Enchiladas* are another standard, composed of crispy tortillas piled high with chopped vegetables, salad or meat, or a bit of each. And finally, the *fiambre* is not a snack but a giant salad of meats, fish, and cheese with assorted greenery, all piled up together, normally eaten on 1 November.

All these dishes (except the last) are served by vendors on the streets and at bus stations, but you would be safer eating them in restaurants, where hygiene is marginally better, or in the markets, where food is freshly made daily. Try them in the *comedores*, typical Guatemalan restaurants that serve a limited range of local food at the cheapest prices.

Hotel restaurants and the more up-market venues rarely serve traditional food, unless they specialize in 'typical' dishes. However there are exceptions to this rule, for example one of the best restaurant chains for Guatemalan fare, only in the capital, is Los Antojitos (*see* listings in the gazetteer chapters). There are also restaurants which serve traditional Maya food, which adds some exotic meats to the standard eggs and beans. For example, you could eat stewed armadillo, turkey (*pavo*) or *tepezcuintle*, a jungle animal that looks like a tiny deer, but is in fact the largest member of the rodent family—delicious when not overcooked. A good alternative to the eggs and beans are *plátanos fritos*, fried savoury bananas.

On either coast, you will also find delicious fresh seafood, usually fish, shrimp or squid, and a special dish you should try here is *ceviche*, which is chopped pieces of fish and onions marinaded in lemon juice, served cold. But it's best to avoid *ceviche* as long as there is a cholera problem here. Tropical fruit of all kinds is sold all over the country, but is best on the coasts, and the local coconut bread (*pan de coco*) is very good; do not eat too much of this unless constipation is the desired effect.

The most commonly available drinks are canned or bottled fruit juices, fizzy drinks or watery local beers. For the climate, the local beer is ideal; served very cold it is refreshing without making you dozy. Gallo or Moza (a dark beer) are the most common; Dorada Draft is also worth a try. Resist the delicious freshly-made shakes made with water (*licuados*) until you feel your stomach can cope with the local microbes. In the better restaurants, fruit juices and shakes are made with sterilized water, but always ask to make sure, since local tap water is generally not safe. Guatemalan wine tastes like a cross between vinegar and petrol, and is best avoided. But the rum is cheap and all right if mixed. Best buy is Ron Colonial, while Ron Botran and Venado Especial will give you a severe hangover (*goma*). Hardened drinkers will appreciate the local firewater, Quetzalteca.

In spite of the fact that Guatemala is a coffee-growing country, the drink here is almost universally weak, normally made of instant powder and tasting like dishwater. This is a pity, because when you get the real thing it is very good. The most likely places to find real coffee are the gringo joints of Antigua and Panajachel, or exclusive restaurants. Tea is also disappointingly weak, but a good alternative is the locally produced hot chocolate.

Prices

When eating out you can expect prices to fall into the following broad categories: snacks and meals purchased from street vendors, in *comedores*, or at markets will cost anything from a few US cents to three or four US dollars. The kind of meal you can expect is the standard egg and beans, a piece of fried meat and rice, or any type of stew, along with tortillas and hot sauce. In the more 'modern' *comedores* you might also find pizza, pasta, hamburgers and chips. Almost every market will include stalls where freshly cooked food is sold and, if you are on a very tight budget, these are your best options.

As a general rule you can expect any restaurant that is obviously geared to Western tastes to charge inflated tourist prices, but even these will be easily affordable for most travellers. The highest prices in the country are found in the gringo restaurants of the capital, Antigua, Chichicastenango and Xela, where you can expect a main meal—such as Thai curry or pizza—to cost between five and eight US dollars. Of course the trendy restaurants in the capital's zone nine and ten would charge a little more, and you could expect a BLT sandwich to cost you a good five US dollars, a main course around fifteen US dollars.

If you have a meal in a luxury hotel or obviously exclusive restaurants, you will still find prices highly affordable compared to what you would pay for the same thing at home. For example, you could expect a main dish to cost between fifteen and twenty US dollars.

Gay Travellers

Homosexuality is as much a part of Latin American society as it is of any other, though the demands of machismo are strongly repressive and it remains confined to a subculture of known bars in the capital cities and tourist towns such as Antigua. Public opinion on the subject is characterized by a mixture of contempt and amusement, and the police and military are known for their brutality against gays; foreign travellers should be careful not to draw attention to themselves. Homosexual and lesbian couples will have no trouble with accommodation arrangements since it is very common for travellers of the same sex to share rooms. Double beds are rare anyway.

Health and Emergencies

Medical preparation for a trip should begin with a visit to your doctor at least six weeks before you plan to go as he or she will be able to offer the most up-to-date information. The standard vaccinations for the region are yellow fever, rabies, typhoid, tetanus, polio, hepatitis, and hepatitis B. Even medical experts advise against a vaccination against cholera as it has little effect and it's simply better to take precautions: drink bottled water and avoid unwashed fruit and vegetables. Sunburn is another problem, and sun screen is not always on sale so do bring your own. Hats are available cheaply everywhere.

Farmácias, as chemists are known, stock all types of drugs, many without prescription, and many that are banned in Europe and North America. Clearly, it is best to bring your own medicines with you, but you should be able to buy most things you need here. If you plan on visiting the jungle, don't forget to bring the relevant malaria pills. Contraceptives such as the pill or condoms are readily available. (Remember that severe diarrhoea can diminish the effectiveness of the contraceptive pill.) Sanitary towels can be bought anywhere in the country, and tampons in the cities. But two items you will have difficulty finding are earplugs and contact lens soaking solutions, and mosquito repellent is also rare. (In the capital you can buy contact lens solution at Optica Moderna, 12 Calle 4–48, Zona 1.) If you intend to do a lot of hiking, remember to bring your own padded foot plasters which make open blisters easier to bear.

Should you suffer an attack of persistent bad guts, you should visit one of the many biological labs, which will analyze your problem and prescribe the appropriate remedy. In most cases these labs will be better qualified to recognize what is wrong than your doctor back home, so do trust them to help you, rather than suffer until returning to your own country. There are good labs in Guatemala City, Antigua and Quezaltenango. Alternatively, go to the nearest private hospital you can find, which will always be better than the state's institution, and not that expensive. Many doctors, and especially dentists, are trained in the US, so you should find plenty that speak English.

If you would like a detailed, personalized vaccination assessment and up-to-the-minute advice, contact the excellent Medical Advisory Service for Travellers Abroad (MASTA), at the London School of Tropical Medicine, ✆ (0891) 224 100. In the UK British Airways run clinics at 32 locations from Aberdeen to Plymouth; their phone numbers are obtainable from a recorded message on (0171) 831 5333. In London, you could also visit Nomad Traveller's Store & Medical Centre, 3–4 Turnpike Lane, London N8, ✆ (0181) 441 7208 (opposite Turnpike Lane Underground Station).

Insurance

Make sure your policy covers both theft and medical expenses and if you're particularly worried about ending up in a local hospital then make sure that the policy includes a flight home should you get seriously ill. Good insurance policies are available through all the main operators, including Thomas Cook and American Express (for their customers only). Specialist travel insurance is also offered by Columbus Direct, 17 Devonshire Square, London EC2M 4SQ, ✆ (0171) 375 0011, ✉ (0171) 375 0022. Their prices are marginally cheaper than anyone else, and they will cover you for individual trips or can offer an annual policy. Children under two years are insured for free, but their names must be on the policy.

Living and Working in Guatemala

This is no easy matter, involving a great deal of paperwork and running around if you want to do it legally. On a casual basis (with no employment rights and minimal pay), you can sometimes get work in the tourist bars and hotels. Bear in mind, however, that local people need the work much more than you do and will certainly work for substantially less. Your opportunities and pay are better if you teach English as a second language in Guatemala City, Antigua or Quezaltenango. For more detailed information see the English language press when you get there.

Voluntary work is quite easy to arrange if you have enough time and money to spare: most programmes require a minimum commitment of three weeks to three months and expect you to pay your own way. For information about highland aid organisations who might need volunteers, contact Mike Shawcross at the Casa Andinista Bookshop in Antigua.

Living in Guatemala long term also involves a great deal of bureaucracy and hassle if done legally. The most common method of securing (unofficial) residence is simply to leave the country at six-monthly intervals.

Maps

Large-scale topographical maps are produced by the Guatemalan military; you can inspect or buy them (US$6) only on production of your passort, at the Instituto Geográfico Militar, Avenida Las Américas 5–76, Zona 13, Guatemala City (*open Mon–Fri, 7.30–4*); it's much cheaper to buy them here than outside the country. *See also* 'Travel Bookshops'.

Markets

If you cannot make it to one of the highland festivals of Guatemala, the country's markets are a close second for colour and interest. Every town and village has a weekly market. The most interesting are in the Western Highlands, where the majority of Indians live. Walking around the stalls and baskets of farm produce and small livestock, you will notice that the atmosphere is refreshingly tranquil. This is because Guatemalan Indians come to market foremost to socialize: to keep up with the latest news from distant hamlets, estabish family ties, and set up potential marriages. Buying and selling is just by the by for these people, who live off the land and are almost outside the money economy of the rest of the country.

Of course the *artesanía* or *típica* markets are quite different: here Indian traders, usually women, drive a tough bargain, and are uncharacteristically pushy in getting you to look at their goods. The best craftware and textile markets are in Guatemala City (daily), Antigua (daily, but weekends are best), Panajachel (daily), Chichicastenango (Thursday and Sunday), Momostenango (Wednesday and Sunday), San Francisco el Alto (Friday), Nebaj (Sunday) and Todos Santos (Wednesday and Saturday). There are many others well worth seeing, and all other market days are listed in the text.

Money Matters

The best currency to bring with you is the US dollar. For safety's sake, you should bring at least half your money in traveller's cheques, which can be cashed at banks, as well as up-market hotels and even selected shops. It's also a good idea to bring some dollar cash for border crossings and emergencies, or to clinch a bargain, or in case you need to change money outside banking hours. Dollar cash, and sometimes cheques, can also be changed on the black market, which is widely tolerated but illegal. Black-market dealers operate in the streets and usually offer a slightly better rate than the banks, although they often indulge in sharp practices and well rehearsed rip-offs. Avoid showing your passport, which could be stolen in the process; don't hand over your cash first; and don't go into an unknown house with a supposed money-changer. Up-market hotels usually accept and exchange traveller's cheques, but at a poor rate. Once in Guatemala it can be very difficult to buy US dollars, and few banks are willing to break down large bills for you, so avoid US$100 notes unless you intend to change that much at each transaction. Credit cards are only useful at top hotels and shops, travel agents, and car hire agencies. American Express, Diners, Visa and Access are the most commonly accepted plastic.

A word of advice: do invest in a money pouch that can be discreetly kept under your clothing; purses, wallets and handbags really are a bad idea, since pickpockets are many and expert. And never leave your valuables unattended—most hotels have safes for customers' money and papers, which you should use.

Local Currency and Banking

The Guatemalan currency is the **quetzal**; one quetzal is made up of 100 centavos. Notes come in denominations of 100, 50, 20, 10, 5, 1 and 0.50. Try to avoid notes of 100 and 50 quetzals, since people do not like changing them; never accept torn or damaged notes because you will get stuck with them. Expect to buy all local currency within Central America; it is hard to get hold of, and nearly impossible to get rid of, elsewhere, except in Miami, where currencies are easily obtained and off-loaded.

Exchange rates are volatile in this region of rampant inflation and regular devaluations, but you can be sure that your money will go a long way here. **Guatemalan banks** do not charge commission for cashing traveller's cheques, but it can take at least half an hour to get your money because of interminable queues and forms. Make sure you are in the right queue. Every town has at least one bank, and often there are a few to choose from, such as the Banco del Ejército, Banco del Agro, Banco Industrial, and Lloyds Bank. The daily exchange rate is displayed, and is no longer fixed by the government so do shop around for the best rate. Banco del Agro often gives the best rate, while Lloyds charge a commission for cashing traveller's cheques. Banking hours are normally Mon–Fri, 9–3, though some open as early as 8am, and others do not close until 5.30pm.

Wiring money from abroad should be avoided if at all possible, since delays and other trouble is virtually guaranteed. If you have no choice, then you will be paid in local currency and can rarely buy back US dollars at the bank. Best use Lloyds Bank International, 8 Avenida 10–67, Zona 1. Another bank that has been known to pay out in US dollars or traveller's cheques is Banco Internacional, 7 Avenida 11–20, Zona 1; telex BANCOIGU; © 518066. Amex card holders can also get dollars at their office, simply by writing a personal cheque. Visa and Mastercard holders can get cash from Credomatic, 7 Avenida 6–6, Zona 1, Guatemala City (*open Mon–Fri, 8–7; Sat 9–1*).

National Holidays

Banks and government offices close on the following public holidays (public transport can always be found even when officially not running):

1 Jan	New Year's Day
6 Jan	Epiphany
Easter Week	(Semana Santa)
1 May	Labour Day
30 June	Anniversary of 1871 revolution
15 Aug	Assumption, celebrated only in the capital
15 Sept	Independence Day
12 Oct	Discovery of America
20 Oct	Revolution Day
1 Nov	All Saints' Day
24 Dec	Christmas Eve
25 Dec	Christmas Day
31 Dec	New Year's Eve

Newspapers and the Media

English-language newspapers—usually *The Miami Herald* or *International Herald Tribune* or *New York Times*—are sold in Guatemala, and you can also keep in touch with international news via CNN which is shown in upmarket hotel rooms throughout the region.

The two most widely available national newspapers are *Gráfico* and *Prensa Libre*; the latter is slightly less populist and celebrity orientated, but both are fundamentally right-wing. As papers critical of the usually right-wing governments get closed down, this is no surprise. *La Hora*, published in the afternoons and only available in and near Guatemala City, has the most balanced news analysis; *Siglo XXI* is on a par with *La Hora* and published in the mornings. The weekly magazine *Crónica* also aims to present a critical and broad analysis of Guatemalan and Latin American events in general.

Visiting the cinema is a favourite cheap pastime in Guatemala, and most large towns have at least one. The programme is often dominated by pornographic, violent or horror films, but most places usually run the latest North American film releases as well. Foreign films are run with subtitles, not dubbed, but the sound and film quality can be dreadful; unscheduled breaks in the programme or sound are frequent.

Television and radio stations abound in Guatemala, where over 60% of the population is illiterate, and many restaurants and hotels have radios and tvs permanently switched on. Satellite and cable TV are also quite common here, and gringo bars and restaurants in Antigua even show American CNN news.

Opening Hours

Most museums are open Mon–Fri, 9–4, with slightly shorter hours at the weekend. Many close over lunchtime, and some are shut on Mondays and weekends. Check opening times before setting out as there is considerable local variation. Archaeological sites are open daily, usually 8–4, though this also varies. Shops tend to open at 8 and close at 5.30; markets normally run from dawn until 4, with most of the action over by lunchtime.

Packing

> *Suitable Apparel: The contents of one steamer trunk and one suitcase, and with a handbag for soiled linen, meet the ordinary requirements of one person.*
>
> *The South American Handbook*, 1925

Before you leave home take another look at your luggage. The chances are you have packed too much; many things such as hats and light clothing can be bought cheaply and easily when and if you need them. If you intend to go walking you should bring sturdy footwear, as suitable boots are difficult to find in Central America. You will also need something to ward off the rain, cold and wind, all of which can strike with a vengeance.

Ideally, use a small rucksack or shoulder bag that can be padlocked. This is no guarantee of security but at least it hinders pickpockets. The advantage of small luggage is that you can keep it with you inside buses instead of having it thrown on the roof. Always keep with you your passport, vaccination booklet, flight ticket, traveller's cheques, insurance papers, photocopies of relevant pages in your passport and the counterfoils of your traveller's cheques. Some people find a pocket calculator invaluable for making sense of fluctuating currency values and assessing prices of goods. Take a money pouch or belt: either a leather belt with a concealed zip, or a wider cotton version that is concealed under your clothing and can fit your money and passport. Pouches can also be sewn on to an elasticated armband and worn under clothing.

A basic medical kit should include insect repellent, flea powder, antiseptic, medicine for diarrhoea including a rehydration powder, antihistamine cream, essential personal medicines, and preferred contraceptive. Foot plasters, sun screen and toilet paper are also very useful. Remember that toilet paper is generally not provided in toilets and should always be carried with you. Flip-flops are excellent for dubious showers and for general use. Also very useful are a small alarm clock for those 4am buses, a torch, a camping knife, and sunglasses. Other things you might want include are: a universal plug; an electrical adaptor; water purification tablets; a pair of earplugs; writing materials; a simple sewing kit; a water bottle.

Photography

The vivid colours of tropical greenery and Guatemalan costumes make the country a photographers' paradise. Bear in mind that the range of light is enormous; in the clear sunshine of the highlands it can be searing, while little light penetrates beneath the canopy of the forest. So bring a wide range of film, as anything beyond the 100–400 ASA range is not available here. Standard slide and black and white film is available, although only in Guatemala City.

Photographing sensitive subjects, including police and soldiers, can easily land you in deep trouble and you should make a point of asking local people if they mind. Photographing Indian religious ceremonies is deeply offensive, unless you are invited to do so.

Post Offices

Post offices (*correos*) open Mon–Fri, 7.30–6.30 in the capital, and 8–4 in every other major town, and often even in the smaller places. When sending letters, it is always best to send them airmail and express—they will still take up to six weeks to reach Europe and four to get to North America. Generally the postal service is slow but safe, and even parcels arrive back home eventually. To send any parcel which weighs over 2kg, you will have to take it still open to the main post office in Guatemala City for inspection, so remember to bring string and sticking materials to finish wrapping at the counter. (Everything you need is usually sold on the pavement outside.) There are strict regulations about the way parcels should be wrapped. If you can afford it, you could use the services of the Get Guated Out agency in Panajachel (*see* p.110, or other couriers in the capital.).

Receiving mail is straightforward via the *lista de correos* at any Guatemalan post office. The central post office in Guatemala City is the safest. Letters from Europe or North America normally arrive in ten days. To avoid mix-ups and delays, make sure letters are addressed to you by your surname only, with no initial or title prefixed—so that there is only one choice of letter under which to sort your mail. The address for the central post office in the capital is: Lista de Correos, Correo Central, 7 Avenida and 12 Calle, Zona 1, Guatemala City.

Members of American Express, or even holders of their traveller's cheques, could have their mail sent to the offices of American Express, Avenida Reforma 9–00, Zona 1, Guatemala City. They keep mail longer than the post office and are probably a bit safer, though there's not much in it.

Sexual Attitudes

Some travellers don't wear underpants under their shorts with the result that when they sit cross-legged on the floor, anyone sitting opposite is subjected to a view of their genitals; this is usually unpopular.

The Tropical Traveller, John Hatt

There is a general assumption among Latin Americans that Westerners are sexually easy, a quality which is both admired and despised. Certainly foreigners are popular conquests in certain circles. Male travellers will find themselves untrammelled by local *mores*, and cheap prostitution appears a real attraction for some. Women, on the other hand, are advised to think carefully about wearing sexy shorts or no bras, since they will undoubtedly attract attention and possibly disgust. Latin American society is astonishingly conservative and the display of naked flesh is regarded as bad manners, with the notable exception of the beach. Men in shorts are often considered to look ridiculous, while walking about barechested is also inappropriate away from the beach. Topless sunbathing is not a good idea in the local context, though it may be accepted in certain luxury resort hotels, far from the gaze of local people. Among indigenous people you should try particularly hard to keep yourself under wraps. To give you an idea of local custom: women often submerge in the waves fully dressed, trousers and all.

Shopping

Undoubtedly the best places to shop are the markets—if you know how to bargain. The Indian hand-woven textiles, made into anything from rugs, blankets, bags, *huipiles* (blouses), skirts and hats, to wall-hangings, are the major attraction. These textiles are elaborately embroidered with the traditional patterns of each region or village.

Hand-made linen tableware is another good buy, with an almost infinite variety of colours and styles available. There is delicate hand-made pottery, which is rather brittle and so difficult to transport; also a large array of carved wooden masks used during the Indian festivals; wooden furniture; wickerwork and rush mats and baskets; leather belts, bags and suitcases; plenty of silver-leaf filigree jewellery, as well as coral and glass bead necklaces; and finally, in Antigua, there is a great deal of Guatemalan jade for sale, made into anything from reproduction Maya statues to pendants. Watch out for soapstone fakes in the markets, and only buy jade from reputable shops.

A 10% government tax is added to most commercial transactions in shops, though almost never in the markets, where you do not get a bill anyway.

Sports and Activities

Amateur Archaeology

Maya ruins are scattered throughout Guatemala and offer a fascinating insight into the area's pre-Columbian history. Local tour companies can take you to almost any site you wish to visit, so there is no need to book from home. *See* p.67 for recommended companies in the capital, or p.195 for companies in Flores.

Hiking

In Guatemala it is possible to hire camping equipment and there are well developed trail systems and national parks. The best place to base yourself is Antigua, where you'll find plenty of inspiration and travel partners too, if required.

Natural History

The best opportunities for ornithology are at Tikal National Park and the Scarlet Macaw Trail nearby; contact Pro Petén, Flores, Petén, ✆ 502 926 1370; or Conservation International, 1015 18th Street, NW, Suite 1000, Washington DC 20036, ✆ 202 973 2264, ✆ 202 887 5188. Another interesting area to explore for its fauna is the Sierra de las Minas cloud forest; contact Epiphyte Adventures, Aptd. 94 A Cobán, Alta Verapaz, ✆/✉ 952 2213

Potholing

Central America's limestone interior is said to provide some of the finest potholing in the world, although as yet the sport has not been developed in any systematic way. Caves in Guatemala have been explored, but if you're planning an expedition you'll still need to bring all your own equipment. Contact Maya Expeditions at 15 Calle 1–91, Zone 10, local 104, Guatemala City, ✆/✉337 4666/947748.

River Rafting

You'll need no expert training for this popular sport, and can simply book a day out once you arrive. The best rafting company in Guatemala is Mesoamerica Explorers, Edificio La Cúpula, 7 Avenida 13–01, Zona 9, Guatemala City, ✆/✉ 501 332 5045.

Telephones

Payphones do exist, for which you will need plenty of 25 and 10 centavo coins, but more numerous are the offices of the national telephone company, Guatel, open daily, normally 7–10pm. Often chaotic places, they are nevertheless the best choice for making local and international calls. Be warned that international calls are very expensive, and just three minutes to Europe will cost you over US$20. Reverse charge (collect) calls can only be made to the US, Canada, Italy and Spain.

The main Guatel office in Guatemala City is near the main post office, at 7 Avenida 12–39, Zona 1 (*open Mon–Fri, 8–4*); a 24-hr office, open daily, is on the corner of 8 Avenida and 12 Calle, Zona 1. In Zona 9 you will find an office at Avenida Reforma 6–29, and at the international airport the Guatel office is open daily 7–7.

For operator assisted calls within Guatemala call 121, for international calls call 171. For collect calls to the USA you can also call 189 for MCI, 190 for AT&T, and 195 for US Sprint operators. For collect calls to Canada call 198.

International telephone calls to the UK, Australia, New Zealand and Europe cost around US$4.50 per minute, plus 10% tax. Calls to the US and Canada cost around US$1.50 per minute plus 10% tax.

To call Guatemala from outside the country, dial 00 followed by the country code (502) and then the seven-digit number. There are no codes for different areas: all national numbers are seven digits only. **Note that the numbers in Guatemala change frequently.**

Tipping

A 10% service charge is sometimes added to restaurant bills, and a 10–15% tourist tax added to hotel bills, although again this by no means rules out an additional tip.

Tips are also commonly given to taxi drivers, porters and chambermaids. However, there are no hard and fast rules and you're free to do as you please, responding to the situation as it arises. Generally speaking the staff in more up-market establishments will expect to be tipped, while those in cafés and cheap restaurants may be pleasantly surprised but will appreciate the gesture.

Toilets

Public toilets are almost unheard of; when you do find them they are likely to be filthy and you will need to provide your own toilet paper. In general, your best bet is to use the toilets in any restaurant, hotel or bar. On the road, you will find petrol stations invariably have clean toilets, which are kept locked for the use of customers only. (Get the key from the attendant or cashier.)

Tourist Information Offices

The national tourist board (Inguat) has an office at the international airport in Guatemala City, although it has a strong tendency to remain closed all day. If staff are there, they can book a hotel room for you or check on availability, as well as provide information leaflets on most tourist attractions.You can be sure of friendly, English-speaking advice at their city office in the Centro Civico building on 7 Avenida 1-17, Zona 4, © 3313075 (*open Mon–Fri, 8.30–4.30*). If calling from abroad start with 502. This is the place to come for anything from maps to bus schedules, hotel booking or advice on tours.

There are also Inguat offices in Antigua, Panajachel, and Quezaltenango and their addresses are listed in the text. Wherever you go, however, other travellers are always a good source of information and in Antigua and Panajachel you will find very useful travellers' noticeboards.

By way of orientation, you should know that all Guatemalan towns, including the capital, are laid out in a grid system, whereby *calles* run east to west and *avenidas* run north to south. Additionally, the bigger towns are divided into different zones, and the street numbers are repeated in each zone, so it is vital to know which zone you need. Addresses are written so that the street the place is actually on comes first, then comes the number of the nearest crossroad, and then the house number. For example, the El Dorado hotel is at 7 Avenida 15–45. This means the building is located on 7 Avenida, between junctions 15 Calle and 16 Calle, at number 45. It's easy once you get used to it.

Travel Bookshops

The longest established travel bookshop in the UK, which also sells maps, is Stanfords Map and Travel Bookshop, 12–14 Long Acre, London WC2, © (0171) 836 1321. Apart from the widest selection of guide books, you will also find literary travel books, usefully ordered according to countries. A short walk away you will find The Traveller's Bookshop, 25 Cecil Court, London WC2, © (0171) 836 9132, which also has a travellers' noticeboard.

Also popular is the Travel Bookshop, 13 Blenheim Crescent, London, © (0171) 229 5260, and Nomad Books, 791 Fulham Road, London, © (0171) 736 4000. Finally, a well laid out travel bookstore is Daunt Books for Travellers, 83 Marylebone High Street, London, W1M 3DE, © (0171) 224 2295.

Anywhere else in the country, your local Dillons should have a decent selection of guides and literary travel books, and they can certainly order any book you require.

Where to Stay

Accommodation in the book is listed under four price bands, which refer to the average price of a double room, including tax. (As everywhere else, single travellers are generally penalized by having to pay almost the same as couples.) Remember that local inflation is rampant and prices change constantly in this region. All prices are therefore quoted in US dollars.

luxury	US$90–US$130
expensive	US$30–US$90
moderate	US$12.50–US$30
inexpensive	US$4–US$12.50

If you are travelling on a budget, keep in touch with the travellers' grapevine: the state of places to stay changes all the time——and the addition of a (working) shower or laundry facilities can make all the difference. Generally speaking, good value accommodation will be found around bus and train stations, markets and truckers' stopping places (near fuel stations). Room prices will vary according to the season (high season is November to May), and it is always worth bargaining about the price, especially if you intend to stay three or more nights. If planning to be around for any of the major festivals, remember to book beforehand by fax, telex or registered mail. Or make sure you arrive at least two days in advance.

There are luxury hotels of international standard in Guatemala City, Antigua, Panajachel, Chichicastenango, near Tikal and on Lake Izabal; first-class hotels in Quezaltenango and Lívingston; and perfectly good standard hotels and guest houses in most of the places you will want to visit. Should you go off the beaten track to remote Indian towns or villages, you find very basic guest houses, or sometimes none at all. Where there is no official guest house, your best option is to find the local *alcalde* (mayor), who will either find you a reputable private house to lodge in, or let you sleep on the floor in the local council building or school. If you plan on visiting remoter places in the Highlands, remember your sleeping bag, since it can get very cold at night.

Prices for even the cheapest hovel are fixed by the national tourist board, so you can always see what the correct price is supposed to be. However, many places neglect to get their annual review, so don't be surprised if the price notice is a few years out of date, and expect to be flexible. Tax at 20% is added to all hotel bills, so always check whether a price is inclusive. Cheap accommodation is normally inclusive. Guatemala has some of the cheapest accommodation in Central America: the most basic double rooms cost around US$3, reasonable guest houses offering rooms for as little as US$8, while slightly up-market hotels charge from US$30 for two.

There are many different names for accommodation, but they basically all mean the same thing and do not necessarily indicate differences in standard. *Hotel, pensión, posada, hospedaje* and *huesped* are standard descriptions that cover the whole gamut of Guatemalan accommodation. Although phone and fax numbers have been listed in the text where available, most places will not accept verbal reservations, and even written ones are difficult to get with any but the most expensive. All you can do is phone to see if rooms are free and then turn up and try your luck.

There are no youth hostels in Guatemala, and only a few places where you can camp with reasonable facilities and safety: Panajachel, El Relleno, Poptún and Tikal. But accommodation is so cheap that there really is no advantage in camping, and the only time you might need a tent is climbing one of the volcanoes or hiking in remote mountain or jungle areas. If you do not want to bring your own, you can hire most camping equipment in Antigua, either from the Casa Andinista or from one of the many tour agencies.

Commercial renting of holiday homes or flats is not an established business here, but you can find long-term lets in the two gringo centres of Antigua and Panajachel, and possibly in Quezaltenango. Again, unless you plan on staying for months on end, you will not save much money by renting, when you can find pleasant, cheap guest houses and meals too.

Women Travellers

Machismo is alive and well in Guatemala, and the concept of sexual equality is generally not even paid lip-service. The traditional roles of women are defined by their place in the family, even though circumstances force the majority of them to work outside the home as well. Men are considered the natural head of the family—though this is often not the case in practice.

However, while sexism has obvious faults, there are also some more positive aspects. Patronage of females means there is always a man around who is willing to help a woman, and even protect her from the advances of other men. Single women travellers often find themselves inundated with advice and help they didn't even ask for, which is often friendly and useful, and offered without any expectation of favours in return.

And women travellers have nothing to fear in Central America that they don't face in any Western country, though they should be sensitive to certain cultural differences. In Guatemala this means being aware that you are in a deeply conservative, Catholic society that is strongly influenced by Latin stereotypes. Women who walk around in skimpy shorts and dresses, or without a bra, are generally viewed as no better than prostitutes. Topless sunbathing is also offensive to local people and should be practised with the utmost discretion.

History

Prehistory

During the last Ice Age, such vast expanses of ocean were frozen that the earth's general sea level was lowered. One effect of this was that Asia and North America were at times connected by a land bridge, known as the Bering Passage, and it is believed that humans first came into the Americas via this route about 60,000 years ago. Radiocarbon dates from polished bone tools suggest that the entire North and South American continents were populated by 11,000 BC.

The people who lived here in those times were hunter-gatherers, who lived a nomadic existence. Small family groups would have roamed the landscape, only occasionally coming together into larger camps in order to hunt the giant mammals of the age, such as mammoth, mastodon or bison. But there were many smaller animals they hunted too, such as rabbits, foxes, squirrels, turtles, lizards and quail.

Between 11,000 and 6000 BC the climate gradually became warmer and drier. Huge lakes dried up, grasslands became deserts, and the woodlands shrank, so that slowly the giants of prehistory became extinct. New kinds of food eventually had to be found by humans, and very, very slowly, people evolved new ways of life, where food came from a greater variety of sources.

In the time from 7000 to 1500 BC domesticated plants played an increasingly important role, and larger camps of people developed in response to the greater numbers needed for effective food gathering. In particular near rivers, lakes and oceans, sedentary groups emerged, who supplemented their fishing culture with gathering a great variety of other food, such as wild cereal plants, fruit, nuts, avocados, squashes, chilli peppers and prickly pears.

The Origin of Agriculture

The evidence for how and when humans first developed agriculture in the Americas is hotly debated. By its nature, plant evidence is hard to come by, and archaeologists have had to make do for their clues with a few cave sites in dry areas, such as in Oaxaca in central Mexico or the Ayacucho basin in the Peruvian Andes. It is at those sites that they have analyzed the ground layers relating to different ages, as well as studying coprolites (fossilized faeces) and human bones. From these combined studies scientists have established that a major change took place in human diet after 4500 BC, and that agriculture was important from this time on.

To look for an exact point at which hunting and gathering stopped and agriculture began is pointless. Development is the key word, and the transition from a nomadic hunting way of life to a sedentary agricultural life was gradual and piecemeal. One of the earliest domesticates was the bottle gourd for carrying water, and other plants were cultivated for dyes. Some plants, such as the tomato, are believed to have been domesticated only when genetic changes in the plant, such as increased size, made it a more important and easily gathered food source.

This must particularly apply to the all-important food plant, maize. Whatever the plant ancestor of maize, its cob would have been no larger than a thumbnail, and its use as a food source cannot have been obvious to early man. Instead, the combined effect of incidental domestication and genetic changes in the plant very gradually made it more and more useful, and eventually people began planting it specifically for food. These changes must have been slow; by 1500 BC maize was still only one-fifth of its present size. What is certain, however, is that man's changed relationship to the environment eventually allowed the first settled cultures to develop.

Early Societies

The earliest evidence for settled communities comes from household objects, such as simple pottery and cotton fibre cloth. From 3000 BC onwards, and certainly from 1500 BC settled communities of up to 1200 people gradually developed a new culture that included ritual and religious belief. Small figurines, believed to relate to ancestor worship or fertility rites have been found from this time. Homes were probably windowless houses made of pole and wattle, with palm-thatched roofs. In the highlands, houses would have been made of mud bricks (adobe), and thatched with straw or coarse grasses. Both types of housing can still be seen in Indian villages today.

Elite centres appeared by around 1000 BC; flat temple platforms from this date indicate ceremonial sites, and unequal burials testify to a stratified society. Some were simply wrapped in a sleeping mat and buried under the family house, while others were buried with great finery and even human retainers.

One of the earliest Mesoamerican civilizations were the Olmec, who existed between 1200 and 100 BC, with their heyday from 900 to 600 BC. However, their territory was almost entirely restricted to the Gulf Coast and the Tuxla Mountains of modern Mexico. The only significant satellite further south was at Izapa, on the Mexican Pacific coast near modern Tapachula. Another Mesoamerican people were the Toltecs, whose capital was the Yucatán ceremonial centre of Tula, and yet another were the Mixtecs, who ruled the area around modern Mexico City after the demise of the nearby city of Teotihuacan. The only Mesoamerican civilization to develop further south was that of the Maya, whose earliest beginnings go back as far as 2000 BC. They are generally divided into three regional groups: the Highland Maya of the Guatemalan highlands, the Lowland Maya of the Guatemalan Petén and adjacent Maya Mountains, and the Northern Lowland Maya of the Mexican Yucatán.

The Maya

The history of Maya civilization is divided into three periods: the Pre-Classic (2000 BC to AD 250), the Classic (AD 250 to 900), and the Post-Classic (AD 900 to 1530). They are generally held to represent the development, maturity and decadence of the civilization.

Pre-Classic Maya: 2000 BC to AD 250

From 2000 BC to around AD 150, Maya ancestors lived in the small communities already described. In particular along the Pacific plain of Guatemala, villages were established to harvest both the land and the sea. Their inhabitants lived off shellfish, crab, fish, turtles and iguanas, as well as maize from cultivated fields. The earliest village culture in this region is known as Ocos, and flourished from 1500 BC onwards. Later came the Cuadros village culture, which lasted until around 850 BC. Both evolved fine pottery skills, making a variety of bowls, pots and figurines. A common artefact of the period was the tripod bowl or jar, often decorated with crisscross and zigzag designs and distinctive patterns made by pressing rope or twine into the wet clay, only found in Central America.

Another important centre of early civilization, Kaminaljuyú, lies in the central valley of Guatemala, and is currently being swallowed up by the modern capital. A significant ceremonial centre from earliest Pre-Classic times, it eventually developed into a huge site of at least one hundred buildings, with political and trading links reaching all the way to Mexican Teotihuacán. Even the inhospitable Petén lowlands show evidence of early cultures, and sites such as Altar de Sacrificios, Ceibal, Tikal and Uaxactún were certainly inhabited by 400 BC.

Eventually, some time between 250 BC and AD 300, these simple village cultures scattered across the Maya territory developed the traits of a great civilization. Monumental architecture, sophisticated art forms, timekeeping and elaborate calendars, writing, and the science of astrology were all components of that development. Society became structured by an official religion and a rigid class system where even slaves were a hereditary group.

Kaminaljuyú developed into a vast and prestigious city. Temple platforms were raised from the ground, reaching up to 18 metres, and on these stood the simple temples of pole and thatch that so disappointed the Spanish in their search for riches. For those were not to be found in the temples, but in the burial chambers underneath them and around the pyramid platforms.

Classic Maya: AD 250 to 900

The Classic Age was a golden age for the Maya civilization, and their sophistication in architecture, art and science matched that of the ancient Egyptians or Greeks. Their astronomers could accurately predict lunar and solar eclipses and had recognized many planets, while the Maya calendar reached far beyond the Christian calendar and the complexity of their writing system has yet to be fully understood (see p.47).

It is during this age that Maya lords built the imposing pyramids of Tikal and Caracol, and sculptural art reached its peak at sites like Copán and Quiriguá. Often these sites are referred to as cities, since as many as 50,000 people once lived in and around them. But that is a misleading term, imposing modern conceptions on the past. It is now generally accepted that it is better to speak of ceremonial centres, since Maya civilization was fundamentally ruled by religious faith and ritual, and all aspects of life, whether the planting season, dates for war, or people's names, were decided by the Maya astronomers and diviners. They were at the heart of all decisions, and the position of every person in society was dominated by their interpretation of the celestial and divine cycle.

Only a very small group of nobles and priests lived at the core of what we see today: the great plazas and pyramids. Nearby there were quarters of artisans, craftsmen and slaves, and spreading out over a much larger area were the dwellings and clustered communities of the peasant majority, who were involved exclusively in food procurement and processing for the central élite, who then redistributed it among the population.

Post-Classic Maya: AD 900 to 1530

Between AD 790 and 889 the Classic Maya civilization abruptly disintegrated. Within a hundred years, the Lowland Maya populations seem to have left, state architecture and monumental building stopped, and even the Maya hieroglyphics appear to have degenerated into simpler forms of pictographic symbolism. Many explanations have been put forward for this collapse: earthquakes or hurricanes, epidemics, ecological disasters, social revolt, foreign invasion or economic decline. Certainly, the warlike Toltecs seem to have moved in from the north around 900, but the evidence from some sources suggests that the decline began before then. Until the Maya script is fully understood, we shall never know more than a fraction of the story.

All we can say for sure is that the Classic Maya civilization did collapse, and from the 10th century onwards, the glorious temples and plazas of most lowland ceremonial centres were left to itinerant squatters, who camped among the abandoned buildings, periodically looting the royal burial chambers or using the masonry for their own building needs. Soon the great buildings were reclaimed by surrounding jungle, and by the time the Spanish arrived, the temples and pyramids of the Maya had been derelict for over 500 years, remnants of a 'lost civilization'. The surviving Maya Indians could not shed much light on the magnificent art and architecture of their ancestors, nor adequately explain their culture's historic knowledge of astronomy, science and writing.

But while southern lowland centres of power, such as Tikal, declined, northern lowland centres, such as Chichen Itzá in modern Mexico, expanded. They developed a new style of art and culture, and traded goods along the coast in canoes. Much of this phase of Central American history remains obscure, though Post-Classic culture may have been a fusion of Maya and Toltec. By the time the Spanish arrived, however, Chichen Itzá was also in ruins. In the Western Highlands of Guatemala, though, the Quiché Maya had their powerful kingdom with its capital at Utatlán, the Mam Maya ruled their domains from Zaculeu, and the Cakchiquel Maya governed theirs from Iximché. All these peoples preserved many aspects of Classic Maya culture, and continued to do so after the Conquest.

baktun

katun

tun

kin

European Discovery and the Colonial Era

Europeans first came to Central America on Columbus' fourth and final voyage in 1502. His ship dropped anchor at Guanaja, one of the Honduran Bay Islands and, much to the excitement of his teenage son, his forces captured a Maya trading canoe, filled with exotic goods such as quetzal plumes, cacao beans, shells and fine pottery. Soon Columbus set sail once more, heading east around the Mosquito Coast, and discovered the Veragua region, which yielded enough gold finds to encourage a steady stream of expeditions to beach on today's Nicaraguan and Panamanian Atlantic coasts.

In 1513, the conquistador Balboa discovered the Pacific Ocean while travelling inland near the Darién forest, and soon Panamá City (1519), León and Granada (1524) were founded. They were some of the earliest colonial settlements in Central America, and flourished as bases from which to explore, as well as exploit local minerals and the Indians. Slavery was good business, and many thousands of Indians were shipped off to South American silver and gold mines. Most died of European diseases and malnutrition before they reached their destination, and those that did arrive proved unsuitable for heavy mine work. It was then that the Spanish began importing the stronger African slaves, thus introducing a significant black society to Central America.

Spanish forces were also penetrating south from Mexico City, soon to discover and conquer the Highland Maya of Guatemala and establish the brutal reign of Pedro de Alvarado. It was he who founded the most glamorous colonial city of Central America: Antigua, in Guatemala, situated in a beautiful highland valley embraced by three volcanoes. Meanwhile Spanish forces also traced the Atlantic coast southwards from the Yucatán, establishing strategic forts near the Honduran ports of Puerto Cortés and Trujillo, as well as inland at San Pedro Sula. These were important in repelling Portuguese and English expeditions, and also as bases from which to exploit the fertile interior for cacao.

After the Conquest, population centres followed the ancient patterns so that the main centre of Spanish rule grew up in the Guatemalan highlands. From there it spread thinly south, neglecting the traditionally 'empty' regions, such as the swampy jungles of the Atlantic littoral, as well as many inland areas, such as the inaccessible Honduran highlands. Much of the interior was left to its own devices by the colonial authorities, with the exception of vital ports along the Pacific, such as Colón in Panamá, and fortifications along the Atlantic, such as Omoa and Trujillo in Honduras.

The Spanish were too preoccupied with extracting the riches of Mexican silver and Peruvian gold to bother much with Central America; its mineral resources were limited, and its largest asset was an enslaved Indian population which did little to increase the wealth of Spain itself. The region was not farmed intensively until after Independence (although indigo and cacao from El Salvador and Guatemala were relatively lucrative exports) and it soon became a colonial backwater. Panamá was lumped in under the jurisdiction of New Granada, ruled by the Viceroy of Peru; the rest became the Captaincy-General of Guatemala in 1543, beholden to the Viceroy of New Spain, the forerunner of modern Mexico. This political division still influences Central American politics today and Panamá retains a unique position, not least because of the US-controlled Panamá Canal.

Unlike the Europeans in North America, the Spanish came as soldiers, not settlers. They did not bring their families, but married and had children by Indian women. The mestizos who resulted from this union soon formed the majority of colonial society. The Spanish crown, however, reserved the positions of highest authority for *peninsulares*—those born in Spain, who brought their families with them—a division that was eventually to spark off the independence movement. Along the Atlantic coast, the presence of African slaves led to a significant society of blacks and mulattos. Added to these peoples were small, tight-knit groups of Chinese, East Indians and white settlers, usually religious groups, such as the Mennonites, as well as non-Maya indigenous groups, for example, the Miskitos or Darién Indians, who survived through their inaccessibility. The Maya themselves succeeded better than any other indigenous people of the Americas in retaining their racial and cultural heritage, and to this day they make up over half the population of modern Guatemala.

Neglect by the Spanish authorities allowed others to make inroads into the territory. English, Dutch and French pirates made their homes along the Bay of Honduras and, by the 17th century, English pirates had even helped their country establish claims to what became known as the Crown Colony of British Honduras. Their legacy still exists in Belize, which has only been independent from Britain since 1981, and in the English-speaking inhabitants of the Honduran Bay Islands.

Independence from Spanish Rule

Central America gained independence on the coat-tails of Mexico in 1821. There was no battle for independence in the region, and there were plenty among the economic élite who remained loyal to Spanish authority. They were virtually let go against their will; once the rest of Latin America had gone, the Spanish colonial authorities had no further interest in a region that had always been one of the least profitable possessions.

It was a confusing time, when such disparate groups as the mine owners from Honduras, cacao planters of El Salvador and cattle ranchers of Panamá found themselves in a territory with no political authority and little common ground. As a result the various regions turned inwards, trying to consolidate their own interests, while sporadic battles raged between forces loyal to Spain and those with ambitions for wider political control of the region. A limited consensus was reached in 1823, when all but Chiapas decided not to become part of Mexico, and instead founded the United Provinces of Central America, whose capital was to be Guatemala City. This union was made up of five newly founded provinces: Guatemala, El Salvador, Honduras, Nicaragua and Costa Rica, whose borders were more or less the same as those of the countries of today. British Honduras remained outside the union, while Panamá became a part of Colombia. It was a recipe for political fragmentation, and the union was soon rent by conflicting economic and political interests, falling apart completely in 1839.

Ever since, Central American unity has been a lost cause. Honduras and Guatemala soon emerged as the original 'banana republics', their economic and political destiny closely supervised by US interests such as the United Fruit Company. Panamá declared its independence from Colombia in 1904, supported by the US to facilitate the building of the canal. Central America's role as the 'back yard' of the US has been a constant theme of its history since Independence, and on several occasions economic and political influence has spilled over into direct military intervention: the US occupation of Nicaragua from 1909 to 1933, the CIA-backed coup in Guatemala in 1954, or the invasion of Panamá in 1989. Admittedly this has produced a level of economic investment which the local governments could never have generated. But the price has been high, and remains the foremost cause of political instability in the region.

A Tragic Heritage

Guatemala's history has always been marred by violence, both natural and human. Earthquakes in the region destroyed the first two colonial capitals, and even Guatemala City has suffered repeated quake damage. Every time buildings and lives were wrecked political change came hot on the heels of physical destruction. The last time was in 1976, when around 25,000 people lost their lives in a huge earthquake in the Western Highlands. In the aftermath of social and economic distress, political unrest grew and the struggling guerrilla groups founded in the 1960s emerged fortified with a new Indian support base. For the first time in centuries, the Indians formed their own armed resistance: the Guerrilla Army of the Poor (EGP) and the Organization of the People in Arms (ORPA). They, and similar organizations, were annihilated by the army in a 10-year counterinsurgency campaign, though the beginning of the 1990s was marked by a small increase in guerrilla activities. In spite of the imminent signing of a peace agreement, the armed forces still claim to have something of a battle on their hands; in the run-up to the most recent elections, in November 1995, the guerrilla forces flexed their muscles again and staged several public meetings urging people to use their vote to prevent the former dictator Ríos Montt from being re-elected.

The country's history is one of the saddest in Central America, beginning with the brutal destruction of Maya tribes in the 16th and 17th centuries, institutionalized slavery in the colonial era, and further loss of land for the surviving Indians, as well as marginalization and continued abuse in the 19th and 20th centuries. The new order of creoles and mestizos (called *ladinos* in Guatemala) treated each other only slightly better, and post-Independence society grew accustomed to warring factions fighting for political control, coups and assassinations. The tradition from earliest times was that the strongest man wins political power, by force or fraud, so that democratic processes have never found fertile ground—or rather, they have always been nipped in the bud. In Guatemala the majority of the population has long been under the yoke of a small, conservative élite of landowners and the armed forces, traditionally kept in power by US military and economic aid.

The Struggle for Power

The aftermath of Independence, in 1821, brought political fragmentation to Guatemala, which was the traditional seat of colonial power in Central America. On the one side were the Spanish-descended ruling class, who under the colonial administration had always held all the positions of power, as well as having the pick of the land and its resources, including Indian labour. They were the conservative bastion of a fading empire, determined to hold on to their power and privileges, by force if necessary. Ranged against this formidable group were the mestizos, of Spanish and Indian blood, who had long resented their enforced subservience to the imperial Spanish Crown and dreamt of complete independence from Spain and her colonial administrators. Deeply influenced by liberal ideology, they too were prepared to back up their convictions with force, and so it wasn't long before conservative and liberal forces were going to battle in various parts of the region. Meanwhile the Maya Indians were at best helpless spectators to the civil war, and at worst forcibly conscripted into a conflict that was not theirs.

In 1829, the liberal forces of Honduran general Francisco Morazán invaded Guatemala, and a year later he became President of the United Provinces of Central America, which had been founded in 1823, though the fighting had never allowed it to develop properly. This marked the temporary end for Guatemalan conservative forces. The Central American federation, however, did not survive, breaking up into separate republics in 1839; Francisco Morazán was executed in 1842.

In the new Guatemalan republic the conservatives once more gained the upper hand, and the country's first *caudillo* (leader), José Rafael Carrera, ruled intermittently from 1844 until his death in 1865. He succeeded in this by playing both factions of Central American politics against each other, and it was not until Justo Rufino Barrios brought down his successor, in 1871, that liberals regained the political centre stage.

The Age of Liberal Reforms

In the mid-19th century, the Spanish-born élite regained some of its former power, but found itself sharing it with the *caudillos* and, increasingly, the limited progress of the country's economic expansion meant that the *ladino* population was forever dissatisfied. Once chemical substitutes had been found for the country's major export crops of indigo and cochineal, a new economic base had to be created, and it was the liberals who seemed to offer the best solutions.

Justo Rufino Barrios (1871–85) instituted a major reform programme that was intended to modernize Guatemala and make it a competitive force on the world market. This included building a national road and railway network, founding a professional army and, crucially, promoting new export crops, of which coffee was the most important. To do this, much Indian land was confiscated, sowing the seeds of widespread rural poverty and popular discontent for the coming century. Church land was also confiscated, which was a convenient punishment for the Church's traditional support for the conservatives.

The government encouraged foreign investment by offering huge tracts of land and no export duties and, by 1900, coffee made up 85 per cent of the country's exports, while the new coffee oligarchy came to dominate not just Guatemala's economy, but also her politics. The Indians were brutally forced off their land and pressed into a system of debt-peonage, whereby they had to work as agricultural labourers with no land of their own to sustain them.

The liberal dictator presidents succeeded in staying in power for many decades, ensuring their survival by forging an alliance with the military. Thus two of Guatemala's most powerful institutions were cemented: the landed coffee oligarchy and the military. State terror ensured that any kind of opposition was crushed, and dictators distinguished themselves by their brutality. A prime example was Manuel Estrada Cabrera (1898–1920), who was such a picture-book baddie that Miguel Angel Asturias used him for the basis of his novel on repression, *El Señor Presidente*.

After the world economic collapse in 1929, the Guatemalan leadership sought to broaden its economic base once more, and foreign investment was further encouraged, especially from the United States. One of the American companies that benefited most was the United Fruit Company, who gained outrageously huge land concessions from both Cabrera and the later dictator president Jorge Ubico (1931–1944). The company came to own more land in Guatemala than anyone else, and controlled not only the Pacific railways, but also the ports, the shipping, and all communications and electric power in its territory. The company's pervasive political influence established another Guatemalan tradition: an economy and government closely tied to North American interests. Under Ubico the government stole a great deal more land from the Indians, and further enslaved them to the new system by creating 'vagrancy laws' which made it illegal for Indians not to work on the coffee and banana plantations for a certain period each year. He also repressed any political opposition, as well as labour unions and rural co-operatives. Death or exile were standard punishments for dissenters, another tradition that has survived to this day.

The Spiritual Socialist

Ubico, however, was overthrown by a military coup in 1944, largely because he lost the support of the US, and also because he made the mistake of alienating sectors of the Guatemalan oligarchy and military, frustrated once more by slow economic progress. The carve-up of riches and power between United Fruit and the landed oligarchy left ambitious young officers and the country's emergent middle class little hope of advancement. Thus Ubico was removed and for the first time elections took place, and Juan José Arévalo was elected.

Arévalo was a teacher and writer who had spent the Ubico years in exile, and returned to his country determined to right the balance of power and welfare. He espoused a doctrine that he called 'Spiritual Socialism', and carried out many reforms during his five-year presidency: social security was established for the first time, as well as a labour code and rural co-operatives, a national educational and health programme was set up, and open elections were encouraged.

His successor, Jacobo Arbenz, continued Arévalo's revolutionary reforms and even legalized the Communist Party and allowed other political opposition to thrive. But Guatemalan democracy was soon challenged by traditionally powerful institutions. The 1952 Agrarian Reform Law, which redistributed land to the rural poor, finally made the Arbenz administration unacceptable. Only uncultivated land was taken, and its owners compensated, but the small group of owners resented every inch taken from them; especially the foreign landowner, United Fruit, who found 400,000 acres of its uncultivated land nationalized in 1953.

The company quickly used its contacts in Washington to lobby the US government and put pressure on the Guatemalan administration. There followed a short period of financial sanctions, diplomatic pressure and covert CIA destabilization tactics. But in the end it was easier to mount a coup and, in 1954, the CIA's 'Operation Success' helped Colonel Castillo Armas take the Presidential Palace. The Guatemalan army refused to defend Arbenz, and so the humiliated president left for exile and democracy was at an end. Castillo Armas was confirmed as president a year later, and three decades of murderous repression ensued.

The Military Reign of Terror

Armas only lasted a couple of years before he was assassinated, but he had already returned all nationalized land to its former owners, dismantled the labour unions and peasant associations, and mounted anti-communist propaganda backed up by an armed counter-revolution in which thousands perished. US foreign aid flowed freely once more, and the traditional alliance between the agro-export élite and the military was soon re-established.

Armas was followed by the hated General Miguel Ydígoras Fuentes, who had been head of the Secret Police under Ubico. The military put him in power after the 1957 elections ended in uncontrollable riots and, from then onwards, the military was firmly in charge of who ran the country. Ydígoras, however, turned out to be too despotic, even for his military supporters, and reformist officers mounted a coup against him in 1960. They failed, but those that escaped the firing squad founded the first armed rebel group in Guatemala: the Revolutionary Armed Forces (FAR). Also founded at this time was the 13th November Revolutionary Movement (MR-13), and both groups turned to Marxism-Leninism and Castro's example for their ideology. Ydígoras was finally overthrown in 1963, and while US military aid increased sharply, so did a brutal counterinsurgency programme, which made any kind of open dissent a life-endangering activity.

In the 1960s, the military tightened its grip on the country and, while presidents occasionally denounced the army's violence, the counterinsurgency campaign remained as virulent as ever. The most notorious campaign of the decade was led by Colonel Carlos Arana Osorio, whose 1968 Zacapa campaign was responsible for the deaths of at least 10,000 civilians. Right-wing death squads also emerged in these years, as certain sectors of the conservative élite became impatient with the army's inability to wipe out armed rebellion completely. Between the years 1966 and 1970, these squads alone are believed to have killed over 30,000 people. Such was the atmosphere of violence and terror that political opposition was all but silenced, and the 1970 'elections' brought the 'Butcher of Zacapa', Carlos Arana Osorio into power.

In the 1970s, the Guatemalan military continued to rule with US support and vital military aid. Only the 1976 earthquake threatened the army's tight control over the country and, with many dead and more homeless and destitute, guerrilla groups re-emerged and found support from the population's Indian majority. Until this time, the revolutionaries had never considered the needs of the rural Indians, nor seen them as natural allies. However, they now began to establish themselves in the Western Highlands and remote north, organizing armed resistance and spreading educational propaganda.

The result of the rebels' move into the countryside was tragic for the Indians. The military implemented a scorched-earth policy, and entire villages were razed to the ground, their inhabitants tortured and murdered. A common practice was to herd the women and children into their local church or community hall, and then set the building on fire, leaving their husbands to listen to their death cries before being murdered themselves. The manner of the army's killings were unspeakable, and the files of Amnesty International are full of horrific eyewitness reports from the few survivors that made it to Mexican and Belizean refugee camps.

In the first months of 1981, 1500 Indians were killed in the Chimaltenango Department alone, and the devastation of land and human life continued. In June 1982, one of the country's most notorious generals took power: General Efraín Ríos Montt. He was installed by the military to reduce corruption and lead the country back towards civilian rule. But instead he launched his 'Beans and Guns' counterinsurgency campaign, and the World Council of Churches reported that the government was responsible for the death of 9000 people between the months of March and July that year. He was an extraordinary character who, while the armed forces were murdering in the countryside, harangued Guatemalans with Sunday sermons on television, telling them not to fornicate or drink, but to lead a Christian life. He was deposed by a coup in 1983, after which he turned to preaching for the Church of the Word in Guatemala City. Now he is once again a major political player, the leader of the country's Congress and presidential candidate for the Guatemalan Republican Front (FRG) in the last two elections. The fact that Guatemala's Constitution does not allow those who have formerly come to power as a result of coups to be presidential candidates has not deterred him; it was only the combined opposition of both the local and international community that kept him from becoming an official contender in 1995.

Civilian Rule

The army finally handed government back to civilian rule in 1985, and the Christian Democrat Vinicio Cerezo Arévalo became the first civilian president of Guatemala in 31 years. Naturally the democratic process was initiated on the army's terms; military offensives in the countryside continued throughout the years of Cerezo's government, and atrocities still occurred, such as the massacre of 22 peasants in the village of Aguacate, near San Andrés Itzapa, in November 1987, and that of 13 Indians in Santiago Atitlán in December 1990.

Cerezo's government was succeeded by Jorge Serrano Elías and the right-wing Movement of Solidarity Action (MAS) in January 1991, who won a resounding victory with 68 per cent of the vote. This result, however, had to be set against a 55 per cent abstention by registered voters, which reflected widespread disillusion with the democratic process in Guatemala and did not augur well. The bad omens were to be confirmed as Serrano—in spite of being an Evangelical—turned out to be astoundingly corrupt. So much so, that he managed to alienate both the country's oligarchy and the military. In a desperate bid to remain in power he staged an auto-coup in imitation of his colleague in Peru, in 1993, but failed to retain enough strong-arm support to succeed. Crucially, he failed to secure US support, and thus quickly found himself deported to Panama, where he is now believed to be developing a golf course with the millions he stole to sweeten his exile.

The constitutional crisis of 1993 revealed that Guatemalan civilian rule was still very much dependent on foreign and military intervention; in fact the democratic process is still little more than a respectable cover for the traditional forces of power. An indication of just how easily Guatemala could slide back into non-democratic ways is the reappearance on the political stage of the former general Efraín Ríos Montt. Not only has he been leader of the country's Congress for some time, but he was also able to gather substantial support for his illegal candidature in the 1995 presidential elections. Forced to withdraw from the official list, he nevertheless campaigned all over the country and, if his stooge Alfonso Portillo of the Guatemalan Republican Front (FRG) had won the elections, he would have become head of internal security—a scenario that doesn't bear thinking about considering his hideous campaign of the early 1980s. The FRG lost, however, and the former foreign minister and mayor of Guatemala City, Alvaro Arzú of the National Advancement Party (PAN), won the second-round presidential elections, in January 1996. Once more, though, almost two-thirds of the electorate failed to vote.

On the other hand, the fact that the 1995 elections concluded in a more or less orderly fashion is positive. With PAN in control, there is a realistic chance of a peace agreement with the guerillas (signed in January 1997). As long as the military can be persuaded to stay out of politics Guatemala will, slowly but surely, progress towards a peaceful and democratic future.

Towards the Year 2000

Guatemala is still condemned by America's Watch and the UN Human Rights Commission for human rights violations and its high number of disappearances. Thus the Guatemalan government is hampered by both the human rights violations of the armed forces and also the resulting constant threat of international sanctions, which will severely restrict the country's economic progress.

The Maya Indians, meanwhile, continue to survive in spite of the genocide of the late 1970s and 80s and their economic, social and political marginalization; and their culture and traditions are still alive in the countryside, especially in the highlands, and a revital-ized tourist industry is taking full advantage of the riches they have to offer. Tourism cannot replace the continuing urgent need for agrarian reform but, in some regions at least, controlled tourism can help Indian communities survive where their traditional economic base has been denied them.

However, tourism is volatile and dependent on many things and does not offer a long-term solution to the needs of Guatemala's rural population, who make up the vast majority of her people. The Maya are well aware of this and have increasingly begun to organize themselves independently of both the guerillas and the official government institutions, who have consistently failed to give them genuine, long-term assistance. The award of the 1992 Nobel Peace Prize to one of their own, the civil rights campaigner, Rigoberta Menchú, gave their cause the international publicity it deserves and, with continued civilian rule, there is a chance they will succeed in establishing a sustainable future.

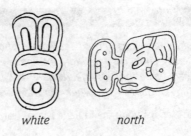

white   *north*

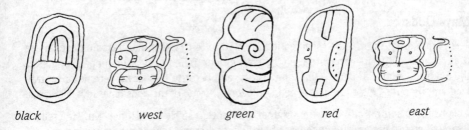

black   *west*   *green*   *red*   *east*

People and Culture

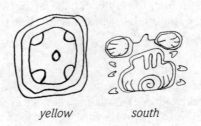

yellow   *south*

> *These are the names of the First People who were made and modelled... Thoughts came into existence and they gazed; their vision came all at once. Perfectly they saw, perfectly they knew everything under the sky, whenever they looked.*

The *Popol Vuh* of the Quiché Maya, translated by Dennis Tedlock

Miraculously surviving the ravages of time and the depredations of the conquistadors, the manuscripts, the stone inscriptions, the pottery, the pyramids and temples, and above all the living tradition itself allow us a glimpse into the extraordinary universe of the Maya.

Maya Gods

The pantheon of the Classic Maya period (AD 250 to 900) has roots stretching back more than a thousand years earlier to the Olmecs, and continued to be worshipped long after the Spanish Conquest. Due to this long history, and because the Maya were not a central-ized empire but a collection of independent peoples, some of the gods have several aliases.

According to some traditions, the original omnipotent spirit was Hunab Ku. He created Itzamná, god of fire and the inventor of writing; and Ixchel, goddess of medicine and the Old Moon. They created all the other gods, including Chac, the goggle-eyed rain god; the four Bacabs, who stood at the points of the compass and supported the heavens; the maize god, an ever-present symbol of renewal; and a rather cuddly character known as the Fat God. The monkey-men gods were the special patrons of the scribes.

Of special importance was 'God K'; he was the wind god and the special protector of the Maya rulers, who carried his image on their sceptres. After the arrival of the Toltecs around AD 900, he seems to have become identified with Kukulkan. God of the primordial wind, he was known to the Quiché as Gucumatz and worshipped by the Aztecs as Quetzalcoátl the plumed serpent.

Among the gods of the underworld (Xibalbá), who sent forth owls to summon mortals to their final ball game, were the skeletal Hunahau, the Death God; his assistants Tatan Holon ('Father Skull') and Tatan Bak ('Father Bones'); the Jaguar God; the long-nosed Ek Chuuah, god of merchants; and Ixtab, the goddess of suicides, who is shown hanging from a noose in Maya manuscripts.

Creation Myths

There are many different accounts of the creation from the Maya lands. One version, inscribed on two stones at Quiriguá in Guatemala and Palenque in Mexico, lay unnoticed for millennia until it was deciphered by two US scholars, Linda Schele and David Freidel, in 1992. On 13 August, 3114 BC, the gods lit the flame from which the universe was created, in a hearth of three stones. The fire can still be seen in the sky today: the red Orion nebula, which hangs between the three brightest stars of that constellation. At the moment of creation, though, the sky lay flat upon the surface of the earth in a two-dimensional universe. The gods then used the Milky Way as a great tree to lift the sky up above the earth.

The creation of human beings is recorded in the Quiché Maya's Book of Creation, the *Popol Vuh*. It took the gods Tepeu and Gucumatz four attempts to accomplish this difficult task. Their first creatures were fashioned out of the earth's mud, but soon disintegrated. The second versions were made of wood, but were stupid and had to be destroyed as unworthy. The third attempt was more promising; the creatures were made of living flesh, and had minds too. Disappointingly, they failed to honour their creators (which was supposed to be their main purpose in life) and were punished by being turned into monkeys. The fourth creations, made from maize, at last proved satisfactory, knowing their place and worshipping the gods.

Itzanná

Maya Society

At the apex of a Maya city was a ruler who claimed to be descended from the gods. At Copán and Quiriguá, carvings show the new king as the sun rising from the jaws of the earth, while his predecessor is swallowed up. To prove that the blood of the gods flowed in their veins, members of the ruling family would shed their blood before their subjects; the men by piercing the penis with a bone spike, the women by dragging a thorn-studded cord through a hole in their tongue. After his death, a ruler would be interred in one of the great pyramids, along with many human sacrifices of men, women and children. Some were undoubtedly captured victims of war, but others would have been kept for sacrifice, especially the children.

Ixchel, the old Moon Goddess

An élite caste of scribes, descended from the Monkey Men gods, recorded every aspect of their society. They kept and consulted the sacred calendars and astronomical tables, which dictated every detail of public and private life. The palace household also included nobles and military officers, who could be sent out to govern conquered cities. Further down the hierarchy were the artisans, artists and traders. Of the ordinary people—builders and farmers, peasants and slaves—we know even less than we do of their ancient Egyptian counterparts.

Sun God

The Maya cities were extremely militaristic, and in a constant state of conflict with neighbouring centres of power. Their aim was not to expand their territory but to capture high-ranking individuals from rival cities, who would then be sacrificed to the gods. This conflict was also ritualized in the 'Ball Game'. The two rival teams were kitted out in helmets and heavy padding, not unlike modern American footballers. The game was played on stone courts with vertical hoops, such as the one

Chac, the Rain God

which can still be seen at Copán in Honduras. The stakes were high: for the losers ended up on the sacrificial altar. In the *Popol Vuh*, two young men are challenged to a ball game with the lords of the underworld. After the defeat and death of the two young men, the severed head of one of them impregnates Lady Blood by spitting in her hand. She gives birth to the Hero Twins, who defeat the underworld gods in a return match.

However, the Ball Game also had important religious significance and has variously been interpreted as representing the battle between light and darkness, or between day and night. Precise interpretation still eludes archaeologists, but it is generally agreed that the ball represented the sun and its flight during the game its daily journey through the sky. Since the Maya believed that the sun's power ensured the survival of their world, it was vital that her daily cycle not be interrupted symbolically during the game: i.e. the ball's flight had to be continuous, and not broken by touching the ground. Players wore heavy padding to protect them from knocks by the ball, which was of hard, solid rubber, measuring 20–25cm. They were allowed to use their bodies but not their hands or feet to keep it in play; the team that failed to keep the ball off the ground lost the game, unless they managed to score a 'goal' by throwing the ball through one of the stone markers either side of their playing field. In the eyes of the Maya, the losers had failed to ensure the continuous cycle of the life-giving sun, thus threatening the survival of the world, and the only way to restore her strength was with human blood—the most precious thing a person could offer. The losers were therefore sacrificed to the Sun God with great pomp, and their graves enriched with special offerings, in particular stone replicas of the players' protective clothing embellished with exquisite carvings and precious inlays.

Until relatively recently it was thought that the game was no longer played by the Maya. In fact, the coastal communities of Indians in western Mexico do still play the game almost exactly as their forebears did. Only the ritual sacrifice and the heavy protective clothing have been dispensed with. To some extent the spiritual significance of the game has also survived, since the game is only played on religious holidays, albeit Christian ones.

Art and Architecture

For the modern traveller in Central America, the most visible remnants of the Classic Maya civilization are the great temples that rise so dramatically from the forests of Guatemala, Honduras and Belize. The characteristic structures are nearly always known as 'pyramids'. This is a somewhat misleading term, however, as it evokes the pyramids of Egypt, which are buildings in their own right. In Central America, they are simply the platform on which a temple was constructed. Sometimes the 'pyramids' are wide and relatively low, as at Copán; sometimes they soar almost vertically, as at Tikal (*see* pp.198–200). They are usually surrounded by a complex of smaller temples, plazas, ceremonial avenues, and sometimes a ball court.

Maya architecture never achieved the carefully worked, accurately interlocking masonry so characteristic of the Incas of Peru. Maya buildings usually consist of a core of rubble and cement, faced with a thin cladding of dressed stone, and they stay up by sheer mass rather than geometry. The cladding, however, was covered with intricate relief carving and mosaics, and where the stone was too hard to be easily worked, stucco was moulded into spectacular relief. The principle of the arch was unknown to Maya architects; instead, they constructed their massive vaults by overlapping stone slabs until they met in the centre of the roof. The peak of the vault was often crowned by a highly ornamented 'roof comb'. We are accustomed to the mellow hues of weathered stone, and it takes some effort of imagination to picture the temples in their heyday: painted blood red, with the relief moulding picked out in bright colours.

A prominent feature of Maya monumental art was the stela. These large oblong stones, rising up to 10 metres above the ground, usually stood planted before a circular altar slab in the temple plazas. The stelae were intricately carved with stylized portraits of noble rulers; the sides or back recorded crucial dates in Maya hieroglyphs. Only a fraction of the stelae have been deciphered, but it is generally agreed that they record royal lineages, and the dates of important battles, accessions to the throne, royal birthdays and other significant events. The Maya 'cities' were home only to the gods, the priests, the ruler, and his dead ancestors. The great mass of the population would have lived nearby, in thatched wooden buildings not unlike the ones that their descendants inhabit today. It was for the dead, too, that the Maya reserved their finest pottery and artefacts of jade, obsidian, crystal and other minerals and precious stones. Many surviving vases illustrate scenes of the underworld, and pottery figurines of gods, humans and animals are frequently recovered from graves. The National Museum of Archaeology and Ethnology (*see* p.71) and the Popol Vuh Museum in Guatemala City (*see* p.70) have excellent collections of Maya ceramics, jade and other artefacts.

The Maya Alphabet

Ever since they were first discovered by Europeans, the complex inscriptions on Maya architecture and monuments have baffled even the most expert epigraphers. We know far less about the Maya script than we do about Egyptian hieroglyphics, but from what we do know, it is even more complicated than Chinese. Maya scribes made virtuoso use of a complex system. They had a phonetic symbol for every syllable, but also used pictographic images—a flame to signify the word 'hot', for example. They would also use pictographs to represent the sound or meaning of individual syllables in a word. Furthermore, there are many homonyms in the Maya script, so that the same symbol can have very different meanings depending on the context. For example, the words 'sky', 'four', 'snake' and 'captive' are all pronounced identically and can only be distinguished in the proper context.

Shield Jaguar

Accession Glyph

Birthday Glyph

Bird Jaguar

Prefix— Female Names and Titles

Many studies have failed because they have tried to bend this system to the concept behind the Western alphabet. Bishop Landa was one of the first to try this, but never realized that his Maya informant was often giving him the name for a letter, but not the variety of meanings it could carry. Eventually the Maya nobleman's patience wore thin, and he wrote 'I don't want to' in the bishop's book.

Among the small groups of symbols whose meaning the experts agree on are the emblem glyphs for a number of important Classic centres such as Tikal, Yaxchilán, or Quiriguá, and the glyphs relating to noble lineages and important events in their dynastic history. The symbols for birth, death, and accession to power have been recognized, and often their dates have also been found in surrounding glyphs or pictures. Symbols found at Yaxchilán, on the river Usumacinta in the Petén jungle, tell us that the city was ruled by the Jaguar dynasty, fathered by the great lord Shield Jaguar, during the 8th century.

The extent of a city's military and political power is often demonstrated by the appearance of its unique emblem glyph at other sites, representing conquest or an advantageous royal marriage. Major advances in Mayan epigraphy have been accomplished in the 1980s and 1990s and those who are interested can learn a great deal more by reading the excellent book *Breaking the Maya Code* by Michael D. Coe (Penguin, 1994).

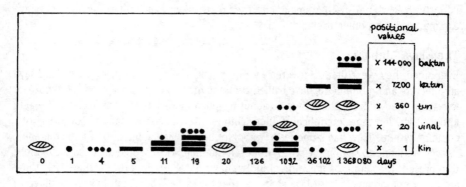

Maya Arithmetic

The concept of zero, so essential to any advanced mathematics, has been thought of only twice in human history: once in India around 600 BC, and once in Central America. Exactly when it first appeared in Central America is not certain, but it was already in use by the time the Maya came on the scene.

The system of Maya arithmetic was vigesimal, based on factors of 20, but had been adjusted to fit in with the calendar. The numerals were arranged in vertical columns, which increased in value from bottom to top. There were just three symbols: a dot signified 1, a horizontal bar signified 5, and a stylized shell signified zero.

The Maya Calendar

The Maya were obsessed with time, and the keeping of time. The fate of each person was ordained by the date and timing of their birth, and the interpreters of the celestial and divine cycles held immense power over the population, including the nobility. One of the four surviving pre-Conquest books, the Dresden Codex, contains an extraordinarily accurate table of the movements and eclipses of the planet Venus.

From Pre-Classic times, the Maya used two different calendars. Who invented them is uncertain, but most believe that it was probably the Olmecs, and that the Maya simply refined the existing systems handed down to them.

The Long Count is a system that hinges on a fixed date in the past, like the Christian calendar, and begins at 4 Ahau 8 Cumku, the equivalent of a day in 3113 BC. According to their belief, this was the beginning of a historic cycle of 13 baktuns (periods of 144,000 days). This cycle is due to be destroyed in the year equivalent to the Christian year of AD 2012, when a new age will begin.

The Maya also used the Calendar Round, which estimated time in cycles of 260 days, each of which held important information for fortunes and ceremonials. This system involved the use of two calendars which ran concurrently. The first consisted of 20 named days with 13 numbers; the second of 365 days, divided into 18 months of 20 days each, with five extra days, called Uayeb, which were considered highly unlucky.

The best way to understand this system in operation is to imagine two interlocking cogwheels of different sizes:

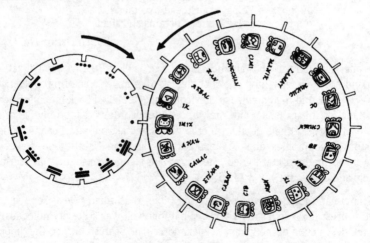

For the two components of this giant cycle to make one completion required 52 solar years, and marked one of the Maya's most important ceremonial dates.

Use of the Long Count was abandoned towards the end of the Classic Age, and the latest dates known from monumental inscriptions match our year AD 909, taken from a stela at the Mexican site of Tonina. The Calendar Round, however, is still in use today.

The Living Heritage

Although much Maya learning has been lost, centuries of persecution have failed to eradicate it entirely. The Maya Indians survive, and their languages, culture and religion are still a part of their everyday lives. The daykeepers or shamans living in the Western Highlands of Guatemala still keep the sacred knowledge of the Calendar Round. Predominantly Indian towns and villages, such as Chichicastenango, Santiago Atitlán, and Momostenango, are well known for their periodic festivals. But since secrecy has been the key to survival, foreigners are unlikely to witness any ritual ceremonies relating to the Calendar Round. In San Andrés Itzapa, however, you can experience the cult of Maximón, a strange hybrid of Maya and Catholic ritual. In a side-street chapel, the cigar-toting effigy of the saint is liberally anointed with rum under the benevolent gaze of the priest. Outside the celebrations continue as fireworks are let off under the auspices of the Maya daykeeper. It is this resilience and power of adaptation that has kept the Maya tradition alive, and makes it one of the most exciting features of Central America today.

Central American Literature: an Introduction

Mis ojos miraban en hora de ensueños
La página blanca.
Y vino el desfile de ensueños y sombras.

It was the hour of dreams. In front of me
A snow-white page outspread I seemed to see.
And a procession came of dreams and shades.

Ruben Dario, *The White Page*

Central American literature has an ancestry at least as old as the Maya civilization itself. The lowland Maya were writing books on deerskin, or paper made from pulverized bark as early as AD 500, and the knowledge they contained stretched back much further. Some, like the Book of Chilam Balam and the *Popol Vuh*, recorded creation myths, prophesies and acts of the gods. Others dealt with crop cycles and astronomical calculations. There were histories, biographies, atlases, almanacs and calendars. Written on sheets of paper anything up to 6m long and folded into pages like a concertina, the manuscripts were elaborately and exuberantly illustrated.

When Franciscan monks arrived bearing the Bible, the Indian priests replied that they preferred to trust their own sacred texts. What followed was a literary holocaust comparable to the destruction of the library at Alexandria. The Spanish burned the 'books of the idolatrous priests' wherever they could find them, often consigning their owners to the flames as well. Only four Quiché Maya manuscripts survive today. The Spanish-Tlaxcalan mestizo Diego Muñoz Camargo recorded the scene in a drawing that accompanies his *History of Tlaxcala*. As two Spanish friars torch a pile of books, gods and animals leap from the flames, as if liberated from the page to inhabit the air.

The Colonial Era

The first colonial writers of Spanish America were the conquistadors themselves and the hard-headed priests who accompanied them. At his house in Antigua, Guatemala, Bernal Díaz del Castillo (1495?–1584), veteran of 119 battles, wrote his argumentative *True History of the Conquest of New Spain* to refute all other accounts. The conquistadors' arch-critic, Father Bartolomé de las Casas (1474–1565), also lived in Antigua for a while. His *Brief Account of the Destruction of the Indies* (1552) described Spanish atrocities in horrific detail, and caused much liberal hand-wringing back in Madrid. To show that the Highland Maya of Guatemala could be converted to Christianity by peaceable means, he composed hymns in their Quiché language.

Early colonial bards penned ponderous epics extolling the feats of Cortés and Alvarado in the heroic style of ancient Rome and Renaissance Italy, while the church churned out devotional tracts, often in Nahuatl and other indigenous languages. The enterprising priests also wrote and staged sacred dramas (*autos sacramentales*). Like the medieval mystery plays, these were based on Bible stories and performed in the native language with singing, dancing, comic interludes and audience participation.

But New Spain was not a propitious environment for the development of literature. All publications had to be vetted by the censors in Madrid, and Spanish printers held a monopoly which allowed them to flood the provinces with their work. Under these conditions it is hardly surprising that the bulk of Central American literature was provincial and derivative. Little poetry of note was written, and no novels at all.

Meanwhile, the gods and animals that flew from the burning pages of the sacred books still hovered in the air. Storytellers handed down ancestral knowledge from one generation to the next. From sympathy or curiosity, some of the Spanish priests began to write down, from the memories of the Indians, the texts they had themselves destroyed. Even Bishop Diego Landa, the most zealous of the book burners, turned his hand to ethnohistory. It is thanks to their activities that the *Popol Vuh* survives today; the earliest copy dates from around 1700.

The *autos sacramentales*, meanwhile, began to assume a life of their own in the hands of their Indian performers. Fables, allegories, parables and satire became important weapons against censorship, and a means of protest against oppression. Brutal landlords could be hidden in animal or mythical characters, ignominiously defeated and held up to ridicule. The comic interludes, often based on Indian folklore, gradually became longer, and in some cases supplanted the Christian element altogether.

One such play, the *Baile del Gueguence* from Nicaragua, was written down in the 19th century, although it is probably older. The knockabout plot concerns a Spanish governor who can't afford to stage the customary songs and dances for the Royal Council. He arrests the *gueguence* (village elder) and tries to extort money from him. After much singing, dancing and bawdy farce, the wisecracking elder outwits his blustering overlord.

From Independence to Modernismo

Just as Central America was slow to be drawn into the independence movement of the early 19th century, it was slow to be drawn into the literary tumult that followed. Writers in the north and south, from Mexicali to Tierra del Fuego, produced a torrent of poems, plays and novels celebrating revolution and erotic love, the Aztec warriors of the past and the gauchos of the present. They lurched giddily from the romantic idealism of Byron and Shelley to the realism of Zola. They devoured the latest European authors while proclaiming *americanismo* in literature.

By the time Central America got in on the act, young writers had found a new creed: *modernismo*. The movement began in Cuba and Mexico, but the Nicaraguan Ruben Dario (1867-1916) became its brightest star and acknowledged leader with the publication of his volume of poems *Azul* in 1888.

Modernismo was a far cry from what the name might suggest to a 20th-century reader. A reaction against realism, it was intended to be 'art for art's sake'. Refined, sensual and otherworldly, it owed much to the French symbolists. But Dario, whose ancestry combined Amerindian, Spanish and African origins, successfully fused the contradictory heritage of the continent into a truly Latin American literature. The beauty of the Nicaraguan landscape suffuses his work, and although Walt Whitman and Edgar Allan Poe were among his literary heroes, this did not prevent him from taking a stab at Yankee imperialism in his poem *A Roosevelt.*

Dario's fame took him all over Latin America, where his prestige was enormous; to France, where he met Paul Verlaine; and to the United States, where he caught the pneumonia that killed him shortly after his return to Nicaragua. He was Central America's first poet of international stature. 'To enter the city of Nicaraguan poetry,' Steven F. White has written in *Poets of Nicaragua*, 'one must first pass the landmark that guards the gates— Ruben Dario'.

The 20th Century: Magic Realism and Political Commitment

Modern Latin American literature conjures up famous names like the Chilean Isabel Allende, the Argentinean Jorge Luis Borges, the Peruvian Mario Vargas Llosa, the Colombian Gabriel García Márquez, or the Mexican Carlos Fuentes. Yet that peculiarly Latin American form of literature we call Magic Realism was invented almost single-handed by the Guatemalan novelist Miguel Angel Asturias (1899–1974). As a young man in Paris, he assisted in the translation of the *Popol Vuh*, which was to influence all his future writing; wrote his first important book, *Leyendas de Guatemala* (Legends of Guatemala, 1930); and completed his novel *El señor Presidente* (The President). He returned to Guatemala in 1933, to spend a miserable decade struggling with political repression, alcoholism and an unhappy marriage. *El señor Presidente* remained unpublished until 1946.

These experiences found an outlet in his best-known book, *Hombres de maíz* (Men of Maize, 1949). This ambitious novel draws on Maya legend, the theories of Marx and Freud, and the literary techniques of Joyce and Eliot, to give a form and a voice to the traumatized subconscious of Guatemala. Like Dario, Asturias conjures up a 'procession of dreams and shades', testifying to the colonization of the spirit as well as of the land; to the loss of identity and masculine pride; and to the powerlessness to keep a woman or refuse a drink. Ariel Dorfman, the Chilean author of *Death and the Maiden*, has described *Hombres de maíz* as 'both the fountainhead and the backbone of all that is being written in our continent today.' Despite being driven into exile by the 1954 coup, Asturias had recovered his confidence as a writer. Many other novels followed, including his *Banana Trilogy*, which satirizes the activities of the United Fruit Company in Guatemala, and in 1967 he won the Nobel Prize for Literature.

Throughout the 20th century, Central American literature has been closely allied to politics. The Nicaraguan poetic renaissance kindled by Ruben Dario soon turned to political protest in the work of Salomon de la Selva (1893–1958) and the group of poets known as the Vanguard. Inspired by the guerrilla leader Augusto César Sandino, the Vanguard combined poetic avant-gardism with the rhythms of popular songs in a celebration of daily lives and work of the *campesinos* (peasant farmers).

One major figure stands outside this mainstream: Alfonso Cortes (1893–1969), affectionately known as *el poeta loco*. After a mental breakdown in 1927, Cortes inscribed his startling, otherworldly poetry on minute pieces of paper while chained to the wall in the house, which had once belonged to Ruben Dario, where he lived with his sisters.

When the Sandinistas came to power in 1979, it seemed as though the poets had actually become the acknowledged legislators, if not of the world, at least of Nicaragua. The vice-president was novelist Sergio Ramirez (1942–), whose compelling tales of the influence of North American culture on his country, *Stories* and *To Bury our Fathers*, were published by Readers International in 1976 and 1984 respectively. The internationally respected poet Ernesto Cardenal (1925–), a veteran of the Vanguard movement, was minister of culture; their ambassador to Brazil was the poet Ernesto Gutierrez (1929–); even the president, Daniel Ortega, was a published poet.

Among the fine poets who emerged during these years were Giaconda Belli and Vidaluz Meneses. The daughter of a general in Anastasio Somoza's National Guard, Meneses attempted to come to terms with this painful relationship in her poem *Last Postcard for my Father*.

Throughout Central America, writers have continued to publish clandestinely in the face of state repression. Quite a few have been the target of assassination or forced into exile. Some, like Salvadoreans Manlio Argueta (1935–)—the author of *One Day of Life* and *Cuzcatlan*—and Jacinta Escudos (1961–) or the Panamanian Bertalicia Peralta (1939–), have been translated into English. Many others have not. *And We Sold the Rain*, edited by Rosario Santos (Ryan Publishing, 1989), provides a good general introduction for English-speaking readers. This collection of short stories offers a glimpse into the lives of the men, women and children of Central America: Maya Indians, Marxist guerrillas and *campesinos*, living through war and poverty.

An excellent introduction to contemporary Guatemalan issues, as interpreted by the country's writers, poets and artists can be found in *Guatemala: The Right to Dream*, published by The Association of Artists for Guatemala (AAG) c/o Reggie Norton, The Hideaway, Hatford Down, Faringdon, Oxon SN7 8JH.

Music

Central America's natural history is an interesting blend of the immediate north and south, but its musical roots are far more eclectic, combining the rhythms of Africa, native America, the Caribbean, Europe and the US to create a series of unique and energetic hybrids. The entire isthmus is rocked by rhythm, and whether you are in a café, on a bus or walking down the street you'll never be far from the sound of a radio. Central Americans have a passion for music and and a great talent for dance. Their various tastes reflect the region's main historical and cultural divisions. From the steamy dance-floors of Managua to the misty villages of Guatemala, music is a means of communication and self-expression, an essential ingredient in daily life.

Music also played an important role in the region's pre-Columbian cultures, although few details are known. The only surviving instruments are small clay ocarinas which make a high-pitched whistling sound. Nevertheless, archaeologists believe that animal-skin drums, rattles and flutes were all in use and that music enhanced the impact of religious ceremonies, increasing the sense of awe upon which the power of the religious élite depended. It is a theory supported by the murals at the Maya site of Bonampak (on the border between Guatemala and Mexico), which clearly show an assembled orchestra alongside the portrait of a ruler and his assistant.

These ancient traditions feed the music of today's Indian groups, who still use music in their fiestas and religious ceremonies, although these days they have absorbed a wide range of influences. Most Indian bands still include drums, flutes and whistles, but the principal instrument is now the marimba, a long xylophone-type instrument sometimes played by three or four musicians. The marimba features in most Central American styles, favoured by Indian groups and farmers from Guatemala to Costa Rica and sometimes accompanied by guitars and singers. It's a soft, lilting style of music, appropriate enough to the highlands and to local fiestas, but rarely heard in the cities. Meanwhile, in the wilds of Panama they have developed a unique and haunting style called *típica*, in which a wailing woman is accompanied by a furious African drumbeat. To an outsider the music might seem disturbing but local people seem to enjoy it, picking out enough rhythm to dance enthusiastically.

The marimba is, in fact, of African origin, having arrived in Central America via Jamaica and the slave trade, although Central America's black communities, based on the Caribbean coast, have now moved on to the more modern sounds of calypso and reggae. Many of the local bands sing in English, taking their lead from heroes such as Bob Marley. This is most evident in Belize; the local variation is *Brukdown* which is firmly rooted in Creole culture and features the guitar, banjo, accordion and drums. Also popular in Belize is *Punta Rock*, a rhythmical blend of salsa, rock and reggae whose favourite artists include Andy Palacio, Chico Ramos and Santino's Messengers.

Classical music has never really taken off in this part of the world, although the Costa Ricans have strived to introduce high culture to Central American listeners. Back in the 1940s President Figueres declared 'why have tractors without violins?' and Costa Rica now has the only National Youth Symphony in Latin America. It's not a musical style that has spread to the streets but musicians from around the world perform at a series of concerts every year in San Jose's *Teatro Nacional,* undoubtedly the most beautiful theatre on the isthmus.

Back in the world of mestizo popular culture, *salsa* and *merengue* are the great Latin sounds, booming out across the dance-floors from Guatemala to Panamá. A lot of the big hits come up from Brazil, Venezuela and Colombia, while other styles, including traditional *mariachi*, which is sometimes played in the streets, come south from Mexico. Modern rock and pop music from Europe and the US is also extremely popular with the likes of Madonna and Michael Jackson competing for air-time. Songs come and go here as quickly as anywhere else and the pervasive influence of radio ensures that they are widely known. On a typical dance-floor contemporary Latin sounds are mixed evenly with pop and rock.

A Traveller's Guide to Maya Textiles

The astounding diversity and exquisite quality of Maya textiles will be one of the most vivid memories of your trip. Patterns and images appear in infinitely varied shapes and sizes, while materials and colour schemes are chosen according to ancient traditions.

Of course, the costumes you see today are not the same as those the Maya would have worn during pre-Conquest times. Then only the nobility would have owned embroidered and finely woven cotton, with the most elaborate decorations reserved for the headdresses, which were festooned with shimmering feathers, animal skins, coloured ribbons and masks. You can see these on ancient monumental carvings, usually the most striking feature of any ruler's portrait, and almost completely obscuring the head.

Originally only nobles were allowed to wear cotton. The great majority had to wear rough tunics woven from *maguey* (cactus) fibres. Ordinary men would have worn a loincloth

and a square cloak thrown over the shoulder to protect them from the sun or cold. On their feet, they wore leather sandals very similar to those in use today, though modern Maya have added a heel support and some are made entirely of old tyres instead of leather. Women originally wore long tunics with a slit for the head and arms, or a shorter version worn loose over a wrap-around skirt, more like the modern costume.

From very early on, however—at least since 300 BC—weaving was a fine art practised on the same hip-strap looms that women still use all over the Guatemalan highlands. Maguey and cotton were cultivated for this purpose, threads used in their natural browns and whites, but also dyed indigo blue and a whole range of reds and purples with dye from the cochineal insect and the purpura mollusc. Silver and gold thread was also used, although this practice was later banned by the rapacious Spanish.

When exactly ordinary Maya men and women began wearing the colourful costumes you see them in now is still disputed, but the most enduring suggestion is that it was initiated by the Spanish in the 16th century. It was their task to organize and control their subject population and the best way they could keep tabs on people's movements was by forcing them to wear uniforms that indicated which tribe and settlement they came from. Thus each town and village developed its own distinctive costume using a mixture of traditional images and dress codes, as well as imported Spanish fashions.

Naturally styles and designs evolved over the centuries. For example, Maya women began tucking their shirts (*huipiles*) into their wrap-around skirts (*cortes*) after the 18th-century Spanish fashion of tailored bodices appeared. The bolero-style jackets worn by men in Sololá, and the knee-length breeches worn in Chichicastenango recall 19th-century European style, while the long woollen tunic still worn by some men in San Juan Atitán was probably inspired by the cassocks of Spanish monks. (Incidentally, wool was unknown in Guatemala before the Spanish imported sheep. Yet now the woollen blankets of Momostenango are highly treasured throughout the land, as well as by tourists.)

In this century, with the introduction of inexpensive man-made fibres and cheap clothing factories, Mayan styles and use of materials have changed dramatically, and often cheaper, western dress is substituted for traditional costume. Even in remote villages, such as Nebaj, where tradition is strong, you will find the women's skirts are made from cloth

imported from Germany. This tendency is more a
concession to dire economic circumstances than a
rejection of their heritage. But there are also more
sinister reasons for abandoning traditional dress, namely
discrimination by the country's *ladino* culture. Sadly, this is
why you will very rarely see Maya men in traditional
clothing. Only the very old or those who have little or no
contact with the outside world still wear their customary
dress, with a few notable exceptions. The men and boys
of Todos Santos, for example, never wear anything
except traditional clothing, their red and white stripy
trousers and elaborately embroidered shirts marking them
out wherever they go. Others will usually wear their traditional
trousers as long as they are in or around their own village. The
men of Sololá, Nahualá, San Antonio Palopó, Santa Catarina Palopó,
and San Juan Atitán belong to this group.

The best chance the visitor has of seeing men in their finery, however, is during traditional
festivals, when the local religious brotherhoods (*cofradías*) hold their processions and
everyone turns out in their best costume. One of the finest of these is the Santo Tomás
festival in Chichicastenango; the men wear very smart woollen breeches and jackets and
head scarfs beautifully embroidered in floral designs of gold, orange and green.

The patron saint of weaving is the Moon Goddess, Ixchel, and many images in Maya
weaving are from the traditional religious pantheon. For example, a tiny bird on a tobacco
plant recalls the story of the Sun God turning himself into a humming-bird to court the
Moon Goddess. Stylized monkeys, bats, deer, jaguar and eagles are also popular figures
from mythology, while other images are taken from everyday life, such as corn, tobacco,
fish, birds, and other plants and animals; the all important sun and moon also feature
strongly. Some images, such as horses, peacocks and chickens date from the post-
Conquest era and were not originally seen in Maya art.

The most widely used patterns are geometric: chevrons, triangles, diamonds, squares, dots
and zig-zag lines detailed with extraordinary invention and in unique Maya style. Usually
decorative patterns are woven into the material, but they can also be embroidered on.
Sometimes the design is so intricate that a tapestry is formed, totally obscuring the cloth
beneath and making it very heavy to wear. In another technique, seen in the village of
Chajul, single, large geometric shapes are sewn onto a plain red background.

The materials used are a mixture of traditional and modern, ranging from locally produced
cotton, wool and maguey, to acrylic, silk, and metallic thread. Increasingly, machine-
woven cloth is also being used, which seems a shame to outsiders, but which is part of an
inevitable process. The beautiful striped bedspreads you find in many markets, however,
are woven by men on large foot looms, the first of which were imported by the Spanish in
the 17th century. Great bands are woven and stored on rollers, to be cut and sewn
together to the required size.

Even the pseudo-traditional weaving passed off on some tourists is often beautiful, and will no doubt one day be considered just as worthy as the genuine article. For those who want to learn the difference, an ideal starting point is the **Ixchel Museum** in Guatemala City, where you will not only see some of the finest historic examples of Maya textile art, but also learn more about traditional weaving methods and which costumes are indigenous to which town or village.

Guatemala City

Guatemala City is unlikely to win your heart. A polluted urban sprawl, it is home to 2 million people—nearly a quarter of Guatemala's population. It is a city which has both benefited and suffered from rapid industrial and commercial growth, where modern technology and the imported 'American dream' are in stark contrast to the poverty faced by many of the struggling workers and unemployed.

There is little reason to spend much time in Guate, as it is known to the locals. The fact that foreigners soon dub it 'Grotty' gives you a good indication as to why. For most travellers it is simply a point of arrival or departure: those in the know head straight to the charming colonial city of Antigua, only an hour away by shuttle bus.

That said, Guatemala City does have a few museums, churches and other sights of interest, including the colourful chaos of the Mercado Central. For some people, however, it is worth visiting purely for the insight it provides into the harsh urban reality faced by a significant percentage of the population, many of whom have been forced to abandon the countryside in search of work. The unemployed and street children roam the city, resorting to begging, prostitution and petty crime in their desperation. Armed guards are a common sight—even McDonalds has security.

The city is essentially divided into two parts. The old part of the city is in the northern half: here you will find Zona 1, where mid- to low-budget hotels, restaurants and shops are chock-a-block, and the main streets are teeming with traders under the neon glare of fast food joints and cinemas. The southern half of the city, by contrast, is modern and more spacious. The wealthy residential districts dominate Zonas 9 and 10, with the city's most exclusive hotels, restaurants, bars and boutiques in the *zona viva*. The south is also the main focus for trade and transport: here you will find the airport (Zona 13) and main bus terminal (Zona 4).

History

Guatemala City was founded in 1776, after the country's previous capital, Antigua, had been destroyed by an earthquake. In spite of the desolation and disease which racked Antigua, many survivors had no desire to up and leave. The ecclesiastical and government bodies were loath to start a city from scratch, while the townfolk and Indian peasants had nothing to gain by moving away. However, the government made it compulsory to move, and so the country's new capital was reluctantly filled. Slowly, a new city was built, designed on the standard Spanish colonial grid system, which has gradually spread out to cover the entire plateau the city is perched on. Today its edges teeter on the brink of dusty ravines that cut the sandy earth like giant wrinkles. As the shanty towns grow, even these steep gashes are being filled, rubbish and shacks clinging desperately to the sides.

Guatemala City has always been a visually monotonous place. The threat of earthquakes means that most buildings are squat and no higher than a few storeys, though 20th-century technology has allowed some skyscrapers to raise their glassy shoots. Most architecture dates from this century, since Guatemala City has not been spared any more than its predecessors: the massive quakes in 1917 and 1976 have ensured that little remains from earlier centuries. What you find is a modern city with the occasional old church or municipal building, the finest of which is the cathedral on the central square.

Getting There and Away
By Air

There are regular flights to and from the following Central American and Caribbean cities: San Salvador, Tegucigalpa, Mexico City, Belize City, Managua, San José, Panamá and San Andrés. Most flights from South America are via Panamá/San José. There are no direct flights from Peru or Ecuador. Note that there is a US$10 departure tax (payable in dollars or local currency) for all international flights. Some aircraft, especially those coming from Belize via the Petén jungle, land at the city's domestic airport, which is in a distant corner of the Aurora complex but even closer to the hotels of zones 9 and 10. There is no special arrivals or departure hall here, but a handful of taxis usually meet incoming flights. *See* p.192 for flights on to Flores (for Tikal).

airlines

Aerovías, International Airport, 2nd floor, ✆ 3347935

American Airlines, Hotel El Dorado, 7 Avenida 15-54, Zona 9, ✆ 3377187, 📠 3346940

Aviateca, Domestic Airport, Avenida Hincapié 12-22, Zona 13, ✆ 3317450, 📠 3317401. Also in the Hotel Camino Real and at 10 Calle 6-39, Zona 1, ✆ 2511791.

British Airways, 1 Avenida 10-81, Zona 10, 6th floor of Edificio Inexa, ✆ 3327402, 📠 3327401

Continental, International Airport, ✆ 3312051, 📠 3312055

Copa, 1 Avenida 10–17, Zona 10, ✆ 3611567

Delta Airlines, 15 Calle 3–20, Zona 10, ✆ 3370642, 📠 3370588

Iberia, Avenida La Reforma 8-60, Edificio Galerías Reforma, office no.204, Zona 9, ✆ 3320911, 📠 3343715

Jungle Flying, Domestic Airport, Hangar 21, Avenida Hincapié and 18 Calle, Zona 13, ✆ 3604917-20, 📠 3314995

KLM, 6 Avenida 20-25, Zona 10, Edificio Plaza Marítima, ✆ 3370222, 📠 3370227

Lacsa, 7 Avenida 14-44, Zona 9, Edificio La Galería, office no.3 and 4, ✆ 3310906, 📠 3312284

Mexicana, 13 Calle 8-44, Zona 10, Edificio Edyma, office no.104, ✆ 3336001, 📠 3336096

Taca, 7 Avenida 14-35, Zona 9, ✆ 3322360, 📠 3342575

Tapsa, Domestic Airport, Avenida Hincapié and 18 Calle, Zona 13, ✆ 3314860,
📧 3345572. Also at the International Airport, 2nd floor.

Tikal Jet, Domestic Airport, Hangar 8, Avenida Hincapié and 18 Calle, Zona 13,
✆ 3345631, 📧 3345631

By Bus

Tica Bus is the only trans-Central American bus company with daily connections
between all Central American countries except Belize and Mexico. Daily arrivals
and departures take place outside their office, 11 Calle 2-56, Zona 9, ✆ 3611773
(*open Mon–Sat 8am–4pm; Sun 8am–2pm*).

The main bus terminal for **local buses** is in Zona 4, where you will find second-
class buses going to almost all parts of the country, as well as nearby places, such
as Lake Amatitlán. These buses are normally in good repair, though they do get
very crowded and the seats are tight. It is best to turn up in the mornings for long-
distance journeys. If arriving here for the first time from outside the capital, allow
yourself to be guided to the nearest taxi, agree on a price of no more than US$5–6,
and get away from the chaos. (If intending to reach the terminal by municipal bus
from zones 1, 4, 9 or 10, just take the first one that has a sign in the window
saying 'terminal' and double check with the driver.)

Zona 1 bus terminal is on a square, on the corner of 18 Calle and 9 Avenida.
Here you will find 2nd-class buses and pullman-style buses arriving and leaving for
destinations in the Eastern Highlands and the Atlantic coast. All tickets, except
those for long-distance pullman buses, can be bought on the bus. (You can travel
on the pullmans without buying a ticket first, but, because seats are booked, you
will most likely have to stand for the whole journey.)

If you are heading for Antigua, one hour away, you will find buses leaving every
half an hour (5am–8pm coming from Guatemala City, but 5–5 coming from
Antigua), from the junction of 18 Calle and 4 Avenida in Zona 1.

There are also a number of **private**, air-conditioned shuttle-bus companies operating between the capital and major tourist destinations in Guatemala. All will
deposit and collect you from your hotel or guest house and charge you about ten
times the price of local buses, which works out at anything between US$10 and
US$25 for a one-way ticket. The best for routes between the capital and the
Caribbean coast and Petén jungle is **Izabal Adventure Tours**, 12 Calle B 36–91,
Zona 5, ✆/📧 3350244. For the Western Highlands you will find leaflets adver-
tising the latest offers at your hotel or guest house. If not, the tourist office will be
able to advise you.

bus companies

The following **pullman** companies are recommended; more comfortable than the
second-class buses, but much cheaper than any tourist shuttle. Please note that the

journey times are approximate, and it is a good idea to check out the timetable the day before you wish to travel. Buses leave from outside the company offices:

To **Cobán** or the **Quetzal Reserve**: Escobar/Monja Blanca, 8 Avenida 15-16, Zona1, ☏ 2511878. Daily services 4am–5pm; the journey to Cobán takes 4hrs, to the reserve 3hrs.

To **Esquipulas**: Rutas Orientales,19 Calle 8-18, Zona 1, ☏ 2536714. Daily services every half hour, 4am–6pm; the journey takes 3hrs.

To **Flores** (for Tikal): Fuentes del Norte, 17 Calle 8-46, Zona 1, ☏ 2513819. Daily frequent services 3am–9pm, officially a 12hr journey, but normally nearer 24. Reservations are essential. Also Maya Express, 17 Calle 9-36, Zona 1, ☏ 23 21914. Daily services 4pm, 6pm and 8pm. Reservations essential.

To **Huehuetenango**: the best company is Transportes Velásquez, 20 Calle 2-43, Zona 3, ☏ 4726005 (office at new bus terminal in Huehuetenango). Departures daily 5.20am–5.30pm.

To **Puerto Barrios**: Litegua,15 Calle 10-42, Zona 1, ☏ 2538169. Daily frequent services 7am–3pm; the journey takes 6hrs. Their best pullman service, which should be non-stop, leaves for the coast at 10am and 5pm daily.

To **Panajachel**: Rebuli, 21 Calle 1-34, Zona 1, ☏ 2513521. Daily services every hour, 6.30am–4pm; the journey takes 3hrs.

To **Quezaltenango**: Lineas Américas, 2 Avenida 18-74, Zona 1. Avoid the Galgos bus company, which has virtually derelict buses and irresponsible drivers; journey takes 4hrs.

To **San Salvador** (El Salvador): Melva Internacional, 3 Avenida 1-38, Zona 9, ☏ 310874. Buses depart daily every hour 5.30am–4.30pm; the journey takes 5hrs. The Salvadorean borders are open daily, 6am–8pm. Or take the Tica Bus mentioned above.

To **El Florido** (for the Copán Ruins in Honduras): Rutas Orientales,19 Calle 8-18, Zona 1, ☏ 2536714. Buses depart daily, every half hour, 4am–6pm; the journey takes 4hrs as far as Chiquimula. There you must change buses for El Florido, taking a Vilma bus, which leaves from the back of the market. Last bus from either Chiquimula or the border leaves at 4.30pm and takes around 2hrs. From the border, a Honduran minibus will take you to the town of Copán Ruinas in 40mins. The Honduran borders are open daily, 6am–6pm.

To **La Mesilla** (for Mexico): five direct buses are offered by Transportes Velásquez (see Huehuetenango above), departing from the capital at 5.30, 8.30, 9.30, 10.30 and 11.30am.

There are also bus routes to the Mexican border towns of **Talismán** and **Tecún Umán**, run by Fortaleza, 19 Calle 8-70, Zona 1, ☏ 2323643. The Mexican borders are open daily, 6am–6pm.

By bus: There are **municipal buses** (*buses urbanos*) running to all parts of the city from around 6am until 8pm. Fares are ridiculously cheap, so it is always worth having small change in your pocket to save you having to bring out high denomination notes in public. Unfortunately, there is no such thing as a bus timetable or even a brochure outlining which bus goes where. The whole system changes constantly, and nobody can claim to know its logic or routes. The good news is that there are probably only four buses you will want to use; remember always to confirm with the driver that he is going where you want to go.

Bus no.5 not only connects the Zona 13 airport to Zona 1, but also connects the centre with the city's most important complex of state-run museums. If you are coming from the airport, you want to make sure the bus says 'Parque Central' in the window. Another bus connecting Zona 1 with the airport is **no.100**, which is usually orange.

If coming from Zona 1, the best place to catch this and the other buses, is beneath the hilltop Teatro Nacional, which is on the continuation of 6 Avenida, beyond 18 Calle. The **no.5** is normally dark green, and if it is going to the airport it should say 'Aeropuerto' in the window. It will also take you to the cluster of the Museo Nacional de Arqueología y Etnología, the Museo Nacional de Arte Moderno and the Museo de Historia Natural, all next door to each other. Best ask to be dropped off here, otherwise you are likely to miss it first time.

Bus no.2 is also normally a green colour, and stops at the same place underneath the Teatro Nacional. This one will take you from Zona 1 to Zonas 9 and 10, travelling along Avenida la Reforma, the main dual carriageway through the southern quarters of the city. (Any bus with the word 'Reforma' in the window should have the same destination, but always ask the driver.) Returning from Zonas 9 and 10, the bus drops you off just past the city's **tourist office**, Inguat, one street east of the Teatro Nacional. If you are heading further into the centre of Zona 1, stay on the bus and it will most likely take you all the way to the Parque Central. Any bus stopping at the Teatro Nacional which says 'Terminal' in the front window, will take you to the city's main bus terminal in Zona 4.

Bus no.65 connects Zona 1 with the domestic airport, travelling south along 6 Avenida once in Zona 9, which you can easily walk to from Avenida La Reforma. South of the Parque Independencia, the bus will travel along Avenida Las Américas, parallel with Avenida Hincapié, and you need to ask the driver to drop you at the corner of 18 Calle to bring you level with the airport entrance, a short walk away on Avenida Hincapié—you can recognize the turning for 18 Calle by the large sculpture dedicated to Christopher Columbus (Cristobal Colón in Spanish), situated on the central grassy verge of Avenida Las Américas.

By taxi: Taxis can be flagged down anywhere, but there are two regular stands worth knowing about, both in Zona 1: on the **Parque Concordia** and the **Parque**

Central. There are also always taxis at the airport and around the bus terminals. If in Zonas 9 or 10 a convenient taxi rank is situated on the corner of Avenida La Reforma and 14 Calle, outside the Hotel Camino Real. Always agree a price before getting into the car, as there are no meters. If you cannot face the buses, and do not wish to hire a car, you can use taxis for journeys as far as Antigua. You should not pay more than US$25 one way for the journey to Antigua, while inner-city journeys should never come to more than US$5-US$6 for a long run.

Tourist Information

Instituto Guatemalteco de Turismo, **Inguat**, Centro Cívico, 7 Avenida 1-17, Zona 4, ✆ 3313075, ✉ 3314416 (*open Mon–Fri, 8.30–4.30; Sat 8.30–1*). The very helpful staff speak English and can offer a limited range of brochures and listings, make hotel bookings and assist in route planning around Guatemala.

The **immigration office** (*open Mon–Fri, 8–4*) is at 41 Calle 17–36, Zona 8.

In a **medical emergency**, contact your embassy for a list of doctors who speak your language and best hospitals, or visit the private Centro Medico, 6 Avenida 3-47, Zona 10. The **police** occupy a large building on 6 Avenida and 14 Calle, Zona 1; emergency ✆ 120.

The main **post office** is on 7 Avenida and 12 Calle, Zona 1 (*open Mon-Fri 7.30am–6.30pm*). International **telegrams** can be sent from the Guatel office at 8 Avenida and 12 Calle, Zona 1 (*open daily 7am–midnight*), or any other Guatel office.

Apart from the banks and exchange offices, there is a **daily exchange service** at the airport (*open weekdays 7.30am–6.30pm; weekends 8am–11am and 3pm–6pm*). Shop around for the best rates from the local **banks** or, if you prefer, use Lloyds Bank, 6 Avenida 9-51, Zona 9, ✆ 3327580. Cash advances on Access or Mastercard can be had at Banco Credomatic, 7 Avenida 6-26, Zona 1 (*open Mon–Fri, 8am–7pm; Sat 9–1pm*), next to the entrance of the Europa Bar. The American Express office is at Banco del Café, Avenida La Reforma 9-00, Zona 9, ✆ 3340040. The **black market exchange** operates on the streets around the central post office, in Zona 1. Best to use cash only, and get them to hand over the money before you give them yours. Remember that the exchange rate here is always negotiable and should at least match the bank's. You can also change dollars at the receptions of large hotels.

The Instituto Geográfico Militar, Avenida Las Américas 5-76, Zona 13 (*open Mon–Fri, 7.30am–4pm*) is the best place to look at or buy detailed **maps** of the country. Bring your passport and expect to pay around US$6 per map. For **car hire** *see* p.5.

The best in the capital to do your **laundry** is the Lavandería Obelisco at the most southerly end of the Avenida La Reforma, next to the Samaritana supermarket: Avenida La Reforma 16-30 (*open Mon–Fri, 8–6.45; Sat 8–5.30*), where you can wash and dry a full load for around US$3, or leave it for a service wash for a little more.

Clark Tours has representatives in the Camino Real Hotel, 14 Calle and Avenida La Reforma, Zona 10, ✆ 3682056, 🖷 3374313.

Discovery Tours, Edificio Plaza del Sol 211, 12 Calle 2-04, Zona 9, ✆ 3310213, 🖷 3315919

Maya Expeditions, Edificio Tauro 104, 15 Calle 1-91, Zona 10, ✆/🖷 3374666

Mesoamerica Explorers, Edificio La Cúpula, 7 Avenida 13-01, Zona 9, ✆/🖷 3325045

Panamundo, Guatemala Travel Service, 3 Avenida 16-52, Zona 10, ✆ 3683010, 🖷 3681315

STP Tours, 2 Avenida 7-78, Zona 10, ✆ 3346235, 🖷 3346237

Tropical Tours, 4 Calle 2-51, Zona 10, ✆ 3393662, 🖷 3323748

If you have more money than time, you should consider using the excellent services of **Jungle Flying** (*see* 'Airlines'), whose speciality is day-trips to the ruins of Copán (Honduras), but they will also fly to the ruins of Quiriguá, Caracol (Belize), Tikal, Ceibal, Yaxchilán (Mexico), Zaculeu or Palenque (Mexico).

Around the City

Guatemala City is not that large, but because it is on a grid of numbered streets, it can be a confusing place at first. The city is divided into zones, and the system for numbering avenidas and calles is repeated in each zone so that the same number of avenida can be in very different parts of the city, and very different kinds of neighbourhood. Consequently you must first find the right zone before you look for the right street. Occasionally street signs are missing, but if you always keep counting as you walk, you will have a rough idea where you are. *See* p.26 for an explanation of Guatemalan addresses, under Tourist Information.

Zona 1: the Centre

Zona 1 is an oblong box of streets defined by the Parque Central to the north, 18 Calle to the south, Avenida Elena to the west, and the railway track to the east. It takes about half an hour to walk its length, so even if you do get lost, it will not take long to find a familiar spot. The main arteries of commerce are Avenidas 5, 6 and 7, as well as 18 Calle.

The hub of the city's life, this zone has everything from seedy bars and strip joints near 18 Calle and 9 Avenida, to shops and stalls, cinemas and hotels, to street performers and shoeshine boys around the Parque Concordia on 6 Avenida and 15 Calle; and finally there is some interesting architecture, not only the Palacio Nacional and cathedral, but also the churches of San Francisco and Santa Clara on 6 Avenida.

Heading up 6 Avenida, you come to the courtyard of **San Francisco** church on the junction with 13 Calle. It is not a large building, yet the chunky colonial Baroque columns of the entrance are attractive, and as you pass the wrought-iron gates you find yourself in a peaceful gloom. The most famous sculpture here is the 'Sacred Heart', which was brought from Antigua. Across 13 Calle, the church of **Santa Clara** is even smaller and more unas-suming, a quiet haven for tired beggars, not often visited by anyone else. Other churches in Zona 1 worth visiting include **La Merced** (11 Avenida and 5 Calle), which has a very fine interior brought from ruined Antiguan churches—note especially the organ, pulpit and altars—and the **Santuario Expiatorio** (26 Calle and 2 Avenida), which is extraordi-nary for its exterior, shaped like a fish, as well as for the modern mural on the inside.

As you reach the **Parque Central**, you get a refreshing sense of space after the claustro-phobic streets behind you. It is not particularly attractive: a large expanse of concrete surrounded by the washed-out colours of modern buildings to the west and older architec-ture to the east. The most important modern building is the **Biblioteca Nacional**, which is situated behind the bandstand and shrub terraces, known as the **Parque del Centenario**, though there is little to separate it from the rest of the main square except a road. Directly opposite is the **cathedral**, its brown façade still valiantly standing despite the cracks. The interior is all whitewashed pillars and dour Passion paintings, though there is a certain Baroque elegance about the place, and hundreds of flickering candles before the altars create a festive atmosphere.

At a right angle to the cathedral stands the **Palacio Nacional**, which suffers from being the pale green of mouldy bread, but is otherwise inoffensive neo-colonial. It was begun by President Ubico in 1939, and completed just in time for his enforced removal from office, in 1944. If you bring your passport, you can enter the palace up the left-hand flight of steps, to find two elegant fountained courtyards, lined by three storeys of balconies. Surprisingly, you can wander about freely, and may just bump into a cavalcade of impor-tant generals or ministers in starched uniforms and dark glasses. On the first floor, facing the street, you may be allowed to take a peep into the reception rooms, with their chande-liers and parquet floors. The stained-glass windows remain shattered from the last bomb attack a few years ago.

Worth visiting while you are up this end of town is the **Mercado Central**, in a concrete bunker immediately behind the cathedral. The lowest levels, which are underground, hold the food market and many *comedores*, where you can eat freshly cooked, local food. The higher level holds the craft market, where you will find excellent examples of Indian costumes from every corner of the country. There are textiles, basketry, leatherware, jewellery, clothes, shoes, trinkets and tat—almost anything you can get in Guatemala's markets can be bought here. Naturally prices are slightly higher than elsewhere, but they are still very reasonable. It would be a shame to buy here when you first arrive, since you would get no sense of the places and people that make these lovely things. But it will whet your appetite for things to come, and if there is anything you wish you had bought before you leave, you can pop back here and buy it then. On Sundays there is also an open market on the Parque Central itself.

Heading south along 6 or 5 Avenida, you will eventually come to Zona 1's best square: the **Parque Concordia**. Slightly elevated above the black air of the streets, a tree-lined prom-enade surrounds a small patch of greenery and a central fountain, where instant photo men, shoeshine boys, preachers, hustlers and street performers vie for your attention. The best time to be here is at the weekends, when you can do some good people-watching or check out the market stalls that cluster alongside. Just a block away, on the corner of 7 Avenida and 12 Calle, the grand, pink, Moorish building is the **Central Post Office**; the **Guatel office** for international calls is next door.

Finally, there are two undistinguished museums you can visit in Zona 1: the **Museo de Arte e Industria**, 10 Avenida 10-72 (*open Tues–Fri, 9–4; Sat–Sun, 9–noon and 2–4; adm*) and the **Museo Nacional de Historia**, 9 Calle and 10 Avenida (*open Tues–Fri, 8.30–4; Sat–Sun, 9–noon and 2–4; adm free*).

Zona 4

18 Calle marks the border of Zonas 1 and 4, where the scene is immediately a mess of dual carriageways, flyovers, and lung-choking traffic easing its way around the elevated fortress of the **Teatro Nacional** on one side, the large indoor food market in the middle, and, on the other side, the highrise buildings of the **Centro Cívico**, which holds the tourist office and various government offices.

There are three places you will want to locate here: firstly, the extension of 4 Avenida past 18 Calle, where the Antigua buses leave; secondly the urban bus stop at the foot of the National Theatre; and thirdly, the **tourist office**, whose entrance is just past the elevated walkway crossing the continuation of 7 Avenida, on the left-hand side. Otherwise you may enjoy exploring the **food market** and hardening your sensibilities with the sights and smells of rotting vegetables and unprettified animal anatomy. Be warned that pickpockets are a constant hazard here, so take nothing with you. Further into the depths of Zona 4, the main bus terminal is best reached by bus or taxi, as there is no particular pleasure to exploring this part of town.

Lastly, and probably least, if you continue past the tourist office on 7 Avenida and turn left on Ruta 6, you will find the **Iglesia Yurrita**. Unfortunately it is closed most days, but the exterior is memorable enough, and surely deserves a prize for bad taste. It was built in 1928, with private funds, to look like a Russian Orthodox church, and is a higgledy-piggledy of mosaics and onion-domed towers, with a bit of Gothic pointiness added for good measure.

Zonas 9 and 10

This is one indistinguishable large area cut down the middle by the spacious Avenida La Reforma, with Zona 9 to the west and Zona 10 to the east. It is a relatively new part of the city and is the favoured home of the capital's wealthier residents, as well as its exclusive shops, restaurants, clubs and hotels. Most of the city's embassies are located around here too, as are some fine private museums.

As you leave Zona 4, the first point of interest on the Avenida La Reforma is the **Jardín Botánico y Museo de Historia Natural** (*open 8–noon and 2–6; closed Sat, Sun and national holidays; adm free*). The best part of this place is the botanical garden, which is small but attractive, while the museum is small and bedraggled; neglected stuffed animals contrast sadly with the living garden outside. Across the road is a slate-grey turreted wall, which encloses a whole block and hides a military training school.

The Avenida La Reforma is a couple of kilometres long, so hop on and off the frequent buses at points of interest. Just off the Avenida La Reforma on 6 Calle Final, you will find the city's best private museum: the **Museo Ixchel**, 6 Calle Final, Zona 10 (*open Mon–Fri, 8–4.50; Sat 9–12.50pm; adm US$2*), housed in the 'cultural complex' of the University Francisco Marroquin. You can't miss it, as the new, purpose-built construction is shaped like a Mayan temple. The spacious interior is designed in such a way that you ascend to the upper floor on a walkway, passing the first major exhibit, a collection of paintings by the indigenous artist Andres Curruchich (1891–1969). He was the first folk painter of Comalapa, a village still famous for its artists and, along with Juan Sisay of Santiago Atitlán, established the 20th-century era of Maya art. He painted mostly domestic scenes, along with images from market days, the slaughter of pigs and religious ceremonies. The pictures give a fine introduction to present-day life in rural Guatemala.

On the second floor you can watch a video about Indian village life, while adjoining rooms contain a number of fascinating displays. The first display features Maya textiles and traditional costume; each figure is set in proper context with helpful texts explaining how the materials are made and where they originate. There are historical annotations on weaving and dyeing: you learn what type of materials have been used down the ages and see displays of the various looms used to prepare them.

The second exhibition recreates a market scene on beautiful Lake Atitlán, where some of the most colourful Maya costumes are worn to this day, with information about the different tribal and linguistic groups that have traditionally lived in this region. Finally, you will find the paintings of Carmen de Pettersen, who spent most of her career painting minutely detailed portraits of people in Maya costume, including depictions of male costume, which is particularly interesting because men have now virtually abandoned their traditional clothes. Good quality samples of Maya weaving and costume can be found in the excellent museum shop, whose prices are surprisingly fair.

If you are interested in Maya sculpture and pottery, a museum you will want to see is the **Museo Popol Vuh** (*open Mon–Sat, 9–5.30; adm US$1*). It has recently been relocated just across from the Museo Ixchel in the Unversity Francisco Marroquin cultural complex.

The main exhibit is a collection of Maya funerary vases, ranging from enormous urns the size of beer barrels, to miniature household ones. The museum has few explanatory notices, making it hard for the layman to appreciate the significance of what is on view. Still, the delicate craftsmanship is obvious, and as beautiful now as it was two thousand or so years ago. Additionally, there is a small collection of colonial religious art and icons, as well as many stone carvings from Maya sites in the Petén jungle and the Pacific lowlands. A tiny, well-stocked bookshop is attached, where you will find excellent publications on many Guatemalan subjects. Access to the bookstore only is free.

Travelling southwards on Avenida La Reforma, you will find the most exclusive quarter of Guatemala City—called the **zona viva**—beginning east of the Reforma, between Calles 10 and 14, and extending up to 4 Avenida. There is really nothing much to set it apart from the other streets, except that the huge number of luxury boutiques, hotels and restaurants bunched together. For relaxed eating and drinking on all budgets, though, this is the place to head at any time of day (*see* p.74).

The end of Avenida La Reforma, and Zonas 9 and 10, is marked by the large busy round-about called **Parque Independencia**, beyond which the road becomes the Avenida Las Américas, heading into Zonas 13 and 14, ever more exclusive and residential, until it ends up at the **Plaza Berlín**. This is more or less where the city comes to an end, and if it wasn't for recent building and the smog, you could see Lake Amatitlán directly to the south, and the rumbling Pacaya volcano beyond.

State Museums in Aurora Park

On the western edge of **Aurora Park**, which is a vast expanse accommodating the airport, a military base, the national hippodrome, a zoological park (depressing and filthy), and an artisan market (tourist trap), there is also a cluster of three state-run museums. The whole complex of Aurora Park is located just southwest of Zona 9, and is best reached on bus no.5 from the city centre.

The **Museo Nacional de Arqueología y Etnología** (*open Tues–Fri, 9–4; Sat–Sun, 9–noon and 2–4; adm*) is without doubt the best state museum in the country. This is the place to introduce the uninitiated to Maya history and art. Rooms are laid out in chrono-logical order, starting with an assortment of theories on the original population of the Americas, moving swiftly on to the emergence of Maya culture, to pottery, tools, and decorative art from each era. Archaeologists have established three phases for Maya cultural history, and as we encounter each one, we see the increased sophistication in art, pottery and sculpture. Major sites, such as the jungle city of Tikal, coastal Quiriguá and highland Utatlán, are rebuilt in miniature, giving the visitor an idea of what these places once looked like. One room (*closed at weekends*) is wholly dedicated to Maya jade arte-facts and jewellery, including the famous mosaic mask from Tikal. Also on view is a collection of Indian costumes, craftwork and utensils from various parts of the country. As you head for the exit, you pass a pleasant circular patio with a fountain in the middle, where ancient stelae stand tall and enigmatic. They are large stones and sculptured slabs, covered in Maya hieroglyphs, still only partly deciphered.

The **Museo de Arte Moderno** (*same opening times; adm free*) is opposite, and well worth a quick visit; although the museum is small, its collection includes a good variety of Guatemalan painters and styles. The earliest paintings are from the 19th century, begin-ning with a rather distasteful anonymous picture of Mary, her heart stuck full of daggers. The exhibition quickly moves on into the 20th century; a couple of artists are particularly memorable. Roberto Ossaye died very young and painted most of his pictures in his twen-ties, which makes his breadth of technique and use of materials all the more impressive. Rolando Ixquiac Xicara has only three of his works on display, but they are enough to show his haunting talent. Finally there are about twenty sculptures in metal, stone and wood. One of the best, an odd assemblage of female torsos and other anatomy, boxed in compartments, is by Roberto Cabrera.

The **Museo Nacional de Historia Natural** (*same opening times; adm free*), just around the corner from the other two, is not worth visiting. Almost none of its glass boxes of flora, fauna and Palaeolithic collections originate in Guatemala, or even Central America.

Parque Minerva and Kaminaljuyú

If you would like a graphic idea of Guatemala's geography, then why not head out to the Parque Minerva, where you will find a giant relief map of the country. It must be said, however, that this is no beauty spot, and the horizontal and vertical scales differ considerably. To get there, take bus no.1, which runs along 5 Avenida in Zona 1.

Kaminaljuyú, today engulfed by one of the capital's western suburbs, was formerly an important Maya city. In fact, it was once the largest city in the country's highlands, with a sophisticated level of art and writing as early as 400 BC. In later centuries, the city is believed to have had close links with the great city state of Teotihuacan, and declined around the same period that city did, soon after AD 600. The archaeological remains of Kaminaljuyú have only been partly excavated, and the present-day visitor unfortunately gets little sense of the site's scale or importance because what you see is mainly mounds of overgrown earth. The site is open daily from 8am to 6pm, and can be reached by taking bus no.17, which runs along 4 Avenida in Zona 1.

Shopping

The **central market** behind the cathedral has an entire floor of native textiles and crafts. **La Placita** by Guadalupe Church at 5 Avenida and 18 Calle is recommended; **4 Ahau**, 11 Calle 4-53, Zona 1, is good for textiles and crafts; and **Pasaje Rubio**, 9 Calle, near 6 Avenida, Zona 1, has antique silver trinkets and coins.

In Zona 9, the best street for souvenirs is 14 Calle, where you will also find **Sombol**, which makes quality clothing using traditional materials and patterns.

The best bookshop in the capital is **Librería del Pensativo**, 7 Avenida and 13 Calle, Edificio La Cúpula, Zona 9 (*open Mon–Fri, 10am–7pm; Sat 10–1.30pm*). English literature can also be bought at **Arnel**, in the Edificio El Centro, 9 Calle and 8 Avenida, Zona 1. International newspapers and magazines (American usually) are found at the exclusive hotels in Zonas 9 and 10.

Where to Stay

The full range, from sleazy to first class, can be found in Zona 1. If you prefer to stay away from the city centre, or require a luxury hotel, then your choice will most likely be in Zonas 9 and 10. Note that it is almost impossible to get a room for the price of a single, especially in the budget range, even if such prices are listed at your choice of accommodation. If staying more than three nights, however, you should certainly try to bargain for a lower price, whether you're travelling alone or in a group. Note also that the top-range hotels usually add tax to your bill.

El Conquistador, Vía 5, 4-68, Zona 4, ✆ 3312222, ✉ 3347245, is conveniently located, but surrounded by noisy roads. **Cortijo Reforma**, Avenida La Reforma, 2-18, Zona 9, ✆ 3322713, ✉ 3318876, offers better quality in a more pleasant location than the nearby El Conquistador—at a cheaper rate. **Hotel Princess Reforma**, 13 Calle 7-65, Zona 9, ✆ 3344545, ✉ 3344546, is an excellent small hotel, with good service and cosy rooms. **Camino Real**, 14 Calle and Avenida La Reforma, Zona 10, ✆ 3334633, ✉ 3374313, is the capital's most favoured exclusive hotel, matching the highest international standards, in a region of the city which is much quieter, less polluted and also safer. Prices are at the top end of the scale, plus tax. **Hotel El Dorado**, 7 Avenida 15-45, Zona 10, ✆ 3317777, ✉ 3321877, rivals the Camino Real in every way, and charges the same prices. **Fiesta**, 1 Avenida 13-22, Zona 9, ✆ 3322555, ✉ 3322569, is near the *zona viva*; a good hotel at the lower end of this price range.

Hotel Stofella, 2 Avenida 12-28, Zona 10, ✆ 3346191, ✉ 3310823, is a pristine businessman's hotel, though the rooms are rather gloomy due to bad lighting. **Crowne Plaza Las Américas**, Avenida Las Americas 9-08, Zona 13, ✆ 3390676, ✉ 3390690. South of Zonas 9 and 10, the city's newest luxury hotel gleams with white marble and the latest in hotel services, but it's a little out of the way; you'll need to take a taxi to the *zona viva*.

Pan American, 9 Calle 5-63, Zona 1, ✆ 2326807–9, ✉ 2326402, is the best hotel in the city centre. Run by friendly staff, it has traditional Guatemalan décor, and the standard of the rooms and restaurant is very good. **Ritz**, 6 Avenida A 10-13, Zona 1, ✆ 2512115, ✉ 2324659, is a modern hotel of international standard, conveniently located, but nothing special. **Posada Belén**, 13 Calle A 10-30, Zona 1, ✆ 2534530, ✉ 2513478, is overpriced, but nevertheless the most beautiful and secure guest house in this price range. Look out for the street number as there is no sign. **Colonial**, 7 Avenida 14-19, Zona 1, ✆ 2326722, ✉ 2328671, has a guard at the entrance, and clean rooms ranged around a pleasant courtyard.

Hotel Plaza, Vía 7, 6-16, Zona 4, ✆ 3327626, ✉ 3317824, is a medium-range hotel, with secure parking and restaurant; clean but close to noisy roads. **La Casa Grande**, Avenida La Reforma 7-67, ✆/✉ 3320914, is not as grand as it appears. A beautiful villa set back from the road, this is a small hotel with personal service and a good restaurant. **Mr Tony B&B**, 4 Calle 4-27, Zona 9, ✆/✉ 3348416, on a quiet residential street, offers rooms with private bath, cable TV and friendly service.

Hotel El Aeropuerto, 15 Calle A 7-32, Zona 13, ✆ 3323086, is within walking distance of the international airport if you have very light luggage. If you ring them, they should come to pick you up, a service they advertise as free to customers. **Hotel Hincapié**, Avenida Hincapié 18-77, Zona 13, ✆ 3327771, ✉ 3374469, is under the same management and is conveniently located for early morning flights to the jungle, as well as within easy reach of Zonas 9 and 10. Free transport to and from the airports is included.

moderate

Hotel Excel, 9 Avenida 15-12, Zona 1, ✆ 2532709, is a clean, modern place with secure parking, and all rooms have private bathrooms and TV. Best in this range is **Chalet Suizo**, 14 Calle 6-82, Zona 1, ✆ 2513786, ✆ 2320429. Spotless and safe, this place is always oversubscribed. Even if you do not stay here, the restaurant is a haven of peace and an excellent choice for breakfast and picking up the latest English language newspapers. **Hotel Continental**, 12 Calle 6-10, Zona 1, ✆ 2305806, is on the second floor of a building with an armed guard at the entrance, so definitely safe, but otherwise nothing special. **Hotel Fortuna Royal**, 12 Calle 8-42, Zona 1, ✆ 2303378, ✆ 2512215, is a Chinese-owned hotel offering all rooms with TV, private bath and air-conditioning.

inexpensive

Hotel San Francisco, 6 Avenida 12-62, Zona 1, ✆ 2325125–28, is central and good, but noisy because of its location. **Hernani**, 15 Calle 6-56, Zona 1, ✆ 2322839, is well kept and close to Parque Concordia. **Lessing House**, 12 Calle 4-35, Zona 1, ✆ 2513891, is friendly and secure and offers rooms with private bathroom. It's good value and in a useful location. **Fénix**, 7 Avenida 15-81, Zona 1, ✆ 2516625, is basic but clean and very reasonably priced. **Pensión Mesa**, 10 Calle 10-17, Zona 1, ✆ 2323177, lives on the old rumour that Che Guevara stayed here once. Basic but relaxed and friendly in a casual hippy style, with a sunny courtyard. **Centroamericana**, 9 Avenida 16-38, Zona 1, ✆ 2518160, is close to the Zona 1 bus station. It offers dingy rooms and sagging beds around a light, covered patio. It is safe and convenient, though the surrounding area is the red-light quarter.

Eating Out

Guatemala is no place for great food. But it is possible to find perfectly good international cooking. Vegetarians are not generally catered for, and will often find themselves restricted to eggs and beans, or pasta. The cheapest restaurants and *comedores* are in Zona 1, with literally hundreds to choose from. Fast food joints are everywhere; hamburgers and hotdogs are always to be found. **McDonald's** (10 Calle 5-30, Zona 1; 7 Avenida and Vía 3, Zona 4; 14 Calle and 7 Avenida, Zona 9, etc.) and **Pizza Hut** (6 Avenida between 13 and 14 Calles, Zona 1, and on Avenida La Reforma, near the Camino Real Hotel in Zona 9) are represented here, as well as many local chains, such as **Pollo Campero** and **Los Pollos**.

In Zona 1

The best restaurant for trying Guatemalan cuisine is the **Arrin-Cuan**, 5 Avenida 3-27, which offers dishes similar to those found in the central market, behind the cathedral, only with better presentation and fancier prices. If you want something special, treat yourself to a meal at the **Hotel PanAmerican**, 9 Calle 5-63, where you'll get the full works, including waiters in traditional dress.

A good Italian restaurant in the centre is the **Piccadilly**, 6 Avenida and 11 Calle, which has a sister restaurant on the Plaza España, 7 Avenida 12-00 in Zona 9, charging the same prices. Three more worth trying are: **Bologna**, 10 Calle 6-20; **Giovanni Canessa**, 12 Calle 6-23; and **A Guy from Italy**, 12 Calle 6-33, and also 5 Avenida 5-70.

A popular Mexican restaurant is the **El Gran Pavo**, 13 Calle 1 4-41. Spanish restaurants to try are **Altuna**, 5 Avenida 12-31; **Isaisas**, 9 Calle 3-59; **Posada de Toboso**, 11 Calle 6-35; and especially **Meson Don Quijote**, 11 Calle 5-27. Chinese food is widely available in Zona 1, usually greasy and cheap. **Fu Lu Sho**, 6 Avenida 12-09, is recommended.

For North-American-style food, try **Danny's Pancakes**, 6 Avenida 9-45, or the **Europa** bar and restaurant, 11 Calle 5-16, a reasonably popular gringo bar with cable TV. Also **American Doughnuts**, 5 Avenida 11-55.

The best place for breakfast—other than the Chalet Suizo mentioned under accommodation, is **Delicadezas Hamburgo**, 15 Calle 5-28, which faces onto the Parque Concordia, popular with gringos and locals alike. Others recommended for breakfast snacks or afternoon breaks are: **Pastelería Austria**, 12 Calle 6-58; **Pastelería Bohemia**, 11 Calle 8-48; **Pastelería Lins**, 11 Calle 6-12; and **Pastelería Los Tilos**, 11 Calle 6-54.

In Zonas 9 and 10

For traditional meals this end of town your best option is **Los Antojitos**, Avenida La Reforma 15-02, Zona 9 (*open daily, noon-10pm*), which does delicious steaks and plenty of Guatemalan dishes at reasonable prices. Try also **Restaurante Tipico el Parador**, Avenida La Reforma 6-70, Zona 9, for typical meals.

Some of the best restaurants in Guatemala City are steakhouses, and a well-priced one is **El Rodeo**, 7 Avenida 14-84, Zona 9. If you want something more special, try **Hacienda de los Sanchez**, 12 Calle 2-25, Zona 10. There are plenty of others, such as: **Gauchos**, 7 Avenida 10-65, Zona 9; and **La Estancia**, Avenida La Reforma 6-89, Zona 10.

Four very good Italians are: **Vesuvio Pizza**, 18 Calle 3-36, Zona 10; **Ciao Italia**, 15 Calle 3-48; **La Trattoria**, 13 Calle 1-55; and **Luigi's Pizza**, 4 Avenida 14-20, Zona 10.

Fancy French food at fancy prices can be had at **Estro Armónico**, 15 Calle 1-11, Zona 10, and **La Bohème**, 3 Avenida 10-41, Zona 10. Vaguely French and easily affordable is **La Crêpe**, 14 Calle 7-49, Zona 9, which does a huge variety of crêpes, both sweet and savoury.

Fish and seafood specialities are served at three recommended restaurants: **Puerto Barrios**, 7 Avenida 10-65, Zona 9; **La Mariscada**, 6 Avenida 9-64, Zona 9; and

Marina del Rey, 16 Calle 0-61, Zona 10. If you enjoy eastern flavours and style you should head for the capital's newest Japanese restaurant: **Sushi**, 2 Avenida 14-63, Zona 10.

If you do not want to travel to Nicaragua, but would still like to taste its national dishes, why not visit **Caprichos**, 1 Avenida 13-74, Zona 10.

You have a wide choice of Chinese restaurants in this part of town. Some of the favourites are: **China Queen**, 6 Avenida 14-04, Zona 9; **Palacio de Oro**, 8 Calle 6-01, Zona 9; **Palacio Royal**, 7 Avenida 11-00, Zona 9; and **Real Capitol**, 6 Avenida 9-11, Zona 9.

For international cuisine of the highest standard and sweets to die for, you should not pass up a visit to **Jake's**, 17 Calle 10-40, Zona 10. The service and meals are impeccable and the prices reflect that. Less exclusive, but not necessarily cheaper, is **Tu Tu Tango**, 2 Avenida 14-74, Zona 10.

If all you want is an American-style snack, head for the authentic but expensive delis: **Maitreya's Deli**, 13 Calle 4-44, Zona 10; or **Señor Tenedor**, 15 Calle 3-52, Zona 10.

Cafés and cake shops are plentiful, and if you cannot find one, you can always try the luxury hotels, of which the Camino Real has the best café. A personal favourite is **Los Alpes**, 10 Calle 1-09, Zona 10, which combines tranquillity with old-fashioned quality. Almost as delicious are the sweets at **Pastelería Zurich**, inside the shopping centre at 4 Avenida 12-09, Zona 10. Other good places to try are: **Pumpernik's**, 2 Avenida 13-17, Centro Commercial Vivacentro, Zona 10 (*open daily from 7am for early breakfasts*); **Palace**, 10 Calle 4-40, Zona 10; and **Patsy**, Avenida La Reforma 8-01, Zona 10.

Entertainment and Nightlife

Guatemala City at night can be a dangerous place, especially in Zona 1, and it is not a good idea to walk the streets alone whether you are male or female. Zonas 9 and 10 are quieter, but even there it would be best to take a taxi to your destination, unless it is just around the corner from your hotel. Having said this, the capital is strangely quiet very early on. Public transport becomes rare after 8pm, and there is a distinct lack of obvious nightlife other than the girlie bars around the Zona 1 bus station.

Your choices for nightclubs are almost entirely restricted to the ones attached to the exclusive hotels of Zonas 9 and 10, which are predictably middle-aged in atmosphere, and have nothing Guatemalan about them. The best music bar is **El Establo**, Avenida La Reforma 14-34, Zona 9 (*open daily 10am–1am*). If you enjoy the company of middle-aged ex-pats, then head for the American-run **Shakespeare's Pub**, 13 Calle 1-51, Zona 10 (*open Mon–Fri, 11am–11.30pm; Sat and Sun 2pm–midnight*). Much more lively, with bands on Saturdays, is **Danny's Mariscobar**, Avenida Las Américas 8-24, Zona 13 (*open daily 11am–late*).

Favourite discos in town are **Kahlua**, 1 Avenida 13-29, Zona 10; **Le Pont**, 13 Calle 0-48, Zona 10; **Dash Disco**, 12 Calle 1-25, Zona 10; **Basco's Disco**, 16 Calle 0-55, Zona 10; and the city's newest hotspot is **Sherlock's Home**, Avenida Las Américas 2-14, Zona 13. Please note, however, that nightclubs are notoriously short-lived and you should ask if they still exist before venturing out into the night.

There are numerous cinemas throughout the city, including four on 6 Avenida in the centre. Films are usually in English with Spanish subtitles.

Day Trips from Guatemala City

Lake Amatitlán

Guatemala City is not a place you will want to spend much time in, and it is highly unlikely that you will use it as a base for your whole trip. However, Lake Amatitlán, just half an hour away, by bus or car, certainly merits a visit to see the views of the Pacaya and Agua volcanoes, or enjoy a relaxed boat trip across the waters. If you turn up during a weekend, you also have the opportunity to take the **bubble-lift** up to the **Parque de las Naciones Unidas** (if it's working), where you definitely get the best views of all.

The lake is just west of the main highway connecting the capital with the Pacific lowlands, and there are frequent daily buses that leave from the Zona 4 bus terminal, or you can flag down the appropriate bus on the corner of 20 Calle and 3 Avenida, in Zona 1. You could also go on an organized tour to the lake (*see* p.67).

On the southern shores of Lake Amatitlán rises the small but active cone of the **Pacaya volcano**, which takes its name from a type of palm with prickly fruit, as jagged as the edge of Pacaya's crater. The volcano still erupts regularly, occasionally hitting careless tourists over the head with bits of flying debris. At night, the orange haze from its bubbling mouth is particularly mesmerizing, most dramatically visible if you camp out near the summit. Organized trips are the easiest and safest way to explore Pacaya, and there are plenty of agencies that do both day trips and overnight tours (camping equipment can be hired), though most of them are based in Antigua. The **Agua volcano**, also visible from the capital, is an hour's journey into the highlands from Guatemala City.

Mixco Viejo

If you have time and money for just one tour from the capital, however, you should definitely make it a visit to the important Maya ruins of Mixco Viejo, about 60km north-west of Guatemala City. Shared between two or three people, the cost of a tour or vehicle hire should not be too expensive, and you will see one of the finest Post-Classic Maya sites in the country. Strangely, considering its significance, Mixco is not generally offered as a day-trip by commercial companies, but all will be ready to go if you can agree on a price. Ideally you need a four-wheel-drive vehicle because the last 15km are on a deeply rutted dirt-track. Getting there and back by public transport in one day is difficult, but not impossible. It involves taking a very early bus from the Zona 4 bus terminal, heading for

Pachalum, making sure that its route will pass near the entrance road to the ruins, and being back at the pick-up spot in time for the last bus back to the capital. (Ask the driver when that will be before you leave Guatemala City.) In spite of the relatively short distance, the journey can take between two and three hours one way by bus, though if you go at the week-end, you have a good chance of hitching a lift back in a private vehicle, especially on Sundays. In your own vehicle the journey will take no more than two hours each way. Take a picnic with plenty to drink, and toilet paper. Note that there is nowhere to stay nearby.

Mixco Viejo was the magnificent final stronghold of the Pokomam Maya, a Post-Classic site built in the 13th century AD and continuously occupied until its fall to the Spanish in the early 16th century. The early centuries were marked by heavy tribal warfare and, as the Pokomam were vastly outnumbered by the neighbouring Quiché and Kakchiquel tribes, they chose this remote highland location to build a large fortified 'city', covering a series of ridges 880m high and almost one kilometre long, jutting out above steep ravines. It made an ideal military fortress, virtually impregnable except through a narrow pass from the west, and guards stationed on the towering cliffs could easily see anyone approaching long before they became a danger.

The earliest settlers, around 1200, only constructed temple platforms on each mountain ridge and observation platforms close to the edge of the ravines. But their successors gradually built up the available land and surrounded the more important districts with tiered walls, cutting into the ridges to make the ravines even steeper and reinforcing them with stone. By 1525 Mixco had become one of the finest and largest highland Maya fortifications, both a military and religious centre. There were no fewer than nine major temples with many altars, two ball courts and dwellings for the population of several thousand, which was swelled by an influx of the surrounding inhabitants to eight or nine thousand on special ceremonial occasions.

Naturally such a centre of Maya power could not be ignored by the conquering Spaniards, and the tragic fall of the site is recorded in the writings of Francisco Antonio de Fuentes y Guzman. No less than Don Pedro de Alvarado himself led the assault, besieging the fortifications in 1525, with the help of 200 Mexican Indians from Tlaxcala. His first attempt, though, ended in failure, serving only to provoke a counter-attack by a Pokomam army from Chiantla that came to defend Mixco. By all accounts that battle was a bloody affair, but the Spanish succeeded in coming out tops in the end, and persuading the Chiantla force to betray their brothers. A secret cave entrance in the hillside was known to lead straight into the heart of Mixco; the Spanish guarded this passage while their fellows made one more serious attack via the western approach. As the battle raged, the Pokomans began to flee via the cave and were promptly slaughtered by the awaiting enemy. Once victory was his, Alvarado ordered the fortress burnt to the ground and forced the survivors to settle far away, in another province. Their village, near the present capital, was called Mixco, and the people who live there still speak Pokomam to this day.

The Ruins

Mixco, which means 'amongst the clouds', is open daily (*8–5; adm free*); the entrance is through the narrow cut in the rockface that was the public way in all those centuries ago. Fifty metres to the left there is a relief map of the site and a geographical orientation of its location, a useful place to begin your visit as well an excellent spot for some great views across the highlands. On a ledge above are covered barbecue spots, with a water tap directly below the shelters. The oblong building to the left is due to open as a museum shortly; the collection will include artefacts found at the site, and there will be trinkets and postcards for sale. (Note that the toilets are likely to be out of order due to lack of water.)

Directly opposite the barbecue area, on the right-hand elevation, is the first temple and courtyard complex (complex A) and if you walk behind the long oblong structure you see another, separated by one of the many ravines— or *barrancas*—that characterize the site. A long and lumpy stone staircase leads out of the depths of the ravine, but an easier route is to follow the high ground around the top. The most important structure there is the **ball court** (Ball Court A), which is 37.21 metres long and was built using small slabs of thin stone from the local river beds. It is the older of the two you will see here, a very simple design, with little public seating and a grassy floor.

From here, a path leads straight over a flight of steps up the fortified wall supporting the main plaza, where the **twin pyramids** make up the most important structures of Mixco Viejo. Their west-facing façades each have a single, very steep staircase, in front of which used to be small altars. The style of these temple platforms, and of all the buildings here, is of a unity rarely found in pre-Columbian sites; this is due to the relatively short inhabitation period. No structure is over ten metres

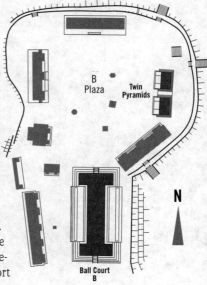

high and there is very little sculpture to be found, as most decoration was painted stucco, which has been lost long ago. In fact, the only decorative features still visible today are the stone markers at the **Ball Court B** nearby, representing open-jawed snakes, each with a human head inside; these are copies of the originals, which are now at the Museo Nacional in Guatemala City. Slightly longer than that of its companion, the stone floor of the Ball Court B indicates Mexican influence.The whole structure was beautifully restored in 1954 by the Franco-Guatemalan Archaeology Mission.

A huge guanacaste tree can be seen growing in the next plaza and, as you climb the steps towards it, you get a superb view of the whole site, as well as of the ravines that must have made even the Spanish attack a daunting enterprise. Sadly this complex was badly damaged by the last major earthquake, but you can still find fragments of original plaster clinging to the walls, and the grassy plain here makes a wonderful picnic site often used by visiting Maya, who still come to celebrate special occasions. The final outcrop of Mixco Viejo is reached by irregular paths that meander up and down beyond this plaza, where the last **courtyard** stands in crumbling isolation and offers very little you have not seen already. Returning to the entrance is made easy, though, by taking the well-trodden path leading off to your left, which follows the contours of the mountain back to the entrance of the site.

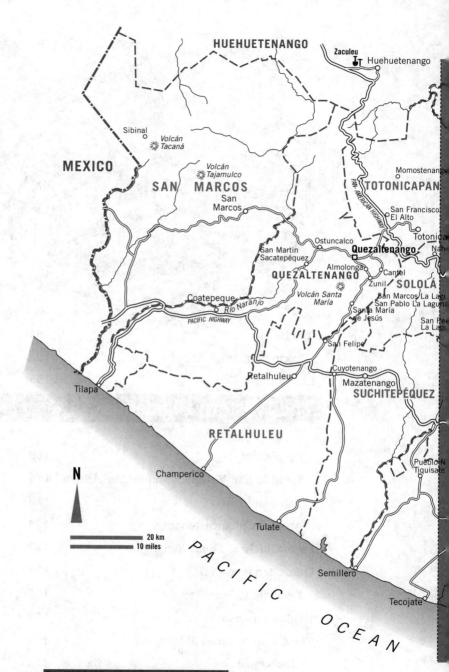

The Western Highlands

QUICHÉ

BAJA VERAPAZ

Santa Cruz
del Quiché

Joyabaj

Chichicastenango

Pachalum

icapán

Los
Encuentros

Mixco
Viejo

Río Grande o Motagua

Nahualá

SOLOLÁ

Concepción

Santa Cruz
La Laguna

SOLOLÁ

CHIMALTENANGO

GUATEMALA

Marcos
aguna

Panajachel

Comalapa

San Juan
Sacatepéquez

blo

Santa Catrina Palopó

San Pedro
Sacatepéquez

Pedro
guna

San Antonio Palopó

Lake Atitlán

Chimaltenango

GUATEMALA
CITY

Santiago
Atitlán

San Lucas
Tolimán

San Lucas
Sacatepéquez

Volcán
Tolimán

Antigua

Santa Maria
de Jesús

Volcán
Atitlán

San Miguel Dueñas

SACATEPÉQUEZ

SUCHITEPÉQUEZ

Alotenango

Amatitlán

Volcán
Fuego

Volcán de
Agua

Cocales

San Vicente Pacaya

Santa Lucia
Cotzumalguapa

Volcán de
Pacaya

PAN-AMERICAN HIGHWAY

lo Nuevo
sate

Siquinalá

Escuintla

SANTA

ROSA

ESCUINTLA

Río Pantaleón

La Democracia

cojate

Sipacate

San Jose

Río Marie Linda

Taxisco

Monterrico

83

The Western Highlands is without doubt one of Guatemala's most beautiful regions. A wonderful landscape of mountains is punctuated by volcanic peaks and expansive lakes, forming a ridge along Western Guatemala from Mexico to El Salvador, with the Pacific Lowlands to the southwest, and the Eastern Highlands and dry valleys towards the Caribbean coastal plain.

This is the most populous region of Guatemala and home to the Maya Indians. Towns and villages are clustered between rolling fields of corn and vegetables, and burst into life on market days and during annual festivals. In spite of brutal oppression in the past, the Maya have clung tenaciously to their culture and traditional way of life. Each tribe has its own language and dialects, and they still weave and wear distinctive traditional costume, with patterns and colours unique to different villages. Pagan rituals and religious rites have been combined with Catholicism, resulting in extraordinary rural communities which are fascinating to witness.

The majority of people in the Western Highlands are descendants of the Maya tribes that have always lived here: the Quiché, Mam and Pokomam, but there are many other smaller, related tribes. Virtually all Indians can speak some Spanish in Guatemala, but bear in mind it is their second language, and it may be as difficult for an Indian from a remote village to speak Spanish as it may be for you. Do note that the Spanish word *indio* is considered a term of abuse by most Indians in Latin America, who prefer the word *indigena*.

The road network in this region reaches almost everywhere you will want to visit: from the enchanting colonial city of Antigua to the stunning Lake Atitlán, with its surrounding volcanoes and villages, and the highland towns, such as Chichicastenango in the Quiché region, with its colourful market and festivals. For the more adventurous, the remote towns and villages of the Ixil triangle, up in the Cuchumatanes mountains, offer stunning scenery and an insight into Guatemala's recent turbulent history. Antigua and Quezaltenango, the commercial hub of the south-west, are ideal bases from which to explore these places.

Antigua

After the frenzy of Guatemala City's traffic, Antigua is a real haven: the air is clean, the town is peaceful and bursting with pleasant places to stay, eat and drink. Cobbled streets are lined by chunky colonial houses, with ornate wooden window grilles and inviting entrances giving on to green-clad courtyards. The surrounding area is equally compelling: Antigua (altitude 1530m) nestles in a fecund valley close to the volcanoes Agua, Fuego and Acatenango, with stunning views beyond its tiled roofs.

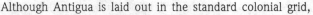

Although Antigua is laid out in the standard colonial grid, finding your way around can be a bit of a puzzle, since there are very few street signs—but it only takes 20 minutes to walk from one end of town to the other, and wandering about is a pleasure in itself. The majority of 'sights' are ruined churches, of which there is an abundance. But even if you are not interested in ruins, the atmosphere of Antigua will undoubtedly make it one of your favourite places.

Inevitably, Antigua is a magnet for gringos, not least because of the 40 or so language schools here. If you do want to learn Spanish, or refresh your existing knowledge, you are spoilt for choice; and in some ways, the preponderance of gringos is very comforting. Antigua is an excellent place to recover from rigorous travel or ease yourself gently into the Guatemalan environment. After a while, however, the place can seem a little artificial, so overtaken by gringo needs and tastes that one is remote from Guatemalan culture and life.

History

Handsome, blond, brave and deeply ruthless, Don Pedro de Alvarado was the archetypal conquistador, tearing through Central America in search of gold. Alvarado arrived in Guatemala in 1523, sent south by Cortés to claim Central America for the Spanish. Although instructed to 'preach matters concerning the Holy faith', once in Guatemala Alvarado adopted his own approach. From 1524 until his death in 1541, Alvarado ruled Guatemala as a personal fiefdom, rewarding his followers with vast tracts of land and the right to use the Indians as they saw fit. He was a brutal ruler, and the indigenous Maya were abused and exploited without mercy.

Establishing a permanent colonial capital city, however, was not a simple affair. Pedro founded Santiago de los Caballeros in 1524, near the former Cakchiquel capital of Iximché east of Lake Atitlán. Difficulties with the unruly Cakchiqueles led his brother Jorge de Alvarado to move the capital in 1527, to the valley of Almolonga, close to the Agua and Fuego volcanoes. The new city, now present-day Ciudad Vieja, took the name of its predecessor, and flourished for almost 20 years before disaster struck. Following Pedro's death in 1541 in battle in Mexico, his grieving wife, Doña Beatriz, swiftly showed her own ambition by proclaiming herself 'Governess of the Americas'. She was only 22, and her reign was to last just one day. On 10 September 1541, two earthquakes, accompanied by torrential rains, triggered a massive landslide which smothered the capital and killed Doña Beatriz along with many of her subjects. *La sin ventura* (the unlucky one), as she had called herself, was the first and last female ruler of the colonial Americas.

This was the end of the administrative body's second capital. Two years later Antigua was finally inaugurated as the new capital. It was to become one of the most glamorous and sophisticated cities of Spanish America—a place where clergy and nobility vied for social status and power, and the most ostentatious convents, churches and palaces were built;

where schools, hospitals, and government buildings provided excellent services for the colonial residents and life was eased with cheap Indian labour.

Violent earthquakes continued throughout the 17th century, but this only increased the building boom. The great Baroque churches and palaces were built with ever thicker walls and better reinforcements. By the end of the century, there were no fewer than ten convents, three parish churches, five hermitages, four churches, a university, and the cathedral, which was the grandest in Central America. All this for a city designed for 5000 inhabitants.

By the mid-18th century, there were nearer 50,000 inhabitants, living in the greatest comfort imaginable at the time: Antigua was enjoying its Golden Age. But the 1773 earthquake brought this to an abrupt end: Antigua was reduced to rubble, with many dead buried underneath and epidemics soon claiming those who survived. The authorities decided the city must be abandoned and the capital moved to a safer location. The subsequent dismantling of Antigua caused yet more destruction. Despite this double disturbance, a great deal of colonial Antigua remains and, in spite of continued seismic batterings and 20th-century architectural sins, the opulent atmosphere of the 18th century remains intact.

Getting There and Away

By bus: Antigua is about 1½hrs from Guatemala City by bus. You will be dropped off at the main bus terminal on 4 Calle Poniente on the west side of town, within easy walking distance of most hotels and guest houses. There are usually plenty of 'guides' hovering about, who will direct you to your accommodation or straight to one of the language schools (who pay them a small fee for this service).

There are frequent daily buses from the local bus terminal to the capital, surrounding villages and nearby towns from dawn until about 3pm. By late afternoon, you have little chance of catching a bus to anywhere except the capital. When planning any journey, even to nearby villages, it is always a good idea to ask about times the day before, and to find out when the last bus returns to Antigua.

There are buses to **Guatemala City** every 20 minutes from dawn until about 5. There are buses every hour to **Chimaltenango** and all destinations along the Pan-American Highway and to the rest of the Highlands. The journey takes about 40 minutes, and you must ask to be dropped off at the junction with the Highway, in order to catch the appropriate bus onwards into the Highlands. Buses coming from the capital are frequent, and you should not have to wait more than half an hour for a connection to such destinations as Panajachel, Chichicastenango, Quezaltenango or Huehuetenango.

Hotels (in black discs):
1 Hotel Casa Santiago de los Caballeros
2 Hotel Cristal
3 Posada de Doña Marta
4 Posada La Merced
5 Posada Asjemenou
6 Hotel Convento Santa Catalina
7 The Cloister
8 Hotel Casa Santo Domingo
9 Posada de Don Rodrigo
10 El Placido
11 Posada El Refugio
12 Hotel del Centro
13 Quinta Maconda
14 Hotel Descanso
15 Posada San Sebastián
16 Hotel Aurora
17 Hotel Panchoy
18 Hotel Confort
19 Doña Angelina
20 Hotel San Francisco
21 El Pasaje
22 Posada Landivar
23 Posada San Vicente
24 Hotel Cortéz y Larraz
25 Casa de los Cántaros
26 La Casa de Santa Lucía
27 Posada Las Rosas
28 Hotel Antigua
29 Ramada Hotel
30 El Rosario Lodge
31 Mesón Panza Verde

Antigua

400 metres
400 yards

1 Bus Terminal
2 Mercado (Market)
3 Correos y Télegrafos (Post Office)
4 Guatel (Telephones)
5 Inguat (Tourist Office)
6 Cemetery
7 Iglesia Y Convento Santa Catalina
8 Iglesia La Merced
9 El Arco Y Convento Santa Catalina
10 Palacio del Ayuntamiento
11 Palacio de los Capitanes Generales
12 Parque Central
13 Catedral
14 Universidad de San Carlos
15 Convento de Capuchinas
16 Convento de Santo Domingo
17 Convento de Concepción
18 Casa Popenoe
19 Convento de Santa Clara
20 Iglesia de San Francisco
21 Iglesia del Calvario
22 Cerro de la Cruz
23 Museo Colonial
24 Museo de Santiago

There are two daily buses to **Escuintla** on the Pacific Highway, leaving at 6 and 7am. The route is a rough dirt road, skirting the Agua volcano, and the journey takes around 2hrs.

There are regular buses to surrounding villages such as San Andrés Itzapa, San Lucas Sacatepéquez, Alotenango (for Ciudad Vieja), Duenas (nearest village to starting point for climbing Acatenango and Fuego), Jocotenango, Santa Lucía Milpas Altas, San Antonio Aguas Calientes, Sumpango, San Juan del Obispo, Pastores, Santa María de Jesús (for climbing Agua), San Pedro las Huertas, and San Luís de las Carretas.

There are many **private bus shuttle** services operating daily between Antigua and the airport in Guatemala City, as well as to Chichicastenango, Panajachel and the Río Dulce area. For prices and timetables, see noticeboards that are found at the tourist office, Casa Andinista, and many hotel reception desks and restaurants, or check the ads in *Classifieds Revue*. The vehicles are normally air-conditioned minibuses, which offer a faster, more convenient and comfortable way of getting to the main spots. They also pick you up from your accommodation and drop you off exactly where you wish to go. If you have the time and mental energy, though, local transport will get you to the same place for a fraction of the price, and possibly more safely as tourist buses do occasionally attract highway robbers—they are obvious targets and have a conveniently dependable timetable.

By taxi: You should have no trouble getting a taxi to take you all the way from either of the Guatemala City Airports (or any part of the city) to Antigua for around US$20–25. Don't worry if you have no local currency, your driver will be delighted to take American dollars.

Getting Around

Antigua is too small to have its own municipal transport, and most people get around on foot. Bicycles, motorbikes and cars can be hired for excursions, as can horses (*see* 'Tourist Information'). There is one taxi stand by the bus terminal and one on the main square, in front of the cathedral.

Tourist Information

The local **Inguat** office (*open 8–noon and 2–6*) is located left of the main entrance to the cathedral. The office not only provides brochures and general help but can also advise on which language schools are currently the best value. Remember that when it comes to language schools personal recommendations are always the most reliable. An excellent source of information on anything from accommodation to tours and travellers' messages is the noticeboard in the courtyard of **Doña Luisa's**, 4 Calle Oriente 12. Another board worth checking is at the **Rainbow Reading Room**, 7 Avenida Sur 8.

The tourist office can recommend English-speaking **medics**, or anyone local will be able to direct you to the San Rafael private hospital, © 8320317, which offers 24-hr emergency care.

Banco del Agro on the main square is the best place to change **money** during the week. The Banco del Agro branch on Alameda Santa Lucía is open Mon–Sat, until 6pm. For exchange outside banking hours, try the travel agents or any of the large hotels. Lloyds Bank International have an office on the main square at 4 Calle Oriente. Note: you can only change US$200 per day, so if you need more, you'll have to make several transactions at different banks.

The **post office** (*open Mon–Fri, 8–4.30*) is on the Alameda Santa Lucía, virtually opposite the bus terminal. The **Guatel** telephone office (*open daily, 7–10pm*) is on 5 Avenida Sur, just off the main square. Many places offer a **fax service** in Antigua: Eco-Intertel, 5 Avenida Norte 30, ✆/✉ 8322640; Turansa, 5 Calle Poniente 11B, ✆/✉ 8323316; Fax Depot, 3 Avenida Norte 3, ✆/✉ 8323293 (behind the cathedral). Also Conexion, La Fuente Commercial Centre, 4 Calle Oriente 14, ✆ 8323768, ✉ 8320602, which offers to match or beat any other price you can find in town for fax, e-mail or phoning. They also sell computer time.

A wide selection of **books** on many Guatemalan subjects, both in English and Spanish, is available at Casa Andinista Bookshop, 4 Calle Oriente 5 A; another good place is the Librería Pensativo, on 5 Avenida Norte 29, though most of their books are in Spanish; or try La Casa del Conde, the gallery and book shop fronting the Café Condesa, on the west side of the main square; last choice, because of bad prices and abrasive staff is Un Poco de Todo in the shopping arcade on the main square. Second-hand books can be bought at the Rainbow Reading Room, 7 Avenida Sur 8. CIRMA: The Centro de Investigaciones Regionales de Mesoamerica, 5 Calle Oriente 5 (*open Mon–Fri, 8–6; Sat 9–1*), is an excellent research library open to the public, where you can find all types of publications in both English and Spanish. The Biblioteca International de Antigua, 5 Calle Poniente 15 (*open Tues–Sun, 11–1 and 2–6*), is the town's largest lending library for both Spanish and English editions.

There are two places to do your **laundry** on 5 Calle Poniente, near the main square: Lavandería Central, 5 Calle Poniente 7 (the most popular) and Lavandería Colonial, 6 Avenida Norte 41 (*both open Mon–Fri, 8–5.30; Sat 8–noon*).

Unfortunately, **tourist crime** needs to be mentioned at this point. Since Antigua is so very popular with visitors it also attracts all kinds of criminals, from petty thieves to armed muggers, and you should take extra care here. There is no need to be paranoid, simply use basic good sense: avoid walking alone late at night, and if you venture out of town, on a volcano hike for example, make sure you are accompanied day or night. Leave valuables in hotel safes.

Car and Bike Rental

Ahorrent, 4 Calle Oriente 14 (in the La Fuente Centre) hire cars, 4-wheel drives or vans; **Avis** have an office at 5 Avenida Norte 22, ✆/✉ 8322692. **Tabarini** car hire are located at 2 Calle Poniente 19 A, ✆ 8323091. Mountain bikes as well as ordinary bikes can be hired from **Maya Mountain Bike Tours**, 3 Avenida Norte

3. Worth checking out is the **Bike Center**, 6 Calle and 6 Avenida Sur 21, which also does sales and repairs.

Language Schools

The most prestigious and expensive of the lot has long been the **Proyecto Lingüístico Francisco Marroquin**, 7 Calle Poniente 31, ℂ 8322886, whose clientele is overwhelmingly North American. **Maya**, 5 Calle Poniente 20, ℂ 8320656, is equally good, and for some reason favoured mostly by a European clientele. Another establishment that is repeatedly recommended is **Tecún Umán**, 6 Calle Poniente 34, ℂ 8322279. More recently popular is the **Sevilla Academia de Español**, 6 Calle Oriente 3, ℂ/◉ 8323609, with courses starting at US$70 per week (4hrs daily).

There are many more schools to choose from, offering every kind of teaching option you might want, as well as accommodation with a local family, if required. Prices are $60–120 per week for standard one-to-one teaching; full-board accommodation with a family usually costs US$30–45 per week extra. If you hire a private teacher, you should expect to pay around US$2.50 per hour.

Other than gathering information from fellow language students and from the tourist office, you could also drop in at the offices of AmeriSpan Unlimited, 6 Avenida Norte 40, ℂ/◉ 8320164 (headquarters in the USA: PO Box 40513, Philadelphia, PA 19104 0513, ℂ 800 879 6640). This American company works with six language schools in Antigua, and also sells many other tourist services, including phone and fax service.

Travel Agents and Tour Operators

Antigua is the foremost tourist centre in the country, and selling tours of every description is big business. A lot of cowboy operators work here; you should take care to shop around and, ideally, go by personal recommendations. Prices are kept low by fierce competition, but check to see what you are getting for your money.

Viajes Tivoli, above Un Poco de Todo bookshop, on the main square, is the best agent in town, and can book any type of international flight for you, as well as tours (including trips to Tikal). And you will find very friendly service at **Centro de Viajes**, on 5 Avenida Norte 15 A. There are many others to choose from. If you are looking for sailing trips, the place to head for is the **Adventure Travel Center**, 4 Calle Oriente 14 (inside La Fuente commercial centre); **Gran Jaguar Tours**, 4 Calle Poniente 30, is known for reliable airport shuttle services and safe Pacaya volcano tours. An enjoyable option for those fit enough is a bicycle tour with **Maya Mountain Bike Tours**, 3 Avenida Norte 3.

Information, maps, hiking equipment and guides for trips to the **volcanoes** can be found at **Casa Andinista Bookshop**, 4 Calle Oriente 5A, which also sells photocopies of topographic military maps to the northern Ixil region and can provide the latest news on travel and safety. Or you could try **Club Chigag**, 6 Avenida Norte

34, though it gets very mixed reports. Note that day trips to Pacaya normally have armed guards at weekends only.

The Plaza Mayor

The heart of Antigua is the main square, the Parque Central, from which calles and avenidas spread out in straight lines, in typical colonial style. In former times it was an open expanse where festivals and market days were held. These days you find a landscaped park, centred around a fountain. Visitors relaxing on the park benches and cathedral steps are frequently accosted by the charming but persistent Indian hawkers. *Compra algo* (buy something) will soon become a familiar refrain, or even *toma una foto* (take a picture)—but be warned, your subjects expect to be paid.

Around the square are ranged the grandiose buildings of the cathedral on the east side, the City Hall (*Ayuntamiento*) on the north side, the Palace of the Captains General on the south side, with Agua's volcanic cone towering behind, and an arcade hiding a bank, shops and cafés along the west side. The square is quite small, and the whole effect is almost cosy.

The whitewashed façade of the **cathedral of San José**, completed in 1680, shows the scars of many tremors and quakes, and the interior is mostly ruined. What you see on the east side of the square are the remnants of the grandest cathedral in Central America and a magnificent Archbishop's Palace. The original cathedral had 12 naves, two of which, restored, make up the present Church of San José; the palace is now no more than fallen masonry and broken columns, some of which still retain their intricate stucco. Wandering among the debris, you might come across the odd human bone from one of the many crypts underfoot; Alvarado and his wife lie buried here, as well as the famous chronicler of the conquest, Díaz del Castillo. Entrance (*small adm*) to the ruined palace is through the gate on 5 Calle Oriente.

The **Palace of the Captains General** stands at right angles to the cathedral. It is now home to the local police headquarters and municipal offices. The covered arches provide welcome shade as you walk around to the commercial west side of the square, where street vendors and shoeshine boys gather.

The elevated walkway that fronts the **Ayuntamiento** on the north side of the square is shaded by 18th-century covered arches. The two-storeyed Tuscan columns neatly mirror those of the palace opposite. In fact, they are the only part of the square's buildings that survived the earthquake of 1773. Originally, this building not only housed the city hall but also offices of the police and the 'Jail for the Poor', which had a chapel where death row prisoners were given their last rites before being hanged in the square. Today the building houses two museums: in the former prison is the **Museo de Santiago** (*open daily, 9–4, small adm*); and part of the former city hall now houses the **Museo del Libro Antiguo** (*same times, adm free*), with a replica of Central America's first printing press and a selection of early religious and scientific books. The Museo de Santiago is set around the old

prison courtyard with impressive four-foot-thick walls and heavy iron-grilled doors. There is a small collection of colonial uniforms, and the walls are hung with various portraits, rusty spikes and war regalia, including Alvarado's sword.

East of the Plaza

Walk along 5 Calle Oriente, past the cathedral, and you will see one of Antigua's finest colonial Baroque buildings, once the University of San Carlos de Borromeo. The ornate stucco around the entrance is best viewed from the elevated entrance to the Archbishop's Palace opposite. Today it houses the **Museo de Arte Colonial** (*open Mon–Fri, 9–4; Sat and Sun, 9–noon and 2-4; adm free*), which you should visit just for its beautiful inner courtyard. The nine rooms inside contain a range of 17th- and 18th-century colonial art and statuary, as well as an example of the type of dyed sawdust carpet Antigua is decked out with during Easter Week.

Turn right down 3 Avenida Sur and you soon come to Antigua's most picturesque square: two columns of palm trees lead the way to a chunky fountain and arcaded wash basins, where Indian women come to do their laundry. As you reach the square, the **San Pedro church** immediately in front of you gleams in freshly restored splendour. Next door is the **San Pedro Hospital**. Founded for members of the clergy in 1663, it has long since been open to the general public, not least because of the recurrent need to tend earthquake casualties, most recently in 1976. At the other end of the square, behind the washing arcade, is the **Church of Santa Clara** and the ruins of the attached convent. Founded in 1699 by nuns from Puebla, Mexico, the convent was built up to its present proportions after the 1717 earthquake, only to be destroyed in 1773. What remains are the cloisters ranged around a spacious plaza and elegant fountain.

Past Santa Clara, heading east on 7 Calle Oriente, you come to the high walls hiding the **San Francisco Church**, by far the most impressive of the town's churches—no plain wooden altars here, but ornate affairs with gold-leaf and intricate carving. Founded by the Franciscans in the late 16th century, the attached monastery was once an important centre of religious teaching, and also included a printing press, hospital and rooms set aside for music and art. Along the left aisle, plaque upon plaque testifies, in good Catholic manner, to the intervention of Antigua's favourite saint, **Pedro de Betancourt**. His tomb has been restored and placed on shiny terracotta-coloured marble. St Pedro, originally from the Canaries, lived in Antigua during the mid-17th century. He devoted himself to the poor and sick with such zeal that he is said to have miraculously cured septic wounds by licking them clean with his tongue. Not one to make life easy, he flagellated himself daily and, during Easter Week, he would crawl past the twelve altars of the Stations of the Cross (*see* below) on his knees. He died in 1667. A small museum (*small adm*) adjoins the church; here you can see a few old books and some of the saint's garments, including his ancient underpants.

Continuing on 7 Calle Oriente and turning left on Calle del Hermano Pedro, you come to the ruins of the **Convento de Concepción**, which was the first and grandest nunnery in Antigua. Sadly, the ruins offer little idea of its former splendour, but there are some handsome colonial tiles near its main entrance. Founded in 1578 by a Mexican abbess, it attracted large numbers of nuns from the wealthiest families, and the convent expanded rapidly, becoming the richest and largest of its kind. Over a thousand women lived here at one time, including the numerous slaves that tended the religious ladies' every need. The most notorious inmate was Doña Juana de Maldonado, who brought the convent into disrepute by regularly entertaining a bishop in her quarters. Thomas Gage, writing in the early 17th century, commented: 'here is not only idolatry, but fornication and uncleanness as public as in any place of the Indies.' Gage, however, was an English lapsed Catholic turned fanatical Protestant, and not a very savoury character himself: in 1640s England it was illegal to preach a Catholic mass, and Gage testified so effectively against former Catholic friends that three were hung, drawn and quartered.

Finally, a short walk away, at the corner of 1 Avenida Sur and 5 Calle Oriente, the **Casa Popenoe** (*open Mon–Fri, 2–4*) is an immaculate colonial house, complete with original furnishings, domestic tools and lovely garden. Constructed in 1634, it was home to the royal official Don Luis de las Infantas Mendoza y Venegas. Left in ruins after the 1773 earthquake, it was neglected until the 1930s, when Dr Popenoe and his wife embarked on its lengthy and careful restoration.

North of the Plaza

5 Avenida Norte, easily recognizable by the clock-tower arch that spans the street, takes you north from the plaza, past a number of Antigua's favourite cafés and restaurants. The arch, a few blocks away from the main square, is part of the **Convento de Santa Catalina**, now a hotel and restaurant. It was founded in 1609 by four nuns from the crowded Concepción convent, and the arch was built in 1693, so that nuns could pass

unseen to the connected property across the street. It is one of the most famous landmarks of Antigua, framing the cobbled street and views beyond.

At the end of 5 Avenida Norte is the **Iglesia La Merced**. It has the most ornate stucco of all the churches in Antigua, with twirls of vines, leaves and flower patterns delicately sculpted onto its columns and walls, their creamy colour perfectly highlighted against an ochre backround. On the small square in front of the church, a few Indian women normally sell their textiles under the shade of pine and palm trees. The beautiful fountain nearby dates from the late 17th century, and originally stood in the cloister of the Convento de San Francisco.

Heading one block east, along 1 Calle Poniente, you reach the remains of the **Convento de Santa Teresa**. Originally home to Carmelite nuns from Peru, it is now a gloomy prison for local criminals. Further on, the street opens up into a tree-lined avenue, a peaceful corner of Antigua, where some of the town's most desirable residences hide behind thick wooden doors.

To the right, down one block of 2 Avenida Norte, a deceptively nondescript entrance leads into the **Convento de Capuchinas**. The spacious ruins, in rather better repair than most, now house the National Council for the Protection of Antigua, organizer of regular exhibitions of local artists' paintings and sculptures. The convent was founded in the early 18th century and destroyed by the 1773 earthquake. Part of the remains, a cylindrical structure just north of the cloister, is the subject of fierce debate among the experts. On the second-floor patio, 18 nun's cells are ranged around the central supporting tower, while underneath, there is a mysterious large, bare, open room, with unexplained niches cut into its outside wall, some holding stone rings on their sides. Was this used as a bath house or a store room, or for torture?

After a while, ruin-fatigue may set in, and a refreshing antidote is a stroll up to the Cerro de la Cruz. This is a hill-top cross, perched directly north of town, a half-hour walk away. To get there, follow 4 or 3 Avenida Norte to its northern conclusion, turn right, and then left, up the hill and beyond the last houses. You will come to some paved steps and a path winding through some pine trees to your left, which eventually comes out on to an open clearing, overlooking all Antigua and the surrounding countryside. Although so close to town, this path is dogged by armed thieves and muggers: **never** go alone, and avoid it altogether in the late afternoon or after dark.

West of the Plaza

Leave the Plaza along 4 Calle Poniente and continue for three blocks to arrive at Antigua's lively bus terminal and permanent **market**, beyond the tree-lined road of Alameda Santa Lucía. 'Guate! Guate!', shout the bus conductors, as you approach, and black clouds blast from revving engines. Market stalls spill out from the purpose-built wooden shacks: cigarettes, fruit and vegetables, hardware, Indian *artesanía*—almost anything can be bought here. It is one of the country's best markets for Indian craftwork at reasonable prices, so it is worth taking the time to shop around here.

One block south of the bus terminal, the extension of 5 Calle Poniente crosses the Alameda Santa Lucía, and ends at the entrance to Antigua's **cemetery**. If you fancy a quiet walk among gaudy shrines, complete with plastic flowers and glittering streamers, this is the place to go. You will notice a lot of blue and green paint here; these are the traditional colours of mourning for the Indians. For a slightly less morbid pastime, the **Casa K'Ojom** (*open Mon–Fri, 9–5; adm US$1*) is an excellent museum dedicated to Guatemala's indigenous musical heritage. To find it, turn right into Calle de los Recoletos, just before the cemetery. The museum is a small bungalow, set back from the dirt road, in a well-kept garden. It displays many of the Maya Indians' musical instruments, and shows how some were adapted to colonial tastes after the Spanish arrived. Some instruments, such as the marimba, are still in use today. The museum has an audiovisual show, demonstrating music from many of the exhibited instruments. There are also useful books on traditional Maya festivals and religious ritual.

Continuing past the museum on the dirt road, you soon reach yet another of Antigua's abundance of ruins. This one is known as **La Recolección**, after the Recolect friars who founded a mission here in the late 16th century. Until the 1976 earthquake its remnants, with their one remaining arch, were considered some of the most evocative by conoisseurs of ruins. Now the crumbling walls and weathered boulders tend to get used as a convenient toilet facility or shelter for the destitute.

South of the Plaza

The southern quarter of Antigua has the fewest sights and attracts a smaller number of visitors—a relief after the crowds around the main square. At the junction of 5 Avenida Sur and 8 Calle Oriente, you will see the wonderfully photogenic ruined church of **San José el Viejo**, framed with greenery.

Follow 8 Calle Oriente east, past four blocks, and you will emerge onto the Alameda del Calvario, which runs directly south from the gates of San Francisco. Probably one of Antigua's most unattractive streets, thick with traffic throwing up swirls of dust, Alameda del Calvario becomes a focal point during the famous Semana Santa (Easter Week) processions. Ceremonial floats are carried past the 12 altars along the road representing the Stations of the Cross, ending up at the Iglesia del Calvario. It's quite a sight (*see* below). By the entrance you will see the gnarled old tree that was planted by Pedro de Betancourt on 19 March 1657—another site where the Indians come to pay their respects to him. The altars here are neglected now, but the beautiful, crumbling stone fountain, with some delicate carving still visible, that stands in the road in front of El Calvario makes your trek worthwhile.

One of the best detailed introductions to Antigua's historical buildings and monuments is *Antigua Guatemala* by Elizabeth Bell and Trevor Long, originally written in 1978 and revised in 1990.

Semana Santa in Antigua

Easter Week in Antigua is one of the most dramatic and colourful festivals in the whole of Latin America, and the largest celebration in Central America. Thousands of Guatemalans and foreigners gather to fill the cobbled streets and cram the hotels. Almost all of Antigua's inhabitants are involved in some aspect of the huge processions, biblical re-enactments and religious services that take place throughout the week, and outsiders come to participate as musicians and singers at the numerous concerts and parties. It's a time of wild celebration and joy, when religious fervour mixes with drunkenness and dancing. Fire-crackers blast in the streets day and night, and the crammed squares are decorated with flowers.

The tourist office publishes a detailed programme annually. However, a few additional general points are worth making: events often happen hours later than stated; banks operate a half-day on Wednesday, and close from Thursday to the following Monday; the food market closes down after Wednesday; from Thursday to Sunday, restaurants and bars often reduce their menus to a few items, usually the most expensive ones, and prices can double; all accommodation prices double or even triple. Booking in advance or arriving a few days early is essential.

Palm Sunday: The festivities begin early, with 7, 8 and 9am processions setting off from the major churches after Mass. The main procession of the day starts at around 2pm, from outside the Iglesia La Merced. Jesus' entry into Jerusalem is recreated for the **Jesús Nazareño de la Merced** procession, and his effigy is carried on a huge float (*anda*), which weighs thousands of pounds. The bearers shuffle in slow unison, gently swaying as they shoulder the impossible weight. Eventually, at around 10pm, the procession, many hundreds strong by now, wends its way around the main square and returns to La Merced. This final stage is the most dramatic: the faces of the throng are lit by flaming torches, purple-robed 'Israelites' swing great copal burners, which spread thick clouds of incense, and fire-crackers explode all around.

Monday: See the freshly decked out altars at Iglesia La Merced.

Tuesday: Festivities and worship honouring the city's patron saint centre around San Francisco church, 6am–11pm.

Wednesday: The main action is at Escuela de Cristo church, 6am–11pm.

Thursday: It is on this night that the famous 'carpets' made of dyed sawdust, pine needles, seeds and flowers are delicately sprinkled on to the streets, only to be destroyed by the most dramatic procession of them all: the 3am **Procession of the Roman Soldiers**. They run around the city's streets, announcing the *sentencia*, the death sentence for Jesus. Others gallop on horseback, and behind them come the modern-day Guatemalan military, giving the spectator an almost too realistic sense of the fearful drama. Meanwhile marimba bands play all over town. It really is worth staying up—or rising early—to see this memorable performance of religious theatre. Some restaurants and bars stay open 24 hours to help you get through the night.

Good Friday: The Procession of the Roman Soldiers comes to a bleary-eyed end around 6am, only for yet another procession to set off from La Merced an hour later, passing through town, and eventually returning to its starting point sometime around 3. As a mark of devotion, many of Antigua's inhabitants lay yet more of the perishable 'carpets' before their front doors. At midday, the re-enactment of the Crucifixion takes place at the Escuela de Cristo church; at 2pm, the Song of Pardon is sung in front of the city hall, as part of the La Merced procession that began in the morning. After the singing, a lucky prisoner from the local jail is released. And many other ceremonies take place all over town.

Easter Eve: The streets are quiet and more 'carpets' are laid out; the procession of mourning, **La Procesión de la Virgin de la Soledad,** in the evening, is one of the most moving you will see. Women dressed in black carry enormous floats with images of the Virgin, draped in black and bedecked with long-stemmed red roses.

Easter Sunday: A 'morning after the night before' atmosphere pervades the town as the festival comes to an end and the majority of visitors quickly depart.

Shopping

Antigua's **market**, near the bus terminal, is one of the best for Indian handicrafts. People come from all over the country to sell here, especially at weekends, when most of the action transfers to the corner of 4 Calle and 6 Avenida. Prices at weekends will be slightly higher, but a practised haggler can still get a good bargain.

There are also some superb shops here, where top quality is matched by top prices, but you'll still find prices lower than back home.

An excellent place for household textiles inspired by traditional weaving and decorative styles is **Colibri**, 4 Calle Oriente 3 B; **Quinta Maconda**, 5 Avenida Norte 11, ✆/✉ 8323585, is similar but rather more expensive. For the largest variety of *huipiles*, displayed with helpful information on origins, have a look in **Kashlan Po't**, La Fuente Commercial Centre, 4 Calle Oriente 14, though shopping here is not as cheap as buying at the place that makes your favourite style or at any of the country's major markets.

For contemporary art—Guatemalan and ex-patriate—there are a number of commercial galleries: **La Fuente Galería de Arte**, 4 Calle Oriente 14, holds regular exhibitions; the gallery that fronts the **Café Condesa**, on the main square, always has the most innovative art showings; at **Los Nazareños**, 6 Calle Poniente 13, you can see the latest work by local artists. For antique art and furnishings, visit **Casa de Artes**, 4 Avenida Sur 11.

Craftwork made of glass, iron or wood can be found at **Casa Chicob** (inside Café Barroco), 4 Calle Oriente 22; **Casa Sol**, 5 Avenida Sur 14, produces beautiful, hand-made ceramics. For furniture and interior decorations try **La Casa de los Espiritus**, 4 Calle Oriente 38. Jewellery is sold in many places, though one of the best venues for jade and silver is **Jades S.A.**, 4 Calle Oriente 34, where you can also visit workshops and learn about traditional Maya symbols.

Where to Stay

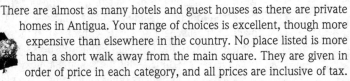

There are almost as many hotels and guest houses as there are private homes in Antigua. Your range of choices is excellent, though more expensive than elsewhere in the country. No place listed is more than a short walk away from the main square. They are given in order of price in each category, and all prices are inclusive of tax. Remember that Antigua is always popular, so you may have to hunt around, and that during Christmas and Easter Week it can be very hard to find anywhere at all. It is best to get there a few days early, or book in advance. Note that not all of the cheaper establishments have a phone.

luxury

Of the large hotels, the **Hotel Casa Santo Domingo**, 3 Calle Oriente 28, ✆ 8320079, ✆ 8320102, is the favourite for sheer glamour and the most exquisite setting, in one of the oldest convents in Antigua. Its beautifully restored rooms are set around courtyards, surrounded by stunning gardens, full of romantic corners, ruined arches and beautiful fountains. The restaurant, however, cannot be recommended for anything but salads and cocktails. The **Ramada Hotel**, 9 Calle Poniente and Carretera Ciudad Vieja, ✆ 8320011/015, ✆ 8320237, offers standard North American hotel facilities in a predictably neutral atmosphere plus a pleasant garden with a pool (open to non-residents for US$3), also a sauna, jacuzzi and steam room. **Hotel Antigua**, 5 Avenida Sur and 8 Calle Poniente 1, ✆ 8320288, ✆ 8320807, is housed in a lovely colonial-type building, with a fragrant tropical garden and swimming pool.

For those who want to splash out on genuine luxury the only place to stay is the **Quinta Maconda**, 5 Avenida Norte 11, ✆/✆ 8323585, a truly magical retreat tucked away behind a discreet door, right in the heart of Antigua. This tastefully restored colonial house has just three guest rooms, ensuring peace and quiet as well as very attentive service, which includes lighting the log fire in your room before bedtime.

expensive

Posada de Don Rodrigo, 5 Avenida Norte 17, ✆/✆ 8320291, is without doubt one of the most beautiful colonial residences in Antigua, with period interior and antique furniture. The cobbled main courtyard has two resident macaws, who lend a tropical flavour; the restaurant in another courtyard is excellent, though expensive. **Casa de los Cántaros**, 5 Avenida Sur 5, ✆ 8320674, ✆ 8320609, is a gorgeous colonial guest house in the quieter southern part of Antigua, where traditional beauty is perfectly blended with mod cons, including a library and a separate TV room. Discounts are available for stays of three weeks or more. **The Cloister**, 5 Avenida Norte 23, ✆/✆ 8320712, is right under the town's landmark arch, and also offers guest house services in a lovely colonial setting.

The **Hotel Panchoy**, 1 Avenida Norte 5A, ✆/✆ 8323919, despite its promising exterior is rather disappointing—though you do get a TV and fridge in every room.

98   *The Western Highlands*

The **Hotel El Carmen**, 3 Avenida Norte 9, ✆ 8323850, ✉ 8323847, has a rather clinical atmosphere, but is perfectly alright. **Hotel Aurora**, 4 Calle Oriente 16, ✆/✉ 8320217, is housed in a fine colonial building, with all rooms looking out on to the courtyard and fountain.

Mesón Panza Verde, 5 Avenida Sur 19, ✆/✉ 8322925, is a small first-class hotel, which offers excellent service and a very fine restaurant. All rooms have fireplaces—and you couldn't do better for the price. **Posada de Doña Marta**, 7 Avenida Norte 100, ✆ 8320261, offers clean rooms with TV, and good views from the first floor.

Hotel Convento Santa Catalina, 5 Avenida Norte 28, ✆ 8323080, ✉ 8323079, is good value and has a great location, though some might find the adjacent bar a bit too noisy in the evening. **Posada San Sebastián**, 3 Avenida Norte 4, ✆/✉ 8322621, is a slightly bizarre combination of antique shop and guest house, but certainly friendly. **Hotel Casa Santiago de los Caballeros**, 7 Avenida Norte 67, ✆ 8320465, ✉ 8325858, is a personal favourite, for being off the beaten track and having a lovely private garden. **Hotel del Centro**, 4 Calle Poniente 22, ✆ 8320657, lives up to its name, but is rather overpriced.

moderate

Posada Asjemenou, 5 Avenida Norte 31, ✆ 8320670, is one of the best value guest houses in this range. Quiet, clean rooms are ranged around a spacious courtyard; don't accept the rooms at the back without a discount. **Doña Angelina**, 4 Calle Poniente 33, has welcoming staff but dark and dingy rooms. **Posada San Vincente**, 6 Avenida Sur 6, ✆ 8323311, is also friendly and offers bright rooms, each with private bath. **Hotel Cortéz y Larraz**, 6 Avenida Sur 3, ✆ 8320276, across the street, is just as good. **Hotel Confort**, 1 Avenida Norte 2, ✆ 8320566, is a small, family-run guest house with a pretty garden, but with only one bathroom. **El Rosario Lodge**, 5 Avenida Sur 36, ✆ 8320336, is great if you want to stay long-term and need a serviced apartment. Guaranteed peaceful spot, but usually booked up long in advance. **Hotel Descanso**, 5 Avenida Norte 9, ✆ 8320142, offers slightly dark rooms with private bath, but the roof terrace and location make it worth staying here.

inexpensive

Posada La Merced, 7 Avenida Norte 43A, ✆ 8323197, is a touch grubby, but very quiet. **Hotel Cristal**, Avenida El Desengaño 25, is very decent for the price and has the added attraction of use of the kitchen. Rooms on the road side can be very loud though. **Posada Las Rosas**, 6 Avenida Sur 8, ✆ 8320644, has gloomy little rooms, but they're fine for the price. **La Casa de Santa Lucía**, Alameda de Santa Lucía 5, is one of the most popular in this category, with clean rooms ranged around a cool, leafy courtyard.

Posada Landivar, 5 Calle Poniente 23, has modern rooms, immaculately kept, and a rooftop terrace. **Hotel San Francisco**, 1 Avenida Sur 15, ✆ 8323383, is a simple budget option, secure and quiet. **El Placido**, 3 Calle Poniente 33, is the latest business run by Doña Esmeralda, one of the landladies most popular among regular budget travellers to Antigua. **El Pasaje**, Alameda Santa Lucía 3, is basic and loud but friendly, with great views from the rooftop terrace. **Posada El Refugio**, 4 Calle Poniente 28, offers accommodation with no frills.

Eating Out

Antigua has some of the best cafés and restaurants in the country, many run by resident foreigners, with a wide choice of local and international cuisine. Make the most of it, especially if you are embarking on a long trip—after a while, even the most seasoned travellers begin to despair at the prospect of yet more of the ubiquitous *huevos y frijoles*. New places are opening all the time, and the following is just a small selection. In addition, all the top hotels and guest houses have restaurants, which are not mentioned here.

For cheap snacks and simple *comedor*-style food, try the market and nearby spots on the Alameda Santa Lucía, past the shopping arcade, but on the same side. **Peroleto** does good snacks and lots of fruit juices. **Panificadora Colombia** and **Antigua Capri**, along 4 Calle Poniente, and **San Carlos**, on the main square, are excellent for simple and cheap local fare.

Some of the best foreign food in Antigua is Italian. **Quesos y Vino**, 5 Avenida Norte 32 A, makes its own fresh pasta on the premises, as well as excellent pizzas and delicious sandwiches to eat in or take away. (*Closed Tues.*) **Asjemenou**, 5 Calle Poniente 4, makes a good calzone, as well as delicious breakfasts and decent coffee. **Restaurante y Pizzeria Catari**, 6 Avenida Norte 52, is the new location of the former Martedino, offering good value, plain Italian food. **El Capuchino**, 6 Avenida Norte, is costly but good. For take-away pizza try **Bianchi's**, 4 Calle Poniente 18. And for a rather strange combination of Tex-Mex or Italian fare, head for **Peregrinos Restaurante** at 4 Avenida Norte 1, around the corner from Lloyds Bank.

Delicious German food, such as *schnitzel*, can be enjoyed to the sounds of classical music at the **Oasis del Peregrino**, 7 Avenida Norte 7. (*Closed Wed.*) Good, but dearer and thin on atmosphere is **Welten**, 4 Calle Oriente 21. (*Closed Tues.*) For Austrian dishes try **Wiener**, Calzada Santa Lucia 8, along the shopping arcade. Enjoy mouth-watering international dishes and immaculate service at **Panza Verde**, 5 Avenida Sur 19, which is very expensive, but worth every *centavo*— smaller pockets could try the lunchtime menu. For something special head for **El Sereno**, 4 Avenida Norte 16, Antigua's most famous top-class restaurant. Competition for that title is increasing, however, and **Restaurante Estro Armonico**, 5 Avenida Sur and 6 Calle Poniente 7, is certainly a contender: eat anything from steak to *tepezquintle* in a beautiful courtyard setting. **Restaurante Luna Llena**, 6 Avenida Norte 32, offers similar elegance, but a less exciting menu.

For mouth-watering Thai meals (vegetarian dishes included) and a friendly atmosphere, try **Café Flor**, 4 Avenida Sur 1. (*Closed Sun.*) **La Casbah**, 5 Avenida Norte

30, offers a colourful environment and great roof terrace, though not a Moroccan dish in sight. (*Closed Mon.*) **Doña Luisa's**, 4 Calle Oriente 12, in a restored colonial house with a beautiful courtyard, is a long-standing favourite in Antigua. It is one of the best places for breakfast, but also serves a few non-breakfast dishes such as chilli con carne or soup. Added features include American cable television and a travellers' noticeboard. A strong competitor for Doña Luisa's business is the **Rainbow Reading Room**, 7 Avenida Sur 8, which offers an interesting variety of vegetarian meals in a charming setting. Portions are generous and the coffee is excellent. Similarly vegetarian, but neither atmospheric nor well-priced is **Sueños del Quetzal**, located in the La Fuente shopping courtyard at 4 Calle Oriente 14. If you're desperate for a bagel, though, this is where you'll find one. A better place for a quick and filling snack—or a full American cooked breakfast—is **La Manzana Grande**, 2 Avenida Norte 3 A. (*Closed Mon.*) Or try **Samba Sub**, 6 Avenida Norte 7, or **Fridas**, 4 Calle Poniente 30 A. On the other hand, if you enjoy waffles, there is no better place than the **Bagdad Café**, across the square from La Merced church. You also get a good choice of homemade bread and rolls.

El Churrasco on 4 Calle Poniente has good cheap steaks. **Los Gauchitos**, on the same street, offers you value for money, but in a fast-food atmosphere. **Las Antorchas**, on 3 Avenida Sur 1, does excellent steaks. For authentic Guatemalan cooking and excruciatingly slow service, try some of the freshly grilled meats at **La Fonda de la Calle Real**, 5 Avenida Norte 5 and 3 Calle Poniente 7. Or just go there for the live music on Fridays, Saturdays and Sundays. The German-owned **Patio de las Delicias**, Avenida del Desengaño 22, is the solitary fish restaurant in Antigua. (*Closed Sun–Tues.*)

There are a few excellent cafés in Antigua, foremost of which is the wonderful **Cafe Condesa**, on the main square, found if you walk through **La Casa del Conde** book shop and art gallery, under the arches on the west side; it has delicious food, served in an enchanting courtyard. Great cakes and cookies, but terrible tea and coffee can be found at **La Cenicienta**, 5 Avenida Norte. Also worth trying is **Café Jardín**, on the west side of the main square. Try **Cookies Etc.**, on 3 Avenida Norte, which also serves good coffee. **Caffé Opera**, 6 Avenida Norte 17, is the closest you'll get to a classy Italian café-bar, expensive but cool.

Entertainment and Nightlife

Antigua's nightlife is rapidly expanding. Apart from restaurants that double as drinking spots, there are several music bars, all open until one in the morning (a law forbids the sale of alcohol after 1am).

One of the latest additions to the nightlife scene is **La Cava** bar, in the same colonial building as El Sereno Restaurant (*see* above), which regularly swings to Brazilian music. Alternatively check out **Babilons**, on the corner of 6 Calle Poniente and 5a Avenida Sur, which serves delicious raspberry cocktails made with fresh berries from the owner George's local farm. **Macondo**, 5 Avenida

Norte 28, in part of the former Santa Catalina Convent, is an established part of any pub crawl, while **La Chimenea**, on 7 Avenida Norte, is known for its comfortable sofas and chairs and its English pub atmosphere. The music is standard American pop. A stumble away, **Picasso's**, 7 Avenida Norte 3, is the long-standing favourite bar in town, and certainly has a good range of taped Western music. The owner-barmen, César and Oscar, also make the best *cuba libres* in town. Almost opposite is **Bota Tejana**, which is a no-frills bar and the only one where you can mix with more local people than foreigners. Out of favour these days is the **El Cabildo**, on 7 Avenida Sur, though it certainly deserves more foreign custom than it gets. For live music check out **La Jazz Gruta**, Avenida Santa Lucia and 3 Calle, open nightly from 9.30pm. Finally, the Ramada Hotel has a small disco.

The cinema is on 5 Avenida Sur, near the main square, and usually shows English language films with subtitles. Programmes tend to be dominated by violence or porn, though, and the quality of the films is predictably poor. Instead try **Cinemala**, 2 Calle Oriente 4 (inside the ALM Language School), which shows three videos a day on a large TV screen, while the **Latin American Film Centre**, Avenida del Desengaño 22, offers an 'inside view of Latin American countries'. Programmes are widely advertised around town, as well as in the free *Classifieds Revue*, a monthly listings booklet available all over Antigua (main office: 4 Calle Oriente 23).

Excursions from Antigua

Excursions from Antigua range from energetic volcano climbing to gentler pastimes such as soaking in hot springs. The highland valley surrounding Antigua is strewn with Indian hamlets and sleepy villages while, in between, rich farming country is covered with crops such as coffee, maize, cereals, vegetables and fruit trees. Towering above are the three volcanoes of Agua, Acatenango and Fuego, the last of which is still active. Nearer Guatemala City, but usually visited on a tour from Antigua, Pacaya volcano is the most dramatic—for years it has been not just fuming but regularly erupting.

The inhabitants of this beautiful area are friendly, but you must still take sensible safety precautions here: take a local guide with you or go in a group, especially on trips to the volcanoes. Find out the latest news on security, either from the tourist office or the local hiking organizations. All villages mentioned can be reached by public transport from Antigua bus terminal or by taxi; remember to agree on a price before you travel.

Villages

San Juan del Obispo is just a couple of kilometres south-east of Antigua, an hour's walk or short bus ride away (catch any bus going to Santa María de Jesús). It is chiefly interesting for the restored palace of Francisco Marroquín, who was the first bishop of Guatemala, in the days of Alvarado. The nuns who now occupy the palace do not mind showing visitors around. The church contains some very fine 16th-century decoration. Travel onwards to **Santa María de Jesús**, just under an hour from Antigua, and you will reach one of the best vantage points from which to survey the whole valley spread out with Antigua at its heart and the spectacular twin peaks of Fuego and Acatenango. The village itself is mainly inhabited by Indians, who sell high-quality *huipiles*, with the best choice on market days (*Mon, Thurs and Sat*).

South-west of Antigua, under six kilometres away, is the village of **Ciudad Vieja**, famous for being near the spot where Guatemala's second capital perished. The ill-fated town of Santiago de los Caballeros was swept away in 1541, when a huge mudslide, caused by an earthquake, came down the slopes of Agua. There are no remains. Also out this way, but clinging to the lower slopes of Acatenango, is **San Antonio Aguas Calientes**, where the Indians sell their superb weaving all along the village street. If you are interested, there are plenty of women here who will give you weaving lessons on their backstrap looms—just ask around if no one approaches you. Trying it yourself, you quickly appreciate the time and skill that goes into Guatemalan weaving.

About five kilometres north-west of Antigua, you can luxuriate in the hot springs of **San Lorenzo el Tejar** (*open daily, 6–5, except Tuesday and Friday afternoons; small adm*). Take any bus heading for Chimaltenango, and ask to be dropped off near the village of **San Luís de las Carretas**, from where it is a short walk along the track to your right. There is a communal pool, or you can wallow in one of the private tubs for as long as you wish. A few kilometres further on by bus is **Los Aposentos**, a tiny lake set amongst a grove of pine trees, a lovely place for a leisurely turn in a rowing boat.

If you only have time to make one day trip from Antigua, go to **San Andrés Itzapa** on a Sunday. The village itself is a dust-blown sort of place that suffered terrible damage during the 1976 earthquake, but you will be fascinated by the local cult of **Maximón**, the most notorious of the Maya Indians' favoured saints, also called St Simón. New World colonists have always tried to suppress the Indians' attachment to this controversial saint, not least because he is supposed to be evil.

Maximón (pronounced 'Mashimon') is most often depicted in Western clothing, with a fat cigar in his mouth and Mafia-type sunglasses. The origin of his reputation for evil is uncertain, and it may have been simply propaganda spread by the earliest conquistadors. One theory is that Maximón was an Indian holy man at the time of the conquest, murdered by the Spanish because they feared his influence over the Indians. As a result of his martyrdom, however, he became one of the Indians' most revered saints—a symbol of their oppression as well as of the power they invoked against it. Today, there are only a handful of villages where he is worshipped, and his chapel in San Andrés Itzapa is one of the least visited by outsiders.

Every Sunday, Indian worshippers flock from as far away as Guatemala City, to pay tribute to Maximón. Their elaborate ritual involves liberal splashings of rum, smoking of fat cigars (by women only), candle lighting, praying and even fireworks. People queue to get to Maximón's altar, where they pray to the saint, splashing him with rum and throwing money into his lap. Occasionally a daykeeper (a shaman) accompanies a devotee, rubbing their head and neck with rum, and stroking their body from head to toe with special laurels. Afterwards the worshipper chooses one of the many stone tables in the chapel on which to light candles. The candles are different colours, signifying prayers on different subjects: red is for matters of love, faith or desire; green is for business or wealth; pink is for health and hope; black is for warding off enemies and jealousy; purple guards against vicious or bad thoughts; blue is for luck in matters of money, journeys or learning and for anything to do with work; yellow is for the protection of adults; and white is for the protection of children. Once outside again, the burning of rum and lighting of fireworks is used to divine fortune with the help of a daykeeper.

To find the chapel, follow the unpaved street that leads off to the right, just past the main square. Anyone can tell you where it is if you get lost. Do not take your camera in case it causes offence.

Volcanoes

Two of the volcanoes, Agua and Pacaya, can be climbed on organized day trips, which cost from $15. To find out about the range currently available take a look at the notice-board at Doña Luisa's. For official information on the latest security situation, reputable guides, and equipment, go to both Casa Andinista Bookshop and Club Chigag before coming to any decisions. Most people prefer the services of Casa Andinista. If you're not planning to stay overnight, strong walking shoes, food and water, toilet paper, sun-cream and sun-glasses are all you need. Remember also that the temperature at high altitudes is very cold, and the wind chill can be severe.

The easiest volcano to climb nearby is **Agua** (3760m), immediately south of Antigua; join the clear path just outside the village of Santa María de Jesús. The slopes of this perfectly symmetrical cone are steep, and the ascent takes a good four to five hours. The high altitude makes it even harder work but, once at the crater, you are rewarded with the extraordinary sight of a football pitch inside the mountain, and views to take away what little breath you have left. The descent is much quicker and, if you set off at 6am, you can do Agua as a tough but rewarding day trip. If you plan to stay the night near the summit, there is a shelter, but you will certainly need a warm sleeping-bag, and preferably a tent. The dawn up here is magical and on a clear day you can see all the way to the Pacific, as well as the surrounding valleys and neighbouring volcanoes of Pacaya, Fuego and Acatenango.

Acatenango (3976m) and **Fuego** (3766m), to the southwest of Antigua, are twin volca-noes that only the toughest attempt to climb. The ascent of Acatenango can take anything up to nine hours but when you reach the top you have views of two craters and a superb panorama stretching from Agua across the valley, to the distant cones surrounding Lake Atitlán. If you have the energy left to climb Fuego as well, you will have to stay the night beneath Acatenango's craters; the next morning, you must descend quite a way before you can start climbing Fuego, and continue for another foot-crunching day. The crater is continuously spouting sulphurous fumes—do not get too close. The return journey is via Acatenango again, so no easier.

Pacaya (2544m), rising above Lake Amatitlán near Guatemala City, is a popular day trip—not least because you can drive a good long way before walking, and then the volcano is pretty small. Up top, you enter a blackened world of burning earth and witches' fumes, lava petrified into strange forms, and the crater spouting clouds of smoke and occasional rocks. The volcano is most dramatic at night, its cone wrapped in a haze of orange light. You need to be careful on Pacaya never to get too close to the eruptions. And the volcano's popularity with tourists attracts bandits; in 1991 tours were suspended after a particularly brutal attack. Note that tour companies tend to use armed guards only at weekends.

Iximché

Capital of the Cakchiqueles, Iximché was once a city of 10,000 people. It was founded by the proud noble families who had seceded from the greater Quiché empire only 50 years before the Spanish arrived. The internal divisions between the Indian nations in Guatemala helped the Spanish in their conquest; the Cakchiqueles sided with Alvarado. He arrived in Iximché in 1524, and declared it the first Spanish capital of Guatemala.

It did not take long for the Spanish to alienate their Indian allies by demanding ever more labour, riches and women, and by 1526 Alvarado had burnt this Indian city, and its inhabitants were forced to flee. It's a depressingly familiar story, and today the site offers few clues to its former appearance. It may have little to offer as a ruin, but it is a tranquil place, set in beautiful countryside. Lying about halfway between Chimaltenango and Los Encuentros, it is an easy day trip from Antigua, or a short detour from the Pan-American Highway.

It is quite easy to get to the site, though if you don't have private transport it does involve a good hour's walk. Catch any bus to Chimaltenango (40mins), and wait there for a Tecpán bus (1hr). From Tecpán, it is then a few kilometres' pleasant walk to the site of Iximché (*small adm*).

Lake Atitlán

The Indians consider the Atitlán basin the navel of the earth and sky, for as one enters it the sky becomes defined by its rim of smoking cones.

Time Among the Maya, Ronald Wright

Lake Atitlán is most extraordinary at sunset: as the cool mountain air turns all the shades from blue to dusty pink to grey, so the waters of the lake vary their hues of greenish blue. Every time you watch it happen, the scene will be different. The lake lies at an altitude of 1562m, and is 18km long and about 10km wide. It is ringed by three volcanoes that pierce the clouds above, their steep rock faces falling straight into the water below. Although dramatic storms can whip up on the lake, the weather here is generally temperate.

Dotted around the lake are a number of traditional Indian settlements, of which Santiago Atitlán is the most famous. But there are plenty of others, less enslaved to tourism, and there are also long stretches of the shoreline that are not inhabited at all, perfect for tranquil hiking or boating.

Getting There

By bus: The **Rebuli** company runs daily buses, 6–3, from its offices at 3 Avenida 2-36, Zona 9, Guatemala City; the journey takes about 3hrs. Coming from Antigua, catch a **local bus** to Chimaltenango, and get off at the junction with the main Highway. From there, flag down any bus with either Panajachel or Sololá on the front window. This journey should not take more than 3hrs either. Bus tickets are very cheap, but always compare notes with your fellow passengers to make sure you are not paying an inflated 'gringo price'.

You can also use the **private bus shuttles** operating out of Antigua. Check the noticeboards there or ask any of the travel agents mentioned on p.90.

Getting Around

The road is paved as far as Panajachel, but after that it becomes a very rough dirt track, extremely steep in places, as it follows ridges above the shoreline. Panajachel is on the north-east shore of Lake Atitlán, and the road curves around the eastern side of the lake, to San Lucas Tolimán in the south-eastern corner, all the way to Santiago Atitlán and San Pedro La Laguna on the south-western shore. The road is so bad that the 55km drive from Panajachel to San Pedro La Laguna could easily take you half a day. There is a new paved road to San Lucas Tolimán, but it leaves the lake, going via San Andrés Semetabaj and Godinez. For an easy day's hike, take an early morning bus from Panajachel to Godinez, and then walk down the mountainside to San Antonio (takes about 1hr), and follow the dirt road along the lake for another 11km, back to Panajachel. Tourist crime is a problem here too, though. Attacks have taken place on this road and on hiking trails around the lake, so do check with the tourist office for the latest security situation.

The best way of reaching the lake's southern villages is by taking one of the ferries or launches that leave from the beach in front of Panajachel every day. There are ferries daily, 8–5, and the boat timetable is always posted at the tourist office (*see* below). The crossing to **Santiago Atitlán** takes 45 minutes, and the price is usually around $3 for a return ticket. This is an inflated tourist price, but it's officially sanctioned by the government, so there is very little you can do about it. Do not buy a return ticket; the return part will only be valid on the boat you went out on, which may not travel back when it suits you. There will be plenty of boats and you can always buy a single if you ask.

Morning ferries direct to **San Pedro** or **Santa Cruz La Laguna** (8–5, but do check at the tourist office), depart from the jetty just before the **Hotel Tzanjuyu**. Follow the road that leads off the main street straight down to the water. The returning ferry drops in at all the villages along the inaccessible western shore, and the two-hour journey is a lovely way to see this quiet part of the lake.

You can, of course, hire a boatman. Agree on a price before setting off and, if possible, go with someone who has been recommended by the tourist office. It is not unknown for the occasional tourist to end up swimming home because of mid-lake renegotiations.

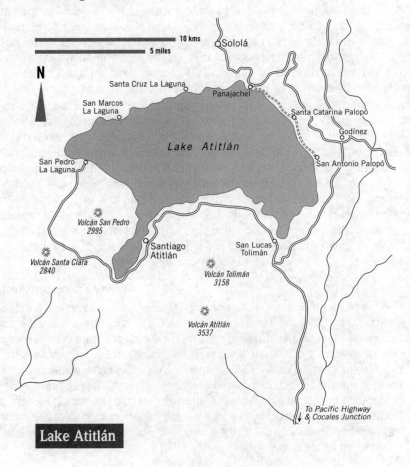

Lake Atitlán

It is possible to travel all the way around the lake by a combination of bus rides, boat trips and walking (not a good idea to go alone). This would take you about four days, and you would need to take your own provisions and tent, though there are simple guest houses in some villages, namely San Lucas Tolimán, Santiago Atitlán, San Pedro La Laguna, and Santa Cruz. To cut this journey by half, you could take a bumpy bus ride from Panajachel to Santiago Atitlán one day (check the time with the tourist office—it is very early), catch a boat to San Pedro La Laguna the next morning, and from there spend two days walking back to Panajachel via Santa Cruz. Beware here too; attacks on walkers have occurred.

Panajachel

The road that turns off the Pan-American Highway for Panajachel (or Pana) and Lake Atitlán is a dramatic short drive. On the way you will come across the bizarre sight of a giant soldier's helmet set on a pair of boots, a sculpture which marks the entrance to a large military base. Before you have time to wonder whether you imagined it, you find yourself transported to Sololá, a small town perched high above the lake's basin. Up to here the road is relatively level, but from now on, you are in for a rollercoaster ride, plunging 500m in 8km, on hairpin bends and along steep ridges, with short flashes of the lake below and superb views of the surrounding mountains and volcanoes. Take your panoramic photos from one of the *miradores* (viewpoints) along the road.

The former Indian village of Panajachel has long been a popular resort for the retired and for visiting foreigners. During the sixties, Panajachel was 'discovered' by hippies, who left an indelible mark on the place. The Indians still sell custom-made waistcoats and skull caps that none of them would be seen dead in, and have even mastered the art of tie-dying. Pana is now a buzzing resort with every kind of accommodation, and a nightlife second only to Antigua's. Restaurants and lakeside stalls cater for a wide range of tastes, offering everything from local fish to Swiss delicacies or health food. All this may sound like rampant commercialism but, although Lake Atitlán is one of Guatemala's foremost tourist attractions, Panajachel is still a comparatively small place and you will find yourself in another world almost as soon as you leave the settlement. With luck, the fact that the entire basin is a national park will help to keep it that way.

Getting There and Away

There are direct **buses** to Chichicastenango (1½hrs) on Thursdays and Sundays, 6.45am–3pm. At other times and on other days take any bus to the Los Encuentros junction and change there. Direct buses to and from Quezaltenango (2½hrs) leave daily, 5.30am–2.30pm, otherwise change at Los Encuentros. Direct buses to and from the capital (3½hrs) operate 5am–2.30pm, thereafter change at Los Encuentros. Connections between Panajachel and Antigua (3hrs) are made by taking any bus to the capital and changing at the relevant junction in Chimaltenango. There are also bus routes to the Pacific coast via Cocales junction on the Pacific Highway. (Check the timetable in the tourist office for the latest schedules for all the above.)

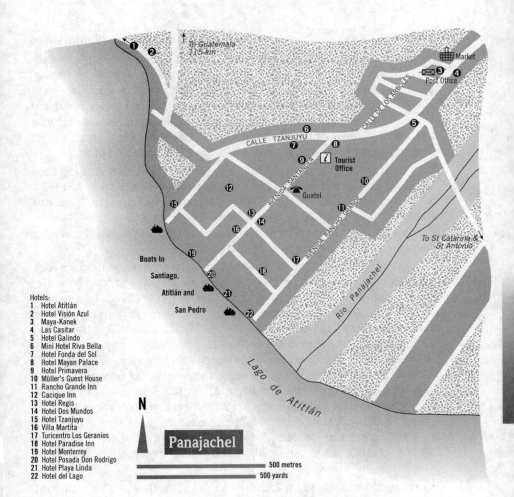

Hotels:
1 Hotel Atitlán
2 Hotel Visión Azul
3 Maya-Kanek
4 Las Casitar
5 Hotel Galindo
6 Mini Hotel Riva Bella
7 Hotel Fonda del Sol
8 Hotel Mayan Palace
9 Hotel Primavera
10 Müller's Guest House
11 Rancho Grande Inn
12 Cacique Inn
13 Hotel Regis
14 Hotel Dos Mundos
15 Hotel Tzanjuyu
16 Villa Martita
17 Turicentro Los Geranios
18 Hotel Paradise Inn
19 Hotel Monterrey
20 Hotel Posada Don Rodrigo
21 Hotel Playa Linda
22 Hotel del Lago

N

Panajachel

500 metres
500 yards

There is a constant flow of **minibuses** between Sololá and Panajachel, or to the Los
Encuentros junction, where you can easily get an onward connection, either back
towards Guatemala City, or west. The enormous size of the crowds waiting for the
early morning buses can be alarming; remember you have a better chance of getting
on to the bus if you wait by the old market, where the early buses stop first. For
local buses around the eastern shore of the lake, check with the tourist office for the
latest schedule. Normally there is just one bus heading towards San Lucas Tolimán,
and the return leaves about the same time from the other end, making it virtually
impossible to return the same day. If just going as far as Santa Catarina Palopó or
San Antonio Palopó you can catch pick-up trucks and minibuses that leave from
outside the Las Golondrinas store, by the police station, 9–4.30 daily.

Tourist Information

The **Inguat** office, © 7621392 (*open Mon–Sat, 8–6.30; Sun noon–6*), is on Calle Santander, in the commercial centre near the main road. Run by the English-speaking and extremely helpful Mr Hector Solis, this should be your first port of call for orientation and information. Details of private bus shuttles are available at the tourist office; you could also wander down Calle Santander and see what **Servicios Turisticos Atitlán** has to offer, outside the Hotel Regis. Expect a single ticket to Guatemala City to cost around US$22, to Antigua around US$12.

The Banco Agricola Mercantil (**BAM**), on the corner of the main road and Calle Santander, changes money at the best rate (*open Mon–Fri, 9–5; Sat 9–1*). For 24-hr cash on Visa cards, though, head for the cash dispenser outside **Banco Industrial**, Calle Santander (*open Mon–Fri, 8.30–3; Sat 8.30–12.30*). There are also always moneychangers hanging around outside the banks. Panajachel is the only place on the lake where you can change money.

The **post office** (*open Mon–Fri, 8–4.30*) is on a small turning off the main road, just after the village church. However, to send parcels out, you have to use **Get Guated Out**, ©/✆ 7622015, which is upstairs next to Al Chisme restaurant on Calle de los Arboles (*open Mon–Sat, 9–1 and 2.30–6*). They will charge you around US$60 for a 5kg parcel to London—US$91, if they use UPS. Normally they use the national postal service, so there is nothing safer about their service; it is just a matter of expensive convenience. The **Guatel** office (*open daily, 7–midnight*) is halfway down Avenida Santander. There are also plenty of **fax services** available. Shop around for the best deals, but you could start by visiting Maya Communications, on Calle Santander, which offers every type of service, from fax and e-mail to computer rental and flight reservations (*open Mon–Sat, 8–1 and 2–6*). Get Guated Out (*see* above) also offer a fax service, and very competitive rates are available at Central American Link, in the courtyard next to Bruno's Steak House.

Bikes can be hired opposite the junction for Calle Santander, on the main road. They cost about $3 per day, but are available by the hour as well. For **motor-bikes**, ask at the tourist office; prices will be around $25 per day. Two places worth checking are Pana Rent and Moto Servicio Queche, on Calle de los Arboles. The latter also rents out **cars**. **La Galeria** (*open 9–noon and 2–6; closed Tues*) has a permanent exhibition of the work of Guatemalan painter Nan Cruz, and also shows locally inspired work by artists from all over the world.

The **laundry** (*open Mon–Sat, 9–6*) is inside the commercial centre on Calle de los Arboles.

Around the Town

Panajachel itself is flat and strung out along a dusty main road lined with hotels, gas stations and restaurants, with almost no traces of the original Indian village. It spills from the main road down to the lake shore in two main thoroughfares with more restaurants and guest houses. There's a bustling street market on Avenida Santander, with an excellent range of well-priced Guatemalan artesanía and textiles. The waterside is newly landscaped, with a tiny stretch of sand, and a number of wooden shack restaurants, where you can eat delicious food right by the lake. The best beach for relaxed sunbathing is beyond the River Panajachel, just east of the main waterfront, easily reached by crossing the pebbly estuary of the shallow river.

Avenida Santander branches off the main road by the BAM Bank, which is also where all buses stop. If you continue straight on, you soon come to the edge of Panajachel and the local market, a traditional affair with no concessions to tourism. This is the place to buy fresh fruit and vegetables. Elsewhere, Panajachel is dominated by the floating population of foreigners, and the place is often referred to as 'Gringotenango'. Nevertheless, as a base for exploring the lake it is ideal and, if you prefer to be away from the crowds, you can stay in villages such as Santa Catarina, San Pedro La Laguna, Santiago Atitlán and Santa Cruz.

Volcanoes

There are three volcanoes around Lake Atitlán, and all of them can be climbed. The easiest is **San Pedro** (2995m), which can be ascended by a steep trail in about three or four hours; begin from the village of the same name. **Tolimán** (3158m), above Santiago Atitlán, takes a few hours longer to climb, while the **Atitlán** volcano (3537m) is a tough one that will take all day. Take a guide: trails are not clear, and there are occasional reports of guerrillas camping out up there. Either book through the tourist office in Panajachel or ask for the *alcalde* (mayor) in the relevant village, and he will recommend someone. Always fix the price first, and remember that you are expected to feed your guide.

Sports and Activities

On the lake, boats, canoes and windsurfers can be hired through the hotels or direct on the Panajachel waterfront. At weekends the water is invaded by speedboats and water-skiers as many wealthy Guatemalans have lakeside retreats here.

A gentler form of activity would be to take a stroll along one of the paths and trails of the 400-acre **Mariposario**, near Hotel Atitlán (*trails open daily 8–5; butterfly sanctuary opens daily 10–3*); founded in 1994, its long-term goal is to provide a refuge for the lake's surviving species of birds, insects and small animals.

Where to Stay in Panajachel and Around the Lake

You have plenty of choices here, and the only times you might have a problem are over Christmas and Easter, when the place is full and prices can double. Equally, prices can sink very low at quiet times—remember, they are always negotiable, even in the top hotels.

On the Lakeshore

luxury

Hotel Posada de Don Rodrigo, ☏/☎ 7622332, at the bottom of Avenida Santander, is a brand-new hotel built in colonial style, and represents a great opportunity wasted. The rooms are dark and poky and the waterslide facing the lakeshore is an eyesore. Far better to stay at **Hotel Atitlán**, ✆/✉ 7621416, the most luxurious hotel on the lake itself, 1km from the village, with all the facilities you would expect, such as private beach, swimming pool and restaurant, as well as plenty of watersports. If you prefer to be near the hub of things in Panajachel, your best option is **Hotel del Lago**, ✆ 3344545 x4420, in the capital, or ✉ 3347518. At the end of Avenida Rancho Grande, this is a largish hotel, with a pool and great views across the lake from the second floor up.

expensive

Hotel Playa Linda, ✆ 7621159, on the public beach, has a lovely garden and verandah, with most rooms facing the lake. The best private beach belongs to **Hotel Monterrey**, ✆ 7621126, off Avenida Santander, on Calle Monterray, though it is becoming rather run-down. Quite a way out, one of the oldest hotels here—and really showing its age—is the **Hotel Tzanjuyu**, ✆/✉ 7621318, with two storeys facing the water, and an atmosphere and décor that recall 1940s Hollywood movies.

On a small bay at the beginning of Panajachel, one dusty kilometre from the centre of town, the **Hotel Visión Azul**, ✆ 7621426, is a pretty little hotel with private beach and pool, near the main road and much cheaper than Hotel Atitlán.

The lakeside hotel in Santa Catarina, **Villa Santa Catarina**, ✆ 7621291, has an excellent location, though the hotel does clash somewhat with the village, arrogantly spreading itself out on the shore, its back to the Indian inhabitants who used to wash their clothes there.

moderate

A fine hotel on the lakeshore in the friendly village of San Antonio Palopó is the **Terrazas del Lago**, ✆ 2328741 in the capital, or enquire at the tourist office in Panajachel. The **Arca de Noé**, below Santa Cruz village (reached by boat only), is a lovely place, which provides excellent meals for guests. Its only problem is the dictatorial woman who runs it. Bungalows with private bathrooms, for up to three people, cost around US$20, and simple rooms, sharing shower and toilets, are much less. Get there early in the morning if you want any chance of getting either a room or a bungalow.

In a less idyllic setting, but with much friendlier management, the **Posada de Santiago**, ✆/✉ 7627167, is just outside the village of Santiago Atitlán (best reached by boat). Accommodation is in individual stone cottages, complete with private bathrooms and open fireplaces. Home cooking is served in a beautiful dining hall. If you book in advance they will pick you up from the village landing point for a small fee, otherwise it's a 20-minute walk from the village.

inexpensive

Below the village of Santa Cruz (reached by boat only) and just the other side of the landing stage from the Arca de Noé, you can stay at the simple but decent

Iguana Perdida, or the even more basic **Hospedaje Garcia**. Up in the village there's the basic but clean **Hospedaje Hernández**, which charges less than US$3 per room.

Panajachel

expensive

Cacique Inn, Calle Real, ℂ 7621205, is expensive for what it offers, but does have a small pool. **Rancho Grande Inn**, Calle Rancho Grande, ℂ 7622255, ✉ 7622247, has immaculate bungalow rooms at a variety of prices, with a breakfast restaurant. **Hotel Regis**, Avenida Santander, ℂ 7621149, is a friendly, well-kept hotel with private garden, right in the middle of town. **Müller's Guest House**, Calle Rancho Grande, ℂ 7622442, has attractive Swiss-style rooms in a peaceful setting. **Hotel Dos Mundos**, Calle Santander, ℂ/✉ 7622078, is an Italian-owned place, with a swimming pool and lovely rooms, right in the heart of Pana. **Mini Hotel Riva Bella**, on the main road, ℂ/✉ 7621353, has simple bungalow-style rooms and secure parking, but is nothing special.

moderate

Hotel Primavera, on Avenida Santander, ℂ 7622052, is an excellent German-owned guest house with pleasant rooms and a good restaurant below. **Hotel Paradise Inn**, ℂ 7621021, on Calle del Río offers motel-style accommodation, as near to the lake as you can be without actually being on it. **Hotel Mayan Palace**, on the corner of the main street and Calle Santander, ℂ 7621028, has bare rooms in a very noisy location: not ideal. **Hotel Villa Martita**, Calle Santander, is a clean and friendly, family-run guest house. **Hotel Galindo**, Calle Real, ℂ 7621168, is on the main road towards the local market. The rooms are very simple; it's not worth the money, in spite of the pretty garden. **Hotel Maya-Kanek**, Calle Real, nearer the market still, is better value. Much more pleasant and friendlier, though, is **Las Casitas**, ℂ 7621224, across the road. **Turicentro Los Geranios**, Calle Rancho Grande, ℂ 7624033, has good value self-catering bungalows for between four and six people. **Hotel Fonda del Sol**, Calle Principal, ℂ 7621162, is expensive for what you get.

inexpensive

Hotel El Centro, Calle Principal, ℂ/✉ 7621353, offers secure parking and plain rooms. **Hotel Panajachel**, opposite Las Casitas by the market, has bare rooms and hot showers downstairs only, but it is cheap. **Hotel Las Jacarandas**, off a side alley from Calle Rancho Grande, has simple, clean rooms and a lovely garden with a spacious lawn for sunbathing. **Hospedaje Country Club**, Calle Rancho Grande, offers rustic, very basic accommodation with secure parking.

Finally, anywhere with a sign announcing 'rooms' offers basic accommodation, sharing cold showers at rock-bottom prices. The best policy here is to inspect a few before making a decision.

San Lucas Tolimán

There are a few basic but clean guest houses here—ask for directions to **Pension Central, Hospedaje El Exito, Pensión Las Conchitas** or **Cafetería Santa Ana**. Better still, try either **Hotel Brisas del Lago** or **Hotel Villa del Lago**, 7 Avenida 1-84, ✆ 7620102.

Santiago Atitlán

First choice must be the **Posada de Santiago**, mentioned above, which was described by one traveller as 'a little piece of heaven'. Meals from the limited menu are excellent if not cheap. In the village itself there is the **Hospedaje Chi-Nim-Ya**, and also the **Pensión Rosita**, a bit cheaper and much grubbier.

San Pedro La Laguna

Chuasinahi is a simple guest house near the waterfront, offering double rooms for around US$6. Adjacent, facing the water, are the wooden shacks that make up **Ti-Kaaj**, favoured by the young hippie set. Also popular with budget travellers is the **Hotel San Pedro**, next door to the Chuasinahi.

San Marcos La Laguna

A quiet village set back from the north-western shore of the lake, San Marcos has become host to the **Eco Campamento La Paz**, with bungalows, rooms, vegetarian meals and relaxation for budget travellers. Also here is the Las Piramides Meditation Centre, which you can easily visit on a day trip using the regular boats that pass by from San Pedro to Panajachel.

Eating Out

The top hotels have restaurants, where you can enjoy expensive meals. Elsewhere the choice is good; one of the best options is **Al Chisme** on Calle de los Arboles, which does great pastries. A good place for breakfast especially is the **Primavera** restaurant (the **Papagayo** snack bar adjacent shares the same management and serves from the same menu). For tasty vegetarian dishes or a healthy (if expensive) breakfast, try **La Unica Deli**, on the main road, towards the market (and **Unica Deli 2** at the bottom of Calle Santander). Other vegetarian options are the **Sevananda** (*closed Sun*) and the **Bombay** (*closed Mon*) restaurants, situated in the commercial centre on Calle de los Arboles. At the beginning of this road, you will also find one of Pana's long-standing favourite bars and pizza restaurants: the **Casa del Pintor**. Try also its sister operation, the **Circus Bar**, on the main road.

For delicious steaks, try **El Patio**, on Avenida Santander, where, as the name suggests, you can sit outdoors on balmy nights. Also excellent for freshly grilled meats is **Bruno's Steak House** on the main road; while the **Casablanca** restaurant, next door, offers candle-lit dinners from an international menu.

There are many more restaurants on Calle Santander, Pana's main drag. If you are on a tight budget, your best option is **The Last Resort** (left after the Guatel office, if you are coming from the main road, down Calle 14 de Febrero), which serves a wide range of filling meals, including breakfast, at rock-bottom prices. The atmosphere is relaxed, as customers listen to the steady beat of reggae or play ping-pong in the back.

Entertainment and Nightlife

For an evening of drinking, the most popular bar these days is still **La Casa del Pintor**, Calle de los Arboles. The **Circus Bar** has live music at weekends. For a mixture of videos and drinking, check out **Ubu's Cosmic Cantina**, in the commercial centre on Calle de los Arboles.

There are also many restaurants and video-bars on Calle Santander that double as drinking venues, so you are not likely to get bored here.

Some Indian Villages Around Lake Atitlán

There are about twelve villages around the lake. The inhabitants are descendants of the two Indian tribes who lived here before the Spanish Conquest. The Tzutujil dominated the western shore, from Santiago Atitlán to San Pedro La Laguna. Their capital was on the slopes of San Pedro volcano, but has long since disappeared; like so many Indian settlements, it was destroyed by Alvarado in 1524. The rest of the shoreline was the domain of Cakchiquel Indians, who collaborated with Alvarado, only to be subjected by him in the end. The descendants of these two tribes still speak their different languages, and each village produces and wears its distinctive textiles.

The villages you are most likely to want to visit are Santiago Atitlán, San Pedro La Laguna, Santa Catarina and San Antonio, as they are the most interesting as well as the most accessible. Of these, Santiago Atitlán is the most visited by tourists, as it is the largest of the villages, and one of the few places where you can witness the cult of Maximón (*see* p.103). For details on how to get there, *see* 'Getting Around' p.107.

Santiago Atitlán

Diagonally across the lake from Panajachel, Santiago Atitlán hides in a protected inlet of the lake, between the volcanoes of Tolimán, Atitlán and San Pedro. Arriving by boat, you pass small reedy islands and fishermen in their dugout canoes, called *cayucos*. By the water's edge, women stoop to wash clothes, while the men and boys work in the neatly kept agricultural gardens beyond. It is an idyllic scene. If you venture up into the village, however, you will be surrounded by women and children trying to sell you their wares, their fierce selling technique only outdone by their ferocious competitiveness.

The reason for the hard sell is obvious. The villagers of Santiago Atitlán wear the most famous 'costume' of Guatemala's Indians. It is very glamorous as well as superbly made, and tourists often pay a lot of money for the weavings and embroidery. (The average wage for agricultural labourers can be less than US$3 a day, yet selling a small piece of embroidered weaving can net US$10.) Traditional dress for males, young and old, is white, knee-length trousers with dark-blue stripes, intricately embroidered with colourful flowers and birds around the knee. A dark-red waistband and white shirt complete the outfit. Today many men wear jeans and modern shirts, but the women often wear traditional dress, including the distinctive headdress or *tocayal*—a red ribbon wound round and round the head, eventually sticking out so far that it looks just like a halo. A *tocayal* is depicted on the 25-centavo coin.

As well as the daily market, another attraction here is the chapel to Maximón, for this is one of the few places in the country where he is worshipped. Maximón does not have a fixed home here, as he does in San Andrés Itzapa. Instead, a different member of the *cofradia* (religious brotherhood) has the honour of keeping him in his house each year.Just ask for the **Casa la Maximón**, and make sure you bring an offering of some rum and a few cigarettes, which will be shared by Maximón and his keeper. Maximón looks quite different here, made of wood and clad in delicate scarves, but still with the dark glasses and cigar. Some have suggested that Maximón is, in fact, a reincarnation of the Maya God, Mam, who also used to be represented as a human figure in wooden effigies.

If you can time your visit to be here on Good Friday, you will witness an extraordinary fusion of pagan and Catholic ritual. The figures of Maximón and Christ are taken down from their respective crucifixes and paraded together, though never facing each other, testifying to the equal importance the Indians attach to Christian and pagan powers, and the Catholic Church's inability to eradicate traditional religion.

The local church on the main square has a plain interior of whitewashed walls and wooden benches, and in recent years has been an important focus of local rallying against army oppression on this side of the lake, notably after the massacre that took place outside the village on 2 December 1990. On that day soldiers at the local army base fired into an unarmed crowd of local residents, killing thirteen and wounding another twenty. The people had come to protest against the fact that the army had forced police to release two officers who had shot and wounded a boy during a bar brawl. It was a tragedy that caused such disgust throughout Guatemala and internationally that the local base was actually closed down—a great triumph and release for the local community; recently, however, there has been pressure to reopen the base. Today a shrine marks the spot where the massacre took place, 100 metres past the Texaco petrol station, on the road heading towards San Pedro la Laguna.

Just northeast of the village, there is a small nature reserve (**Parque Nacional Atitlán**), designated to protect the poc, a kind of grebe. Lake Atitlán was the only place in the world where it existed and, strictly speaking, it is now extinct: the bird you see today is a hybrid of the original grebe with the pied-billed grebe. Visiting the reserve by hired canoe from Santiago Atitlán is a very pleasant way to spend a quiet hour or so.

The environmental changes that led to the extinction of the poc have a lot to do with increased tourism to the region: in 1960 Pan American Airlines, in association with the local tourist board, sponsored the introduction of largemouth bass to the lake to encourage a sport fishing industry. But within five years the voracious bass had eaten their way through just over half the lake's 18 species of fish, and local people, as well as the poc, suddenly found their traditional food source drastically diminished. As if that was not bad enough, the massive earthquake of 1976 caused fissures in the lake's bed, which has resulted in the water level dropping almost ten metres since, and caused many of the reed beds to dry up. All this plus the effect of a rapid growth in the population around the lake and an increasing number of holiday homes meant that by 1991 there were no longer any pocs. The bird, which was only known to exist on this lake, had become extinct because of the destruction of both its habitat and food resources.

If you are interested in finding out more about the lake's precarious ecological situation or would like to do some volunteer work in support of reforestation, local education and training, contact **Amigos del Lago la Atitlán** (Friends of Lake Atitlán), 14 Avenida A 14-76, Zona 10, Guatemala City, ☎ 3374886.

San Pedro La Laguna

San Pedro La Laguna, at the foot of the San Pedro volcano, is a refreshingly quiet place, with none of the frenzied tourism of its neighbour. The main reason for this is no doubt the lack of traditional costume, as most villagers seem to have ladinized. However, the reedy shoreline, dotted with gigantic boulders lapped by gentle waves from the lake, makes for relaxed days and peaceful nights. There is nothing to do except sunbathe, swing in a hammock or paddle in the water. In between these pastimes, you can eat and drink simple fare at one of the three waterfront restaurants.

Santa Catarina and San Antonio

Following the old dirt road east of Panajachel takes you through a beautiful grove of trees and then out into the sun and along the contours of the lake. Reports suggest that walking is unsafe these days; the best way to travel out this way is to catch a pick-up leaving from the road junction near the police station in Panajachel. The first village is 4km away, the second 11km.

The first village you reach is **Santa Catarina** (officially Santa Catarina Palopó), nestling in a tight dip between dusty mountain folds. Nothing much goes on here, but the views of the lake in its mountainous frame are terrific. The women wear intricately embroidered *huipiles* in green and blue, with blue skirts. You may have seen them selling their clothes at the Panajachel market on Avenida Santander.

Further on, the road twists and turns, up and around the craggy shoreline, until it reaches **San Antonio** (officially San Antonio Palopó), its mud houses stacked on the hillside above the lake. A lovely crumbling church perches in the middle of the village and in front of its steps women and children sell fruit and vegetables. As you pass the open doors of some of the homes, you might see one of the giant foot-looms, used exclusively by the men to weave large blankets. The women wear a simple but elegant costume here: red *huipiles* and dark-blue skirts, with plenty of silver-leaf necklaces and coloured beads.

Chichicastenango

The junction of Los Encuentros, on the Pan-American Highway, marks an important turning point for the traveller: the main Highway turns west, passing Lake Atitlán on its way to the city of Quezaltenango, and northwards from there. The equally large branch road heads directly north, taking you to the unique Indian town of Chichicastenango (Chichi), and the nearby departmental capital of the Quiché region, Santa Cruz del

Chichicastenango

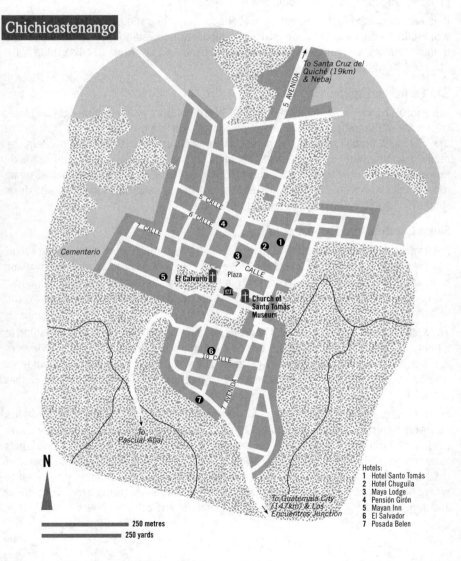

To Santa Cruz del Quiché (19km) & Nebaj

5 AVENIDA

5 CALLE

6 CALLE

7 CALLE

Cementerio

4

2 1

3

7 CALLE

5 El Calvario Plaza

M

Church of Santo Tomás Museum

10 CALLE

6

7 AVENIDA

7

To Pascual Abaj

To Guatemala City (147km) & Los Encuentros Junction

N

250 metres
250 yards

Hotels:
1 Hotel Santo Tomás
2 Hotel Chuguila
3 Maya Lodge
4 Pensión Girón
5 Mayan Inn
6 El Salvador
7 Posada Belen

Quiché. Here the paved road comes to an end; its continuation, a rugged dirt road, takes the hardy traveller on a five-hour bus journey to a remote region known as the Ixil Triangle. This distant area in the northern reaches of the Western Highlands is a wild place, where the landscape has something alpine about it: farming valleys nestle in the wide bowls between forested mountains. The Indians here favour geometric designs on their clothes, and the *huipiles* of Nebaj rank among the country's most stunning.

Getting There and Away

By bus: From **Guatemala City** (3hrs), there are regular daily buses leaving from the Zona 4 bus terminal, from dawn until around 5pm. Most of them will be heading for the town of **Santa Cruz del Quiché**, Quiché for short, and all go via **Chichicastenango**, as do the buses to Joyabaj. Destinations, written in their abbreviated forms, are marked above the front window of all buses.

From **Antigua** (3hrs), there are no direct buses, but the connection is easily made by flagging down passing buses at the Chimaltenango junction. From **Panajachel** (2hrs), there are daily direct buses to Chichi at 7, 8, 9am and 4pm. At other times, catch any bus to the Los Encuentros junction, from where you can pick up buses coming from the capital.

If you are heading for the Ixil region, you will need an early start to catch the **Nebaj** buses leaving Quiché between 8 and 10am. Buses leave roughly every half hour for Quiché, and the journey takes around 30mins. Wait for them passing just past the Pensión Chuguila, at the top of the steep downhill road leading out of town.

There is a direct bus leaving for the town of **Quezaltenango** (it will say Xela on the bus), in the northwestern highlands, between 9 and 10am every morning, journey time 3hrs; wait for it opposite the Pensión Chuguila. Do make enquiries to check that this bus is still running when you are here. If it is not, you can quickly connect with regular buses for Quezaltenango, Panajachel, or Guatemala City, by taking any bus heading for the Los Encuentros junction.

Around the Town

Famous for its fabulous market (*Thurs and Sun*), and the spectacular festival of St Thomas, Chichi has a unique atmosphere: most of the inhabitants are pure Maya, and their traditional culture and way of life informs every aspect of the place. Chichi's cobbled streets meander steeply up and around the main square. Adobe houses huddle together, red-tiled roofs contrasting beautifully with whitewashed walls and the rich green pastures all around.

The Church of Santo Tomás

On the main plaza, the church of Santo Tomás was brutally plonked on top of an existing Maya temple by the Spanish in 1540. It is one of the best places to observe how the Indians adapted to enforced Christianity by worshipping the Christian god alongside their traditional gods and saints in an unorthodox mixture of Catholic and pagan rites.

The steep flight of steps that leads up to the main church entrance is almost always enshrouded with wisps of incense and smoke, as people burn offerings to the gods or to St Thomas, the local patron saint, before entering. Foreign visitors, who have made no offering, should never use the main entrance, but go in by the side door. The perfumed air is even heavier inside the church, where *brujos* (shamans, also known as daykeepers) swing incense burners up and down the aisles. Low altars line the centre aisle all the way to the front. Each one is used for invoking a different blessing: there is the one for the well-being of pregnant women, one for not feeling sad after the death of a relative, another to remember the victims of the 1976 earthquake, one for weddings, one for Maya priests, one for Catholic priests, and several others. Petals are offered and a set number of candles lit on each altar, often in pairs, as a way of communicating with the spirits of the dead: one candle for the living, one for the deceased.

The left-hand side of the church (as you face the main altar) is dedicated to Maya gods and spirits, while the right side is for Christian saints. Both groups are accorded equal reverence, with offerings of candles, flowers, incense and alcohol. On first impression, the altars on either side may look similar, but closer inspection will show otherwise. For example, note the first altar on the left, near the main entrance: the figures are an extraordinary mixture of Christian images and Maya gods. The voluptuous ladies on the far side are, in fact, the patron saints of pregnant women, while the angel-type figures in front, each with an arm missing, represent the god Hunahpu, who had his arm ripped off by Seven Macaw, whom he fought to avenge his father's death:

> *Suddenly Hunahpu appeared, running. He set out to grab him, but actually it was the arm of Hunahpu that was seized by Seven Macaw. He yanked it straight back, he bent it back at the shoulder. Then Seven Macaw tore it right out of Hunahpu. Even so, the boys did well: the first round was not their defeat by Seven Macaw.*

> Popol Vuh, the Quiché bible, translated by Dennis Tedlock

When visiting the church, always keep your distance from the ceremony inside. Busloads of tourists come here every week, and the Indians have become very sensitive to disrespectful behaviour by visitors. Photography is out of the question. If you would like to know more about the interior of the church or the rituals performed, you will always find someone near the side entrance who will oblige for a small fee. Each of these informal guides will give you a very personal (and possibly different) explanation.

El Calvario and the Museum

While both Indians and *ladinos* worship in the main church, the smaller church, directly opposite, is for Indian worshippers only. El Calvario is a whitewashed building with a very plain interior; housing the glass coffin that holds the Black Christ, who is paraded about the streets during Easter Week. To one side, there is a small shrine to the God of Chickens, where the faithful leave eggs or other offerings, when their chickens are not laying well.

The small museum (*open 8–noon and 2–5; may be closed Mon and Tues*) on the south side of the main square, has an interesting collection of Maya jade artefacts and pottery. The collection belonged to Father Rossbach, who was so popular and trusted by the local people that, over a period of 50 years, they made him presents of precious pieces they had kept by their home altars and passed down through the generations. These were left to the town on the priest's death.

The Shrine of Pascual Abaj

Traditionally, the Quiché Indians worship their gods and spirits in many places. These are often open-air shrines, set on sacred hilltops, in forests or by streams. Nature is an integral part of Maya religion, with its own spirit and power that must be respected. The hills around Chichi are full of Maya shrines, most of them secret to outsiders. However, the shrine of Pascual Abaj is well known and regularly visited by foreigners. Find it by descending the hill from the main square and taking the street that leads away from Santo Tomás church. Turn first right and you will come to an open field; take the path leads off to the left, through someone's yard, and up onto a pine-clad hill.

There is usually nothing much to see, other than patches of burnt earth around a collection of stones, where fires have been lit and chickens ritually sacrificed. Tufts of feathers blow around in the breeze and children scurry up to sell you trinkets. But the glorious view of town and the surrounding hills is worth the walk.

The Festival of Santo Tomás

Probably the most famous festival in Central America, apart from the Easter Week celebrations, the *fiesta de Santo Tomás*, December 13–21, includes a large market on the main square and endless processions and firework displays. The last three days are the best time to be here, with the town really packed out on December 20 and 21. The processions begin as early as 6am—some are just continuations of ones from the night before, with the participants, both men and women, distinctly the worse for alcohol.

All through the day the sudden crack of fireworks will blast your eardrums, and the town is a constant hum of music and voices. Traditional dances are performed on the main square, the participants dressed in their finest regional costume. At this time you can see nearly all the costumes of the Quiché region in one place, the Chichi dress being one of the most elaborate: the men wear knee-length trousers and jackets made of dark-brown wool and embroidered with red, pink and green silk around the edges. Their shirts are white; on their heads they wear a triangle of cloth of the same material as that of their suits. The women wear a brown-based costume too, their *huipiles* distinguished by the heavy embroidery of large-petalled flowers of mainly orange, yellow and green.

On the second to last day of the festival all the official dancers assemble on the square to be introduced to the spectators: a couple from each region will perform a short twirl, and then take off their masks to reveal that both of them are, in fact, men. It is an extraordinary transvestite show for deeply Catholic and conservative Guatemala. On the last day the Indians form a massive procession carrying their holy shrines and altars, each followed by candle-holding women and children.

The pole dancers are a rare spectacle you will see throughout the festivities in Chichi. They jump off 20-metre poles in a dance of death, *Palo Volador.* This activity sounds rather more dramatic than it actually is, since the men are suspended by ropes wrapped tightly around the tops of the poles; their body weight slowly unwinds the ropes, allowing them to circle gracefully to the ground. Only occasionally is there some real drama, when one of the participants is so drunk that he falls off his perch before tying the rope on.

Where to Stay

The choices for accommodation and eating out are increasing all the time, though they are still surprisingly sparse considering this is one of the country's most famous tourist attractions. Except during the festival, accommodation is easy to find.

expensive

The **Hotel Santo Tomás**, 7 Avenida 5-32, ✆ 7561061, ✉ 7561306, is the newest hotel in town. Set in a restored colonial mansion with a courtyard, rooms have modern facilities and open fireplaces; there is also a decent restaurant. Prices are wildly flexible so do negotiate. The **Mayan Inn**, ✆ 7561176, ✉ 7561212, is near the main square, on the street leading out past the museum. It is the longest established quality hotel, with a lovely atmosphere of colonial splendour frayed at the edges. Spacious rooms are ranged around a variety of courtyards, complete with macaws and tropical foliage. **The Hotel Chuguila**, 5 Avenida 5-24, ✆/✉ 7561134, has pleasant rooms around its own courtyard and patio restaurant and offers secure parking.

moderate

Maya Lodge, ✆ 7561177, in a colonial building right on the main square, is clean but basic and not really worth the price it asks. Officially singles are US$35, doubles US$40. Out of season they can be less than US$10. **Pensión Girón**, 6 Calle 4-52, ✆ 7561156, is friendly but the rooms, set around a large car park, are bare concrete with ancient beds.

inexpensive

Most popular of the cheapies has traditionally been the **El Salvador**, conspicuously painted blue and white and overlooking the main square from a nearby rise (down the hill, on the street leading away from the church, and then second right turn). Rooms are grubby, bathrooms downright dirty, but the place is convenient. Recently, though, several other places have opened up which might prove more popular: try **Hotel Posada Belen**, 12 Calle, up beyond the El Salvador, which has bare rooms in a smaller, quieter environment and charges the same price.

Eating Out

Restaurant prices are high and their offerings low in quality; you are better off eating the freshly cooked meals made in the market. The top hotels are your safest bet for a decent meal, though the

Tzijolaj restaurant, above the commercial centre on the main square, offers a varied menu and great views across the market. (*Closed Tues.*)

Otherwise try **Tziguan Tinamit**, on the corner of 5 Avenida and 6 Calle, which serves very good pasta dishes; **El Torito**, in the same building as Pensión Girón; or **Tapeña**, 5 Avenida, near Pensión Chuguila.

Around Chichicastenango

Just half an hour's bus journey away is the town of **Santa Cruz del Quiché**, the departmental capital of the Quiché region. If you want to continue towards the Ixil region, you will have to come here for the morning buses. The town itself has little to offer the visitor, except a stroll around the large covered market. However, it is near the pre-Columbian capital of the Quiché tribe, **Utatlán**. The site can be reached by following 10 Calle west out of town, where a dirt road makes for an enjoyable short walk past corn fields, and on to a small hilltop covered in pine trees. The atmosphere is wonderfully tranquil.

Before the Spanish arrived, K'umarcaah, as the Quiché called it, was a relatively new capital, constructed for the élite, and incorporating many fine palaces and elaborate fortifications built of stone and covered in white plaster. Twenty-four noble families lived here, with a great many servants, craftsmen and other employees and a large number of warriors, who patrolled the city.

Yet Alvarado's forces still managed to burn the city to the ground. He came here in 1524, invited by the Quiché king, who planned to ambush the Spaniards. But Alvarado suspected foul play when he saw only men and soldiers in the city, so attacked immediately. The king's sons, Oxib Queh and Beleheb Tz'i were then publicly burned in the main plaza. There is not much left to see today, apart from the main plaza. For a clearer idea of what the city looked like, it's worth visiting the small museum on site, where there is a large model, as well as a helpful guardian to answer questions.

The most intriguing feature of Utatlán is the couple of tunnels below the site. Perhaps they were a secret hideout for the Quiché, or they might have been symbolic entrances to the Underworld, and places of worship. Bring a torch and ask for directions at the museum, since the path is steep and rather obscure. The first tunnel you reach is very narrow, its walls blackened by the Indian shamans, who regularly come here to worship, burning candles and incense. The lower tunnel is more spacious, but the hint of chants and ritual sacrifice teases the imagination, as the smell of burnt copal fills your nostrils.

The Ixil Triangle

> *Beauty cloaks Guatemala the way music hides screams.*
>
> *Time among the Maya*, R. Wright

This area, in the northern region of the department of Quiché, is wild in more than landscape. The northwest of Guatemala was the main battlefield for guerrilla and state forces from the 1970s to the early 1990s. Although the violence waned after 1985, there is still sporadic armed conflict. Some of the most horrific massacres the country has seen took place in the Ixil Triangle, defined by the area between the Indian villages of Nebaj, Chajul and San Juan Cotzal, in the northern region of the department of Quiché.

These crimes were perpetrated by both sides; their victims almost always the innocent Indian farmers, as the two forces alternately try to use them for their own ends, often justifying their violence in the name of the Indians. Many villages were razed to the ground, only to be rebuilt by the government as 'model villages'. Those inhabitants who survived the nightmare of the eighties are deeply scarred by it.

At the time of writing, the area around the Ixil Triangle is peaceful enough, and for those wishing to learn something of Guatemala's recent history, as well as hike in some of its most gorgeous countryside, there are few better places to visit. Remember, however, that peace in this particular region is deceptive, and violence could erupt again at any time, especially if the government's negotiations for a peace settlement fail. Understandably, amenities for visitors are very simple indeed. Before visiting the area, get advice from the **Casa Andinista Bookshop** in Antigua—Mike Shawcross, the owner, used to run an aid programme in the Ixil region.

Nebaj

The approaching dirt road takes you over a cold and windy pass and then twists and turns down towards Nebaj, which lies spread out on the floor of a wide highland valley ringed by steep mountains. It is the largest of the three villages of the Ixil Triangle, and the only one that can offer commercial accommodation for the steady trickle of anthropologists, aid workers and tourists. If you arrive on any day other than the market days (*Thurs and Sun*), you will find a very quiet settlement, where the only noise comes from a chicken scratching in the dirt road, or children chasing home-made hoops.

Nebaj is a beautiful, crumbling village, where most of the residents still cook on log fires, the smoke rising picturesquely above red-tiled roofs. Nearby, the market is housed in an area of purpose-built wooden shacks, full to bursting on Sundays, with an overspill of vendors in the surrounding streets. The villagers of the surrounding mountainsides and valleys come here to sell their vegetables, and small livestock, such as chickens, turkeys and the odd goat. It is then that you can see the full glory of local dress, particularly the women's headdress: a wide band, folded into knots and bows as it is wrapped around the head, ending in bushy pompoms that are piled on top of the turban or hung loosely by the side of the head.

The wonderful countryside here offers spectacular walking and hiking (always check the area is safe at your time of travelling). Take the two-hour walk to the 'model village' of **Acul**, in a neighbouring valley. The original village was razed to the ground by the army, and then rebuilt, gathering the survivors in one easily supervised location. The rows of houses look pleasantly neat and orderly, but in fact they are uncomfortable to live in, and the allocated kitchen gardens too small and too close together. People and animals live in unhealthy proximity, making diseases and infection a recurrent problem. The track is wide and clear, the views reminiscent of the Swiss Alps, and when you get there, you can purchase home-made cheese at a farm that used to belong to an ancient Italian, who nearly made it to a hundred. His homestead is just outside the village; ask anyone for directions.

Another pleasant, less strenuous walk is to a nearby **waterfall** (*las cascadas*). Follow the road heading to Chajul, and turn left before crossing the bridge where a well-worn dirt track will take you to the falls. When you are close, the track takes a sharp bend left and goes steeply downhill before levelling out in front of the waterfall, which shoots off a ledge to pound the rocks 15m below. If you are tempted to picnic in the field near the base of the falls, be warned that the mosquitoes will drive you crazy. If staying longer, you could also visit the markets of San Juan Cotzal (*Sat*) and Chajul (*Tues and Fri*).

Chajul

A 2-hour drive away across gorgeous green valleys, Chajul is the most interesting of the Ixil villages to visit from Nebaj. Perched on a steep hillside, the settlement of adobe houses and mud streets is about as remote as any you'll get on public transport. Its Maya inhabitants follow a traditional way of life: donkeys and horses are the most common form of transport beyond here, though most people are used to covering long distances on foot; few houses have running water or electricity. If you really want to stay overnight, there is a cheap and dirty *pensión* south of the town centre. To make enquiries contact the owner who works at the post office.

If you catch the market bus on Tuesdays or Fridays (4am, returning 11am and noon), the sunrise will reveal mists slowly rising off the corn fields and lonely homesteads dotted around the countryside. Gleaming zinc roofs testify to the recent resettlement of the area and, in Chajul itself, the local church holds a chilling reminder of the bad old times: a great oil painting, *To our Martyrs*, depicts the victims shot by the murderous factions from both sides of the conflict. The church has been beautifully restored since its roof was burnt down, and the altars and attendant sculptures are some of the most interesting you will see anywhere. They appear to be originals, from colonial times. Either side of the altar, meanwhile, you will see two figures clad in traditional Chajul costume, which look suspiciously like Maximón. The local Maya certainly seem to worship them with special reverence, approaching on their knees, clutching candles and murmuring prayers.

The Chajul *huipiles* are some of the most striking in the country: the basic cloth is woven in pillar-box red, deep purple or baby blue, and decorated with lively geometric designs of birds, horses and women, as well as an infinite number of smaller geometric patterns that fill borders and even whole surfaces. Notice also the women's ear-rings, made of ancient coins and threaded through pierced ears with purple strips of cloth. To protect their precious embroidery, the women often wear their blouses inside out.

Getting to and from Nebaj

Two or three direct buses for Nebaj (5–6hrs) leave daily from **Santa Cruz del Quiché**, 8–10am. The journey is long, the ride bumpy, the seating space minimal, but the scenery will be superb. You can also catch a direct bus to Nebaj from Huehuetenango, in the northwest of the highlands, departing daily at around 11.30am. This journey is equally long and scenic.

Buses returning to Quiché leave daily at 1, 3, and 4am, all passing through the town of **Sacapulas**, where you will have to change if you want to take back roads northeast (for **Cobán**) or northwest (for **Huehuetenango**, unless you are on the direct bus of course). If you are heading for Cobán, you can catch a noon bus to Uspantán, where you will probably have to stay the night (for more on this route *see* p.140 & p.169). Don't worry if you get stuck in Sacapulas: the Restaurante Rio Negro offers decent meals and basic accommodation.

Buses to **San Juan Cotzal** leave Nebaj daily at 4am, returning around noon. For **Chajul**, buses depart at 4am on Tuesdays and Fridays only, returning at 11am and at noon. Always check when and where buses are leaving from at the last minute, as schedules can be erratic.

Tourist Information

There is now a branch of **Bancafé**, 2 Avenida 46 (*open Mon–Fri, 8.30–4; Sat 8–noon*) in Nebaj: very close to the market, where you can change cash and traveller's cheques.

You will certainly be hounded by the local women and girls in both Nebaj and Chajul to come and see their wares in their homes. However, you should also look at the **weaving co-operative shops** (on the main square in Nebaj; on the street between the church and the market place in Chajul—just ask around for someone to open the store) which sell very high quality textiles. Their prices are not rock-bottom, but by shopping here you are contributing to a living wage for the local weavers, and helping stop the flow of people from the countryside to the capital, where many end up in desperate circumstances.

Where to Stay and Eating Out

The smartest option is the **Hotel Posada de Don Pablo**, ✆ 7551033, opposite Irene's *comedor*, where rooms have private bathrooms; singles from US$7, doubles from US$10. Next best is the **Hotel**

Ixil, located on the main entrance road to Nebaj, where rooms are clean and simple with shared bath.

Undoubtedly the best and friendliest place to stay, though, is **Las Tres Hermanas**, near the main square. (Only two ancient sisters remain.) A handful of damp, windowless rooms line a pleasantly chaotic courtyard, where a central wash basin stands amongst rose bushes, fluttering washing lines and chicken droppings. Prices are just over US$1 each, and excellent cheap meals are provided on request. A good place to stay if you want use of a garden is **Hospedaje Kariari II**, down a mud track on the way to Acul. Popular because of the hot shower is **Hospedaje Central Nebajense**, 3 Calle and 5 Avenida. Also worth trying is **Las Clavellinas**, which offers simple rooms and also boasts a shower.

The **Maya-Inca**, on 5 Calle, is a restaurant run by a Guatemalan-Peruvian couple. The service is friendly and the meals and freshly made cakes are a treat. **Irene's**, just off the main square, makes good meals but takes forever, so get there before you're really hungry. You can request meals in advance at **Las Tres Hermanas**, or check out the *comedor*-style shacks on the main square. During market day there are always snacks to be had by the market.

From Chichi to Quezaltenango

The drive west, from Chichi to Quezaltenango, or Xela (pronounced 'shella') as it's commonly known, is one of the loveliest in Guatemala. Returning to the Pan-American Highway at Los Encuentros, the road sweeps up and around forests and fields, giving you a brief glimpse of Lake Atitlán, lying deep in its rocky cushion of volcanoes and hillsides. An hour passes, while the landscape unfolds into cornfields and thatched hamlets, the occasional cluster of pines or eucalyptus trees swaying in the ever present breeze.

Nahualá is a small Indian town, easily missed from the main road and rarely visited by tourists, except on 25 November, when the place turns into a terrific chaos of drunkenness and revelry during its annual fiesta. The men here wear distinctive thick, knee-length woollen skirts of brown and white checks, together with pink or red shirts. During the festival you will see them in their very best outfits, but another good time to visit is for the Sunday market. This is a staunchly traditional place, where the Indian cult of Maximón is alive and well, and the saint has his own permanent chapel. The image of the saint here is of a type little known in Guatemala: a two-foot-high wooden sculpture depicts Maximón dressed in a white tunic, with his mouth open and his tongue sticking out.

Beyond Nahualá, the road loops up and onto a windswept highland plateau, where the cold thin air allows only hardy grasses to grow, but the earth is a rich and fertile black. It's a refreshing contrast to the vibrant colours and sunbaked scene so far, providing a short spell of misty clouds and boggy fields before you descend back into the open sunshine of the Quezaltenango valley. It seems almost to be completely flat—a great open plain, ideal for agriculture, and therefore a region busy with towns and villages. At its heart lies

Quezaltenango, Guatemala's second city and an excellent base for excursions to Indian markets and beautiful countryside.

Alvarado fought one of his most decisive battles against the Indians here, and in 1524 slew the great warrior king, Tecún Umán, whose headdress was made up of splendid quetzal feathers; the conquistador was so impressed by its beauty that he declared the city must be named Quezaltenango—Quetzal Citadel.

Quezaltenango (Xela)

Xela is a rather extraordinary place, giving itself the airs of a city while remaining undeniably provincial. The burghers have always considered themselves guardians of a notable cultural and economic centre and, after the earthquake in 1902, set about building themselves a Grecian temple (sadly now derelict), a grand main square surrounded by columns and steps and a huge cathedral. There is a large theatre as well, fronted by columns and its own small square. All the ingredients of a proper city are here, but they look rather incongruous, and most of the buildings are neglected, lending an air of pleasant melancholy. The weather too is rather gloomy: Xela's altitude of 2335m ensures a noticeable chill, and it frequently rains.

Getting There and Away

By bus: From Guatemala City, there are fast and regular pullmans, and the journey takes around 4hrs. The sign in the bus window will always use the abbreviation Xela. Coming from Antigua, Panajachel or Chichi, catch the relevant bus from the nearest junction with the Pan-American Highway. Your best chance of catching a bus like this is in the morning and early afternoon.

When you arrive at the bus terminal in town, walk through the market next to the terminal and cross the main road to find the bus stop for the centre. The buses are an easily recognizable yellow; ask for one going to the Parque Central.

As the capital of the Western Highlands, Xela is a major transport centre, with buses arriving and leaving for almost all corners of the highlands, as well as for the Mexican border and down to the Pacific Coast. **Líneas Américas** (for pullman buses to Guatemala City and all major junctions in between) have their office on Calzada Independencia, between 5 and 6 Calle, which is the main road coming into town from the Cuatro Caminos junction. **Rutas Lima** are on the same road, near 4 Calle. If all the pullmans are full, or you don't mind the chicken buses, then head for the main bus terminal, on the edge of town, where regular buses leave from dawn until late afternoon. On the rare occasion when no bus is heading direct to Guatemala City (or Huehuetenango, if you're heading north), take any bus to the Cuatro Caminos junction, outside town, and wait there.

The main **Minerva bus terminal** is the place to wait for regular buses to Huehuetenango (Huehue; 2½hrs) and San Marcos (2hrs), where you can also change buses for the Mexican border posts of La Mesilla and Talismán respectively. There are frequent buses to regional destinations such as San Francisco el Alto (El Alto; 1hr), Momostenango (Momo; 2hrs), Zunil (45mins) and Totonicapán (Toto; 30 mins); and also to the Pacific towns of Mazatenango (Masate, 1½hrs), Retalhuleu (Reu, 1½hrs), and Coatepeque (Coa, 1½hrs). The quickest way to reach the Mexican border town of Talismán is to take a bus to Retalhuleu, or any of the large towns on the Pacific Highway, and change there.

If heading for any destination past the Cuatro Caminos junction, instead of going to the terminal, you can wait at the Rotunda roundabout at the end of Calzada Independencia. The only drawback with this option is that buses will be very full by the time they get here, and you are unlikely to get a seat.

Getting Around

In spite of being the country's second largest city, Xela has the proportions of a small, compact town and the walk from the bus terminal to the central park only takes half an hour, though the dusty main road is hardly inviting. Everything you will need or want to see is at or close to the main square; the only time you will need to use the bus is to travel between the centre and the bus terminal.

Tourist Information

The **Inguat** tourist office is on the south side of the main square in Xela (*open Mon–Fri, 8–1 and 2–5; Sat 8–noon*), © 7614931. The helpful and friendly staff can offer information on buses and excursions to the surrounding area, in particular hiking trips to the nearby Santa María volcano. They also have a list of the latest authorized language schools.

For **medical attention**, either go to the private hospital in Zona 3 (past the Moza Brewery), or see Dr Lilian Leiva la Mejía, 14 Avenida A 0-27, Zona 3 (*open Mon–Fri, 10–6,* © *7631001; English spoken*).

There are four **banks** to choose from on the main square, but the best rate for cash is at Banquetzal, on 14 Avenida. The **post office** is on the corner of 15 Avenida and 4 Calle, Zona 1. The **Guatel** office (*open daily 7–10pm*) is opposite the post office at 15 Avenida 3-40. **Fax services** are offered by: **The Shipping Center**, 15 Avenida 3-51, Zona 1, ©/✆ 7632104 (*open Mon–Fri, 9–5.45; Sat 9–noon*). They also offer mail and parcel service, courier and phone services. **Maya Communications**, in the shopping arcade off the main square, © 7612832 (*open daily 8.30–15.30*), also have e-mail services and plan to stay open till 1am.

There are three **laundries** in the town: Minimax laundry, 14 Avenida, Zona 1 (*open Mon–Sat, 8–7pm*); Quick Wash 'n' Dry, 7 Calle 13-25 A, Zona 1 (*open Mon–Sat, 8–6pm*); Lavandería El Centro, 15 Avenida 3-40, Zona 1 (*open Mon–Sat, 8–5.30; closed 1–2*).

The **Mexican consulate** is on 9 Avenida 6-19, Zona 1 (*open Mon–Fri, 8–11 and 2.30-3.30*), they accept applications in the mornings and give them back in the

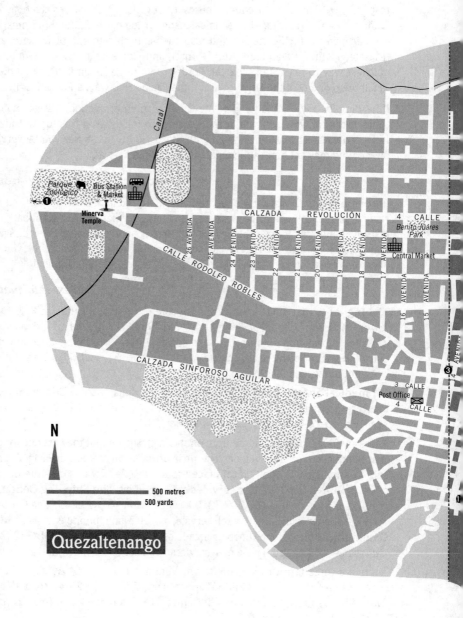

Quezaltenango

Hotels:
1 Los Alpes
2 Hotel Centro Americana
3 Modelo
4 Hotel Río Azul
5 Radar 99
6 Casa Kaehler
7 Villa Real Plaza
8 Hotel Casa Florencia
9 Santa María Guest House
10 Pensión Bonifaz
11 Pensión Altense
12 Hotel El Centro

afternoons. Very helpful on all matters to do with travel is **Guatemala Unlimited**, 12 Avenida C-35, ✆/✉ 7616043. You can also **hire bikes** and **cars** here and get in touch with volcano guides (around US$20 per day). Don't bother with the conducted tours, though—they are outrageously overpriced.

Language Schools

One of the best schools here is the **Proyecto Lingüístico Quezalteco la Español**, 5 Calle 2-40, Zona 1, ✆ 7631061. One-to-one teaching as well as films and discussions on anything from local politics to Guatemalan culture costs US$120–150 per week, living with a family (full board). The same management also runs the **Proyecto Lingüístico la Español Educación para Todos**, at 6 Calle 7-42, Zona 1, ✆ 7630717.

Also recommended are: **Casa la Español Xelaju**, 9 Calle 11-26, Zona 1, ✆ 7612877; and **English Club International Language School**, Diagonal 4 9-71 (at La Cuchilla barrio; take bus no.5). There are many more, with constantly changing reputations; take time to make enquiries locally before making your choice. On the latest information, those schools to be avoided include ALM, Maya Lingua, Santa Maria and Kiebalam.

If you have the time and would like to experience real highland life, try a course at the remote language school, the **Escuela Centro Xoy** in Joyabaj, run by the non-governmental community project SCDRYS (*Sociedad Civil para el Desarrollo Rural Replicable y Sostenible*). The school is next to the health centre (*centro la salud*) in Joyabaj but you must get in touch with their head office in Quezaltenango, 7 Calle 7-18, between Avenidas 24 and 25, ✉ 7616873; the man to speak to is Mr Douglas Sandoval. The Maya in the department of Quiché suffered some of the worst atrocities in recent decades and are still struggling to re-establish their lives. Many of their villages are beyond the reach of the road network and proper services, and receive no assistance from the government. Maya community leaders representing remote villages throughout Quiché have come together to form SCDRYS in an effort to plug into the economic benefits of tourism by offering language tuition along with the opportunity to live with indigenous families and learn about village life (30% of your fee goes to the family you live with, 20% to the local community, 25% to local development projects, 15% to SCDRYS and the rest is spent on administration). The weekly fee is around US$120 per person, less if in a group. To reach the Centro Xoy, either catch a direct bus from the capital's Zona 4 bus terminal or wait for a Joyabaj bus at the Los Encuentros junction on the Pan-American Highway.

Around the Town

The actual sights of Xela can easily be seen in one day. They consist of the cathedral and municipal museum on the main square, the outrageously tasteless San Nicolás church, and the local zoo. Of these, the church is the most diverting: it is a Gothic-style building reminiscent of an over-iced Christmas cake, all pinks, blues, silver and white. The zoo, just beyond the dilapidated temple that stands by the edge of the market, is decidedly unpleasant: desperately bored felines pace around in their own droppings. To get to either, take a bus heading for the terminal via San Nicolás.

One advantage of the pretensions to grandeur here is that there are a number of good restaurants, most notably Chinese, and the hotels are some of the best value for money in the country. Local entertainment consists of three cinemas and the theatre. The most popular films are either violent or pornographic, but you do stand a good chance of seeing an American movie with Spanish subtitles at the cinema next to the theatre. These last two venues are worth a look in themselves; the buildings are slightly bedraggled but still splendid. In all, Xela is a good place to use as a base for exploring the surrounding region—you can easily spend a whole week here, taking a different trip each day. It is also an excellent place to learn Spanish, since there are fewer tourists and thus plenty of opportunities to use your new language.

Volcanoes

The splendid **Volcán Santa María** is visible from all over town. If you are fit, the climb takes about five very tough hours. Your efforts will be rewarded with terrific views of the whole string of Guatemalan volcanoes, including the active Santiaguito just next to you, as well as the surrounding valleys and lush Pacific foothills. Topographic maps for the climb are best bought in the **Casa Andinista Bookshop**, Antigua. Check with the local tourist office for the latest security report and advice on how to hire a guide, if you want one (the ascent is marked, but the path isn't always easy to follow). To reach the beginning of the trail, catch a bus from 17 Avenida and 1 Calle, to **Llanos del Pinal**, and ask the driver to drop you at the relevant crossroads. Follow the dirt road until you see painted signs to a trail off to the left. A resident American-Guatemalan, who is a mine of information on the volcanoes, is Natán Hardeman; ask for him at Aladino's Bar. Or see John Diehl at Guatemala Unlimited.

Where to Stay

expensive

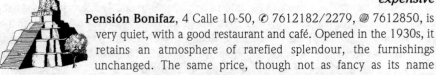

Pensión Bonifaz, 4 Calle 10-50, ✆ 7612182/2279, @ 7612850, is very quiet, with a good restaurant and café. Opened in the 1930s, it retains an atmosphere of rarefied splendour, the furnishings unchanged. The same price, though not as fancy as its name suggests, is the **Hotel Villa Real Plaza**, 4 Calle 12-22, ✆ 7614045, @ 7616780, on the main square.

moderate

Los Alpes, on the road past the Minerva bus terminal, towards San Martín Sacatepéquez, ✆ 7635721, is only worth staying at if you have your own transport. **Modelo**, 14 Avenida A 2-31, ✆ 7612529, @ 7631376, is one of the best medium-priced hotels, with a good restaurant. Try to secure one of the rooms in the new annexe as they're pleasanter and cheaper. Another good choice is the **Hotel Casa Florencia**, 12 Avenida 3-61, ✆ 7612326, just above the main square, with its own restaurant, very decent rooms with TV and bath. **Hotel El Centro**, 10 Calle 11-69, ✆ 7612466, 🖂 7631357, offers clean, decent rooms with private bath and TV, as well as secure parking. **Hotel Centro Americana**, on the corner of 14 Avenida and Minerva Boulevard, ✆ 7618219, 🖂 7618118, looks a bit grubby on the outside, but the rooms are of a good standard. Secure parking is available.

inexpensive

Hotel Río Azul, 2 Calle 12-15, ✆/🖂 7630654, near the main square, has clean, bright rooms and parking facilities. The long-time favourite among budget travellers is the **Casa Kaehler**, 13 Avenida 3-33, ✆ 7612091, very close to the main square and most of the best restaurants. It really does have hot water—important in this cold town. The drawback is its paper-thin walls. Avoid **Radar 99**, next door; it's dirty and very basic. **Pensión Altense**, 9 Calle and 9 Avenida, ✆ 7612811, on the other hand, makes an excellent alternative. Also popular, because of the shared kitchen, is **Santa María Guest House**, 3 Calle 10-24, ✆ 7612660. The only problem here is finding the landlady, who does not live on the premises. There are many more cheap places to stay, so just ask around if the above are full.

Eating Out

Xela is gradually accumulating more interesting places to eat and drink, no doubt due to the increase in language students, but few restaurants stay open past 10pm. A personal favourite is **Cardinalis**, 14 Avenida 3-41, where authentic, delicious Italian fare is served in gigantic portions. The owner-chef is also responsible for **Torre di Pisa**, opposite the theatre. Another good place for large appetites is the **Chicago Grill**, inside the new 'El Portal' commercial centre at 13 Avenida 5-38, which also boasts American cable TV. The restaurant **Royal Paris**, 2 Calle 14 A 32 is ranged around a very pleasant covered courtyard, and offers a varied menu.

A favourite Chinese restaurant is the **Shanghai**, just off the main square, on 4 Calle, where you can also eat international and the odd Guatemalan dish; excellent value. Pizzas are another specialty in Xela, and the best places to eat them (other than Cardinalis) are: **Pizza Ricca**,14 Avenida, and **Don Benito's**, on the corner of Calzada la la Revolución and 15 Avenida. For steaks try **La Rueda**, next to the market near the Minerva temple. The restaurant of the Modelo hotel serves good, though not cheap, meals in a quietly refined atmosphere. The same can be said for the Hotel Bonifaz restaurant. Finally, if you prefer vegetarian food, try the **Café Q**, Diagonal 12 and 4 Calle (push the door open), also a popular gringo bar. Another travellers' meeting point is the **Blue Angel Video Café**, 7 Calle 15-22 (*open daily, 2-11*), where you can eat salads and small snacks while perusing the books and videos.

For breakfast and for excellent coffee, the cheapest in town, try the **Café Baviera**. Alternatively, head for one of the café-restaurants along 14 Avenida, for example the **Gran Hotel Americano** (accommodation not recommended). Another good place is the **Deli Crepe**, further up the road. Or try the **Café Berna**, 16 Avenida 3-25 (on the Parque Benito Juares), which is almost as good as the Baviera. If you feel like being civilized and taking afternoon tea, there's no better place than the **Pensión Bonifaz**, which serves great cakes and reasonable coffee too.

If you just want to buy some pastries, the best bakery in town is **Pan y Pasteles**, 4 Calle 26-19, on the way to the Minerva Bus Terminal (*open Tues and Fri only, 10–4*). It is run by Mennonites, who make everything from rye bread to cream pies.

Entertainment and Nightlife

A friendly bar, right in the heart of town, is the **Salon Tecún Bar** (*open daily 6pm–late*), in the shopping arcade off the main square, underneath Maya Communications. Slicker and with a vast choice of drinks is **Aladino's Bar**, 20 Avenida 0-66, out by the Moza brewery in Zona 3. Probably the best bar in town. If you prefer a more local atmosphere, try **Don Rodrigo's Taberna**, on 14 Avenida, a friendly little place. Otherwise you have a choice of small watering holes near the main square and around the central market at the far end of 15 Avenida.

Excursions from Xela

Zunil and Fuentes Georginas

One of the friendliest markets you will encounter is in the village of **Zunil**, just 20 minutes from the city. This is a small Indian settlement spread around a disproportionately large white church, situated in a lovely valley. The market sells vegetables and there is a cooperative behind the church which offers the unique Zunil textiles, not found in any of the country's other markets. The main pleasure of visiting the Monday market is in seeing the local women in their brilliant pink, purple and puce clothing sitting behind their freshly harvested goods, quietly chatting to one another.

While you are here, you should also have a look in the great Spanish church, its dark interior hiding an unusual ornate silver altar. The annual fiesta is on November 25; another special occasion is Palm Sunday. To reach Zunil, catch a bus from the Minerva bus terminal. The last bus back to Xela leaves between 5 and 6pm.

On the hillside, 8km above Zunil, are the best hot springs in the country, the **Fuentes Georginas** (*closed Mon*). Even though recent reports suggest they are not as hot as they used to be, you'll still enjoy their beautiful location. You can either walk uphill for two or three hours or, for US$4, take a pick-up from the village. The mountain is covered in thick tropical foliage, an indication that you are not far from the steamy Pacific. At the top, a few small bungalows perch on a fern-clad ridge with two steaming pools and a bar-restaurant. There is a small entrance fee if you do not plan to stay the night, but you'll certainly be tempted; each of the bungalow rooms has its own fireplace, bathtub, and barbecue outside. Plenty of firewood is provided to keep the damp out all night, but it is a good idea to bring your own firelighters, sold in any of the markets, and extra blankets. The price is around US$10 per night, singles pay US$7.

If you don't wish to go all the way to the Fuentes Georginas, you could visit the hot baths in the village of Almolonga, on the way to Zunil. These are, however, very much public bath-houses and only worth visiting if you are yearning for a hot soak, rather than a swim.

Lake Chicabal

This small lake is tucked inside the cone of an extinct volcano. The nearest village is San Martín Sacatepéquez, also known as San Martín Chile Verde, on one of the roads leading to the Pacific. You can reach it by taking one of the buses that go from the Minerva terminal to Coatepeque via San Martín; the journey takes about 45 minutes. The last returning bus is usually around 5.15pm, though if you're lucky there may be one around 7pm.

The inhabitants of San Martín speak a rare Mam dialect that isolates them from the rest of the Indians in this region. Maya tradition is strong in this closed community, and the men wear a distinctive white, knee-length tunic, held by a red sash. The nearby lake is considered a holy place, and on May 2 and 3, shamans gather to perform sacred ceremonies by the water's edge. Tourists should keep a low profile here, particularly at this time, and respect the holiness of the place—do not swim in the lake if local people are present.

To reach the lake, take the small path a little way to the right of the church, which leads gently up and past the last homesteads of the village. When you reach a concrete bridge, turn right and climb uphill. Continue through the forest and across a small savannah, and then up through forest again, until the path becomes a wide dirt track. Take a left and follow the large trail, ignoring smaller ones leaving it and, after a couple of kilometres, you will reach the top of the last hill and come to the cone itself. You will often be unable to see the water until you are almost in it because of a milky cloud that sits low on the crater.

It should only take about an hour and a half to reach the lake, but the uphill journey can seem a lot longer. There are not many people up this way, but if you do meet someone, it is worth checking with them that you are on the right path. Sitting in this cool and evocative place, the soothing silence all around, it is easy to understand why the Indians chose it as a place of worship.

Some Local Markets

The short drive to the highland town of **Totonicapán** takes you up to the Cuatro Caminos junction of the Pan-American Highway and to the edge of the great plateau. Leaving the dust and commercial straggle of the junction behind, the bus enters a beautiful avenue of pines and conifers and the road rises gradually to the town itself, tucked at the far corner of a dead-end valley, at a cool 2500m, surrounded by tree-covered hills and craggy outcrops.

The large market (*Tues and Sat*) in Toto is filled to bursting with all shapes and sizes of the distinctive local orange-glazed pottery. This is very brittle, so you are unlikely to want to carry it home. However, you may be tempted by some of the weaving on the second floor of the main market building (though much of it is machine-made). There is also fine wood-work, basketry and ropes. The annual fiesta is held 26–30 September.

About an hour's drive from Xela, **San Francisco el Alto** (2640m) is a small market town, perched on a ledge overlooking the Quezaltenango valley. On the way, the bus crosses a river at the village of San Cristóbal de Totonicapán, remarkable for its huge colonial church, which contains precious altars and fine silver. Market day is Sunday and, since it's somewhat off the tourist track, you may find a good bargain here. Continuing on, the road climbs steeply to the windswept San Francisco el Alto; on Fridays the town is jammed with traders who come from all over the highlands to sell anything from textiles and craftwork to food and animals. San Francisco has one of Guatemala's largest livestock markets; the chaotic scenes of pigs being wrestled by men checking their teeth are quite something, though the way the animals are treated is enough to turn you into a vegetarian. The **Los Altos** guest house (at the top end of the town), is clean and friendly, and a good place to stop over if you are going on to Momostenango. The price is just over US$1 per person and secure parking is available. Otherwise you can stay in the **Vista Hermosa** or the **Hotel Galaxia**.

After San Francisco el Alto, the road becomes a wide dirt-track and the bus bumps slowly up through a pine forest and then down into a remote highland valley. The scenery along the way is fantastic and it is not surprising to discover that this region is full of sacred hilltops and altars. **Momostenango** (Momo) means just that: the place of many altars, and it was here that the American translator of the Maya bible, Dennis Tedlock, spent time as an apprentice daykeeper. Daykeepers ensure adherence to the annual festivals of the Maya calendar, in particular the Maya New Year, celebrated every 260 days. It's very difficult to discover when these festivals will be held, and even if you turned up by chance you would probably not be welcome—these are secret celebrations, jealously guarded from outsiders, who have so often sought to destroy them. (To learn more about the Maya calendar, see Tedlock's *Popol Vuh*, and Michael Coe's *The Maya*.) The church here is similar in atmosphere to the one in Chichi, mixing pagan and Catholic images and worship. The Momostenango market is held on Wednesdays and Sundays (main day)—so it is not possible to combine it in a day trip with the San Francisco el Alto one. In the market are some of the best and cheapest examples of the distinctive woollen blankets that are produced in this town and sold all over the country. The blankets come in a variety of colours, some natural creams and browns, some interwoven with rich dyes of red, blue and green, patterned with traditional Maya images. There are two main types: thick, woven rugs, which can be used as wall hangings, and the long-haired, soft blankets, which make beautiful bedspreads. There are plenty of inspiring walks here and some very simple accommodation if you wish to stay. Try either **Hospedaje Paclom** or **Hospedaje Roxane**; both are convenient but neither has much else to recommend it.

Towards the Pacific

Even if you have no intention of going to the Pacific Lowlands, you should consider taking any Mazatenango bus as far as **San Felipe**, not to see this dilapidated roadside town but to enjoy the journey there. The drive is spectacular, and you get a real sense of climate being tied to altitude as you travel from Xela's early morning chill down to the hot and humid Pacific coast. As the road plunges ever downwards, the vegetation becomes thicker and greener, and the heat and humidity increase. Every now and then, the view stretches out towards the Pacific, and you will see the hazy horizon, the quivering air obscuring the ocean. The Guatemalan Highlands tower behind you and, to the north and south, you may still see the volcanic cones, rising above all.

San Felipe is the first tropically hot settlement you come to and, although still high up, the atmosphere here belongs to the Pacific. Peeling wooden shutters protect its inhabitants from the worst of the heat, and the place has a dusty, neglected character. There's no reason to continue to the Pacific Highway, unless you want to sweat it out in the commercial hubbub of **Mazatenango**, or any of the other dusty towns along there. Plenty of buses pass for Quezaltenango, so you should have no trouble returning.

Huehuetenango

Huehuetenango is the last major town before you reach the Mexican border post of La Mesilla, and the focal point for the northern Highlands. There is little to detain you for more than a day here, but the town is a stepping stone for connections into the remote Cuchumatanes Mountains, the highest range in Central

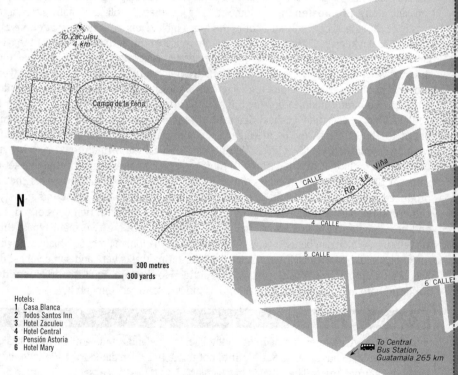

Hotels:
1 Casa Blanca
2 Todos Santos Inn
3 Hotel Zaculeu
4 Hotel Central
5 Pensión Astoria
6 Hotel Mary

America, offering superb scenery and remote Indian and *ladino* villages.
The most famous Indian village is Todos Santos, whose inhabitants have been beautifully portrayed in a black and white photographic book called *Los Todos Santeros* by Hans Namuth. For hiking and walking, there are few places to rival this region, and if you have the time and energy to come here, you will encounter a world quite different from the Western Highlands, wilder and more dramatic.

Huehuetenango, or Huehue, is a small, bustling, provincial town with an economy based on agriculture and some mining. Pedro de Alvarado's brother, Gonzalo, came here to wreak horrible revenge for the plot to ambush the Spanish in Utatlán, said to have been suggested by the Mam leader, Kaibil Balam. Warned of the approach of over 2000 Spanish troops, the Indians barricaded themselves inside Zaculeu. Two inconclusive battles were fought and, in the end, the Mam were beaten in a bitter six-week siege that almost brought both sides to starvation. It is an outrageous irony that the infamous counterinsurgency troops, well documented as the perpetrators of the country's worst horrors, are named Kaibiles, after the Indian leader.

Getting There and Away

From Guatemala City, you face a 6-hr bus drive the length of the Western Highlands, so it is worth booking a seat on a pullman bus (*see* p.64 for the address in the capital). Returning to the capital, the best pullman buses are run by **Transportes Velásquez**, leaving from the main bus terminal outside town; you could also use

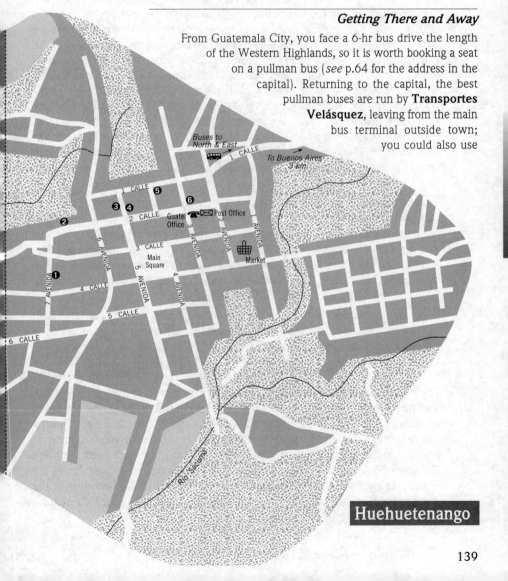

Buses to
North & East
1 CALLE
To Buenos Aires
3 km
1 CALLE
2 CALLE
Guatel
Office
Post Office
3 CALLE
Main
Square
4 CALLE
Market
5 CALLE
6 CALLE
1 AVENIDA
2 AVENIDA
3 AVENIDA
4 AVENIDA
5 AVENIDA
6 AVENIDA
7 AVENIDA
Río Sacuma

Huehuetenango

Los Halcones, whose office is at 7 Avenida 3-62 (buses at 7am and 2pm); alternatively try **Rápidos Zaculeu,** on 3 Avenida 5-25 (buses at 6am and 3pm). If you arrive in Huehue by 'chicken bus', you will be dropped at the bus terminal outside town, from where regular buses and minibuses ferry passengers into the town centre. The yellow bus for Chiantla is the most comfortable one for getting to the town centre, as it has more room for you and your luggage.

From the Minerva terminal in Xela, there are frequent direct buses; or head to the Cuatro Caminos junction. Coming from anywhere else in the Highlands, you can catch a bus to Huehue from any main junction along the Pan-American Highway.

Leaving Huehuetenango, you will find all buses now depart from the terminal outside town. Get there by waiting at the *parada servicio urbano*, just past the Café Jardin, on 6 Avenida. There are buses to many towns and villages in the Highlands and beyond. For example, to Sacapulas (2hrs) heading east; Soloma (4hrs), high in the Cuchumatanes; and La Mesilla (2hrs) on the Mexican border, for which buses depart hourly until 4pm. For Sacapulas and Soloma there are only one or two buses, late in the morning; it's best to check the day before, and buy your ticket then as well. Seats are booked in advance for the local buses, and you may have trouble getting on unless you buy your ticket a few hours before departure. Buses for Todos Santos depart at 1pm daily (returning at 4am), and there are several more in the early afternoon; buses for Nebaj depart at 11.30am daily (returning at 1.45am).

To take the spectacular back road that connects the Western Highlands with the eastern Verapaz range, either catch a direct bus to Sacapulas, or a minibus to Aguacatán, and change there. You will need an early start to make the noon bus from Sacapulas to Uspantán, which is the furthest you are likely to get in one day, and the only place which offers basic accommodation. The bus for Cobán leaves at the antisocial hour of 2.30am, so take your alarm clock. Alternatively, try hitch-hiking on one of the trucks that ply the route regularly.

If you reach Sacapulas by noon, you can pick up one of the buses for Nebaj, coming from Quiché. And if you head down south from here you can catch one of the buses for Quiché, which stop at dawn.

Tourist Information

There is no tourist office here, but hotel staff can be a good source of information. The **post office** (*open Mon–Fri, 8–4.30*) and **Guatel** office (*open Mon–Sat, 7–midnight*) are next to each other on 2 Calle, opposite the Hotel Mary. **Banks** can be found by the main square, but note that no foreign currency exchange is possible on Saturdays. Mexican **visas** or tourist cards can be bought from the Honorary Consul at the Farmacia del Cíd, on 5 Avenida and 4 Calle. If you are continuing north, this is the last place where you will find a **laundry** (in the Turismundo Commercial Centre, at 3 Avenida 0-15; *open Mon–Sat 9.30–6.30*).

Around the Town

The main square, just a few minutes from the busy local market around 1 Avenida, is the most attractive part of town. A colonnaded walkway offers a shady stroll in front of the municipal building while a grand church stands almost opposite. In the middle of the square a neglected relief map of the Cuchumatanes gives you a vague idea of the rugged mountains though most of the flags marking settlements have disappeared.

The town is 5km away from one of the Highlands' more important archaeological sites: **Zaculeu**, ancient capital of the Mam people. (Catch a local bus from the corner of 4 Calle and 7 Avenida.) For some reason all the surfaces were smoothed over with white plaster in the late 1940s, leaving you with a sense of climbing over giant building blocks rather than the remains of Maya temples. The view of the Cuchumatanes and surrounding countryside is some consolation for this crass restoration.

Where to Stay

moderate

Huehuetenango's newest hotel is the **Casa Blanca**, 7 Avenida 3-41, ✆/☎ 7642586, which has modern rooms around a colonial-style courtyard. Try the restaurant and leafy terrace even if you don't stay here. A genuine colonial house with a pleasantly overgrown courtyard is home to the **Hotel Zaculeu**, on 5 Avenida 1-14, ✆ 7641086.

inexpensive

Hotel Mary, 2 Calle 3-52, ✆ 7641618, ☎ 7641228, is a concrete three-storey building, noisy, but with clean rooms and hot water. **Hotel Gobernador**, 4 Avenida 1-45, ✆ 7641197, is a very friendly guest house, with clean rooms and a breakfast restaurant. **Hotel Central**, 5 Avenida 1-33, is an old favourite, with double rooms only, which also has a restaurant attached. Possibly the nicest budget place to stay, though, is the charming **Todos Santos Inn**, 2 Calle 6-74, ✆ 7641241, which comes complete with resident parrot. Other, horrible, accommodation is available, but since tourists are few here, you should have no trouble finding a place to stay among the above.

Eating Out

Outside the hotel restaurants, your choices are limited here. A number of restaurants line 2 Calle, off the main square. One good place is **La Fonda la Don Juan**, which has a good mix of local and international dishes. **Pizza Hogareña** on 6 Avenida, between 4 and 5 Calle, is a popular pizzeria which also has a branch next to the Hotel Mary. Another place worth trying is the **Café Jardín**, on the corner of 6 Avenida and 4

Calle. Finally, the newest eating venue is **Le Kaf** on 6 Calle 6-40, serving decent pizzas and local dishes such as eggs and beans.

The Cuchumatanes Mountains

This distant region of high mountains and desolate plateaus saw unspeakable atrocities during the eighties. Many people, both guerrilla and Indian peasant, fled to its furthest reaches and on into Mexico to live in miserable refugee camps. The remaining Indian men were press-ganged into civil defence patrols by the army. Often armed only with machetes or ancient rifles with hardly any bullets, they were supposed to guard their villages and the roads against insurgents. However, these patrols have now been disbanded, and local people will tell you that all is *tranquilo*, and the bad times over.

In the early mornings, the earth is white with frost; the altitude hovers around 3000m here. In some ways, the landscape recalls the Andes: trees are short and wind-bent, the sparse grassland is strewn with crusty boulders and rocks, and many dwellings are no more than wooden huts thatched with rough grasses.

There is only one major dirt-road that threads its way past Indian and *ladino* towns and villages to Barillas (a frontier town to Mexico) and the mainly uninhabited jungle. There is no road to the border, so there is little reason to travel this far. The furthest Indian village, of interest only on its market days on Thursdays and Sundays, is **San Mateo Ixtatán**. The journey from the Cuchumatanes takes at least six very rough hours by bus, and once there the only accommodation you will find offers straw matresses and very basic food. In your own four-wheel-drive, with provisions and camping equipment, you could have a very adventurous time getting here, with plenty of chances to explore off the beaten track. Even without your own transport, the journey as far as **Soloma** will be plenty adventurous, and the scenery is spectacular.

The Journey to Soloma

Leaving Huehuetenango, the bus takes you past the small town of Chiantla, in colonial times a rich silver-mining town, whose church holds one of the country's most precious altars to the Virgin. Protected in glass casing, she is dressed in priceless silver and adornments and attracts pilgrims from all over the country.

Once past the last checkpoint, you could ask to continue the journey perched on the roof with the luggage, the most exciting place from which to enjoy the scenery. (The driver will think you are mad.) The dusty road turns back and forth, winding up into the mountains, eventually coming out onto a highland plateau, where the distinctive landscape of the Cuchumatanes first comes into its own. The houses are raggedy wooden or adobe, with roofs made of tiles, grass, or wood shingles. Sheep graze in the rocky fields, and if it wasn't for the bus thundering by, all you would hear is the occasional bird, hovering over the stunted trees.

A knobbly pass leads to a steep track that loops around mountainous creases and down into a valley containing several small villages until you eventually reach Soloma, after four hours of having your bones crunched by the bumpy ride. The town is populated mostly by *ladinos* but you will see a few Indian women, who wear long, white *huipiles* that look rather like nighties.

There really isn't anything to do here, except spend half the night in the basic **Hospedaje Central**, by the market square (US$1 each), and get the 4 or 5am bus back towards Huehuetenango. The adventure is undoubtedly exhausting but the scenery is worth the aching bones and little sleep. On the return, you can get off at the Paquix junction (referred to as *cruce*), and wait for transport heading to the famous Indian village of Todos Santos. On any day other than Sunday, you should have a good chance of flagging down a vehicle. Or you can always catch something heading back to Huehuetenango until around 3pm.

Todos Santos

The steep helter-skelter ride down into the valley of Todos Santos is exhilarating now that the road has been improved. The sheer mountainsides are terraced with agricultural fields, in between what is left of the pine forest, and deep gashes of eroded ground bear witness to a serious problem. But the people here need the land for food and the wood for cooking and house-building, and it is the government who should be helping with reafforestation programmes.

Todos Santos is a large Indian village, the heartland of the Mam people. The villagers wear one of the most distinctive traditional costumes. The men are as glamorous as the women, wearing jolly red and white striped trousers held up by hand woven belts with bobbles at the ends. Their shirts of thin white and blue stripes are embroidered around the neck and cuffs with intricate designs in pink, red, purple and blue. They also wear a kind of mini straw bowler, perched above the ears. The women wear gorgeous *huipiles* made of red or purple cloth, embroidered with complicated designs in the same fashion as the men's shirts. Visitors come to buy them in the local co-op shop; prices are rightly high, but still cheaper than in any of the more accessible markets. The crocheted bags, used mainly by the men, are also made by the villagers here. You see them standing in doorways, chatting and never so much as glancing down at what they are doing, while their hands move with expert speed. Market days are Wednesday and Saturday.

Getting There

By bus: Buses from Huehuetenango leave daily from the main terminal at 11.30am. Get there early if you want to be sure of getting a ticket. Alternatively, take any bus heading into the Cuchumatanes and get off at the Paquix junction, where you might be lucky enough to hitch a lift. Be warned, however, that this is the 'middle of nowhere', and many hours can pass without a vehicle in sight. You could always walk—but from the junction it would be a full-day's hike, though mostly downhill.

Buses leave Todos Santos at the painful hours of 3 and 5am; or you could try your luck with the occasional private vehicle that may be leaving for Huehuetenango. By the time you read this, there may also be a midday bus, so it's worth asking about the latest transport schedule. During Easter Week, there are officially no buses at all from Thursday to Sunday.

Around the Village

The village is on a small promontory, overlooking the valley below; the shingled houses are tightly packed and the narrow streets curl steeply up and around the main square, hemmed in by hillsides. The atmosphere is peaceful and friendly, and while there is nothing much to do here, the surrounding countryside offers some fine walks. A language school has recently opened here, so you could spend some time studying. Past students complain, however, that living with Mam-speaking Indians they get little opportunity to practise their Spanish, and the living conditions are very spartan indeed. The school also seems to have a rather doctrinaire attitude, which some people find trying.

The only times the village bursts into action are during Semana Santa, and the more famous All Saints' festival on 1 November, when the men stage death-defying horse races. Bravado dictates that a rider must not just race his horse but drink great swigs of alcohol as well, often with painful results; you may be distressed by the cruelty to the horses too. The most interesting day to be here is Easter Friday, when Romans, dressed in cardboard helmets and what look like pink and yellow bin-liners, run about the streets searching for Jesus. There is much shouting and laughing as the soldiers are pursued by hordes of excited children, until eventually Christ is led away to the Calvario church—in fake beard, rosy cheeks and long white gown. One of the strangest sights of all is a resident family of American missionaries, who seem to think they can blend in by wearing Indian costume.

Where to Stay and Eating Out

The best place to stay is the **Casa Familiar**, 30m above the main road, past the *comedor* Katy. Not only do you get a decent room, but there is also a hot shower, very welcome in this damp and chilly environment. The only downside is that you have to pay extra every time you use the shower. (Anyone can use it, you don't have to be a resident.) The owner, Doña Santiaga Mendoza Pablo, will farm you out to one of her relatives if she can't give you a room herself, but the standard of rooms on offer rapidly deteriorates to wooden shacks lined with plastic.

If you can't get in at the Casa Familiar, you will find basic accommodation and a cold shower at the **La Paz**, on the main street. About US$1 per person, the *pensión* (guest house) is friendly, and the best rooms have a balcony looking out over the street. Third choice is **Las Olguitas** (same price), which is also a *comedor*, but the rooms are in a wooden contraption above the kitchen, and the place is not only noisy but very dirty too.

Favourite for meals of beans, eggs and tortillas is the *comedor* **Katy** (*open 7am–8pm*), on the hill above the main square, beyond the small park. You might get bored with the same food three times a day, but it is certainly preferable to the filthy tables at Las Olguitas, and the menu is the same there anyway. For a bit of variety, on market days, a few kitchens operate inside the market building.

Walks Around Todos Santos

Towards San Juan Atitán (2hrs or 5hrs all the way)

The path leading up the hill past the *comedor* Katy will take you up a steep trail by an open-air shrine hiding among a small group of conifers. There are a couple of crosses here, one of which is not a Christian cross at all, but a Mam cross signifying Holy Earth, made out of ancient wood. Like Momostenango and Chichicastenango, this is a place where the Maya daykeepers still practise their rites and Maya tradition is as strong as ever. Some grassy mounds nearby testify to the remains of the small Maya site, **Tojcunanchén**.

From here the dirt track widens and leads you to a pass where the view across two valleys invites you to take a rest and enjoy the beauty all around. Larks and other birds buzz by, and the fecund fields are riddled with little paths where women patter swiftly past on tough bare feet, usually followed by a gaggle of children and the odd duck. You can either turn back here or continue for another two to three hours of relatively easy walking to the village of **San Juan Atitán** (*market Thurs*). Here the men wear a quite different dress from their neighbours: white linen trousers, covered by a brown, woollen tunic, and a red belt around the waist.

Continue straight ahead down the hill instead of following the dirt track to the right and you will pass the rim of the Todos Santos valley. The path descends and then climbs several ridges, taking you across streams and past flocks of sheep on the sheer mountain-sides. The path is broad and clear, so you should not get lost, but always ask anyone you meet if you are on the right path for San Juan. About two hours after leaving the Todos Santos valley behind, you reach the final ridge before descending into the broad valley where San Juan clings to the hillside, an hour's walk below. You can see it to your left, and here you have a choice: either head straight down the mountain to a dirt-track that eventually connects with a road, which you then follow, turning left; or you can head left at the top of the ridge, following the contours of the mountain before dropping down directly above the village. Note that the village is strung out along the dirt-road for a good two kilometres, and the main plaza is some way from the first houses you encounter.

If you want to walk all the way to San Juan Atitán, bear in mind that you will be too tired to return the same day. You can, however, stay the night there. Just ask for the unmarked **Hospedaje San Diego**, above the main square, run by a very friendly family, who will share their meals with you for a small fee. The next day you can either walk back to Todos Santos or catch a pick-up truck for Huehuetenango at 6am (1hr). Remember that it can be very chilly up here, so do bring rain- and wind-proof gear.

Down the Todos Santos Valley (3hrs)

Following the dirt-road out of the village, past the dentist's and through a straggle of houses, you will come to a large path leading off to the right. Follow this downhill for a while, and you will find yourself walking parallel to the deep ravine that hides a busy river at its base. The route takes you past cactuses and the occasional shepherd with his flock; this is a great way to see the countryside and meet the local farmers too. Eventually, you descend to cross the river and make your way over three more bridges before a dirt track takes you up to the other side of the valley, and to a road leading back to Todos Santos. On this side you will see small homesteads, some of which have roadside stands selling warm sodas.

The Pacific Coast

*Our driver slowed down at last. We were in a street of decrepit
shanties; there were children in the dust and wandering pigs. Then,
suddenly, vast and blank under a glaring white sky, the Pacific.*

Beyond the Mexique Bay, Aldous Huxley

If the idea of the Pacific Coast conjures up in your mind images of palm-fringed white beaches dotted with picturesque towns and villages, then you are in for a disappointment. The coastal plain that stretches some 250km from Mexico to El Salvador is dominated by large-scale agriculture: endless plantations of sugar, cotton and rubber are cut by potholed roads, which end on banks of black volcanic sand at the coast. The settlements along the Pacific Highway are sweaty and choked with pollution and commerce. The villages are some of the most depressing anywhere, populated by underpaid plantation workers.

And yet what the beaches lack in tropical glamour they make up for with their sheer size, the giant sand dunes stretching endless and barren towards the horizon. The area as a whole is in no way developed for tourism, and for travellers keen to get off the beaten track this is an advantage. The fishing villages, with their forlorn streets and neglected huts, have a melancholy appeal and the people are more open, curious to discover what on earth you are doing here. Most are *ladino*, with some migrant Indian labourers, and the markets and festivals are characterized by Spanish heritage rather than Indian.

After the touristic bustle of the Western Highlands, you might find silent days swinging in a hammock just what you want: by day you can watch lizards and iguanas basking in the sun; by night you will witness an explosion of insects around any light and crowds of toads flashing their tongues to catch them. The coast here has been changed beyond recognition through drainage and deforestation for agricultural development: if you want to know what the coast looked like before, head for the Monterrico Nature Reserve. Here you will find the original mangrove swamps and some of the attendant wildlife. If archaeological ruins are what interest you, you can see the unique remains of the coastal civilizations near Santa Lucía Cotzumalguapa. Or you might prefer the energetic sleaze of Guatemala's second port, Puerto San José, where weekend crowds from the capital bring a riot of music and streetlife.

The Pacific Highway runs parallel to the coast, 50km inland, along the foothills of the highlands, so you cannot actually see the sea. It used to be the country's best and fastest road, but lack of funding caused by corruption on a spectacular scale has left it in a terrible state. These days there are significant stretches where nothing but mud remains. The Highway is especially bad between the Cocales junction—where the road coming from San Lucas Tolimán joins—and Retalhuleu. Off the Highway, the roads are abysmal, the bus journeys excruciatingly slow and hot. The only exceptions to this rule are the main roads leading to Quezaltenango (from Retalhuleu, Coatepeque or Mazatenango), and to the ports of Champerico and Puerto San José.

The best time to visit the Pacific is during the dry season, October to April. April to July are the hottest months, and at this time the heat and humidity can reduce even the most energetic to a state of brain-dead panting. At any time of year, mosquito repellent is essential, and during the rainy season you should consider taking malaria pills.

Along the Pacific Highway

The Pacific Highway, connecting with Guatemala City, is a major commercial artery, on which vast plantations truck out their produce, such as coffee (from the foothills rising off the plain), sugar cane, cotton and rubber. The towns along here exist almost exclusively on the commerce connected with these primary products, and their markets are sweet with pineapples, papayas, bananas in all shapes and sizes, coconuts, oranges, and plenty of other fruits. The bus terminals are hectic with traders from all over the country, and the black exhaust fumes sit chokingly low in the heat. None of the towns have much to detain the visitor and most are best seen from a bus window, on your way to somewhere else. If you need to stop over along this route, though, the best place to do it is Retalhuleu, which is a pleasant enough town and is also close to the most rewarding Pre-Columbian ruins on the Pacific: Abaj Takalik.

West Towards Mexico

Coming from Guatemala City, the first major town on the Pacific plain is **Escuintla** (1hr journey from Zona 4 bus terminal), a busy place with a huge market and crowded streets lined with crumbling old buildings. Next to Retalhuleu, it is the best of a ragged bunch—not for its beauty but for its sheer chaotic energy. It is also an important junction for many other destinations, such as the back-road connection to Antigua (7am and 1pm from the main bus terminal; 2hrs). Regular buses leave or pass through for Taxisco (2hrs) and the Salvadorean border (4hrs), and also for Puerto San José (2hrs).

If you should find yourself having to stay the night in Escuintla, try **Hotel Izcuintla**, 4 Avenida 6-7; or **Campo Real**, on 10 Calle. There is a **Lloyds Bank** on 7 Calle 3-9, and a **Banco de Guatemala** on the corner of 7 Calle and 4 Avenida.

Continuing northwest, you pass dusty **Siquinalá** (change for Sipacate beach), and then **Santa Lucía Cotzumalguapa**, referred to as Cotz and only worth stopping in if you plan to visit the archaeological collection nearby (*see* p.157). From here the buses thunder along the Highway, past dusty palms, rows of banana trees and innumerable roadside shacks.

The next large town is **Mazatenango** (Masate in conversation and on the bus windows), which is unbearably hot and sticky, and the only possible reason for getting off the bus here is to change for one heading to Quezaltenango (regular buses 8–5; journey 2hrs), or for one going to the remote fishing village of Tulate, two to three hours away through the plantations (*see* p.152). If you do need to stay over in Masate, try the **Hotel Alba**, © 8720264, on the main highway outside town, to the west. A double room costs around US$25 and there is secure parking. You will also find **banks** and a **Guatel** office in the centre.

Retalhuleu

Cuyotenango quickly follows after Masate, but the Highway cuts brutally through its middle and leaves it behind, taking you to Retalhuleu (Reu, pronounced 'ray-oo', for short), a small distance off the main road, and the richest and grandest of the Pacific towns. Here old colonial splendour mixes with the exclusive new villas of wealthy plantation owners; the road into town is lined with fortified entrances leading to immaculate lawns and tropical gardens. Reu is by no means a beautiful town but the crumbling buildings around the main square are pleasant enough, and the streets around the market are alive with commerce. Unlike the Indian markets, *ladino* ones are definitely there to buy and sell, to spend and make hard cash. Pushing and shoving, shouting and haggling are the norm around here, and it is fun to walk among the overflowing stalls selling mostly agricultural produce.

Tourist Information

Banks, a **post office** and **Guatel** office (*open daily 7–10pm*) are all on or near the main square. A **Mexican consulate** (*open Mon-Fri, 4–6*) selling visas and tourist cards can be found at 5 Calle and 3 Avenida. This is your last chance to purchase these before you reach the border.

Around the Town

The local **Museum of Archaeology and Ethnology**, inside the Municipal Palace on the main square (*open Tues–Sun, 9–noon and 2–6; small adm*), has an amazing collection of Pre-Classic figurines and heads. Some of the figures show a strong Mexican influence (for example, the ear-plugs), not surprising so close to the border; the meaning and background of the miniature zoomorphs remain tantalisingly mysterious. Make sure you have a look upstairs as well, where you will find a fascinating photographic collection, dating back to the 1880s, with photos of Reu during its glory days.

If a visit to the museum gets you interested, why not make time to see the unusual ruins of **Abaj Takalik** (*open daily, 9–4*). Take a local bus to the village of Asintal, and then walk a further 4km; or drive there yourself, though only 4-wheel drives will make it past the village of Asintal, just off the Pacific Highway heading northwest. The site covers nine square kilometres, spreading across three major coffee plantations, though only a small part, on the Finca Margarita, has been excavated so far. The small temple platforms you see are not part of the central plaza and very little work has been done on them; the ancient stone monuments and carvings are the highlight of the visit. The oldest stela found here (no.5) is believed to be 166 years older than the oldest one at Tikal. The imagery here is drawn from the local environment, so there are representations rare in Maya art, such as the alligator on monument no.66, and interesting symbols, many based on the most common local animals, such as frogs and toads. Monument no.68 shows a singing toad, which signifies rain, since toads always come out to sing after rain; monument no.8 shows a monkey escaping from the jaws of a jaguar, signifying life and prosperity. One of the most impressive monuments is the huge Olmec head, almost Asian in appearance. Notice also the river stones used in the pyramid platforms at Abaj Takalik; local people still build with similar stones today.

Where to Stay

There are three central hotels in Reu: the modern **Posada de Don José,** 5 Calle 3-67, ✆ 7710180, 7711179, charges around US$30 for one of the double rooms, set around a courtyard and pool; it also has a decent restaurant. The old-fashioned but very agreeable **Hotel Astor,** 5 Calle 4-60, ✆ 7710475, charges around US$21 for a double with TV and private bath, and also offers secure parking. **Hotel Modelo,** ✆ 7710256, across the street, is quite a bit cheaper—very good value for what it offers. There are a few motels along the entrance road to town. Change buses here for regular connections to Quezaltenango (2hrs), or buses to the small port of Champerico (1hr).

Coatepeque

Almost an hour after Reu, the last town before the Mexican border is Coatepeque (Coa for short). It's not such a bad place to stay if you really have to. Coming from the Mexican border posts of Tecún Umán (34km) or Talismán (60km), this is the first town with **hotels,** a **bank, post office** and **Guatel** office. You can also change here for frequent buses to Quezaltenango, if you are heading for the Highlands. The top hotel is the **Hotel Villa Real,** 6 Calle 6-57, ✆ 7751939, a modern building with clean rooms and secure parking, where a double room with private bath and TV will cost you around US$17. Quite a bit cheaper is the family-run **Hotel Baechli,** 6 Calle 5-35, ✆ 7751483, which is simple but OK, and also offers secure parking. Cheapest of all but not very pleasant is **Hotel Lee**, on 4 Avenida, also with secure parking. There are also a number of more up-market places on the highway, complete with pools and restaurants.

If, for some reason, you get stuck here with nothing to do, you could catch a bus to the seaside village of **Tilapa** (2hrs). Unfortunately, though, the great beach is pretty filthy because a nearby river empties all its rubbish on to the sand and into the surrounding sea. And to reach the beach you have to cross a mosquito-infested mangrove swamp. If there is anywhere on the coast that you have a good chance of catching malaria, it is here.

The **Mexican border post** by **Tecún Umán,** being the nearest, is the busiest crossing, and most of the heavy trucks and private vehicles take this route. Unless you need a visa, you can buy tourist cards for Mexico from immigration officials, and the post is operational

24hrs a day. Buses leave regularly for the six-hour journey to Guatemala City (depending on road conditions), and on the Mexican side the town of Tapachula is half an hour away by bus. On public transport you need to arrive during daylight hours to connect onwards. The border by the **Talismán** bridge (long walk across the bridge) is also open 24hrs, and buses on the Mexican side quickly connect with Tapachula. Heading for the Highlands from Mexico, get any bus to Retalhuleu and connect there for Quezaltenango.

East Towards El Salvador

From Guatemala City, the Highway branches southeast by Escuintla, taking you past the familiar lowland scenery of plantations and dusty roadsides, offering the occasional view of a towering volcano peering through the clouds to your left. About two hours later you come to **Taxisco**, the first town of any note and the place to change buses if heading for the **Monterrico Nature Reserve** (*see* p.156). Shortly afterwards, the bus arrives in **Chiquimulilla**, yet another commercial centre and your last chance to head somewhere other than the border.

From here you can catch a bus south to the fishing village of **Las Lisas**, or go north to the town of **Cuilapa**. The back road twists up through coffee plantations and into the dusty hills of the **Oriente**, Guatemala's heat-cracked, sandy range of hills that extends almost the entire length of the eastern border from the Pacific to the Atlantic. Once here, you can make for the capital again, or travel further into the country's eastern region.

After Chiquimulilla the Highway heads towards El Salvador. The **Salvadorean border** (*open daily 6–8*) is by a small settlement grandly entitled Ciudad Pedro de Alvarado; it's very quiet, since almost nobody uses this route. In El Salvador, regular buses (*until 6pm*) take you onwards to Sonsonate, where you can change for San Salvador. The more usual and faster route for travelling to El Salvador is on a direct bus connecting the two capitals, via the Pan-American Highway.

The Western Pacific

In the 1930s when Aldous Huxley visited **Champerico**, it was Guatemala's third port. Yet even then he wrote about 'the unspeakable boredom of life at Champerico'. These days very little commercial shipping comes here at all, so it is even duller. It would be a good place to drink oneself to death, strolling along the crumbling remains of the port from time to time, sniffing the fishy smells from the occasional small boat, wandering the beach (suitably grey) and then returning to the bar of the Hotel Martita.

The town is easily visited from Xela, with daily direct buses from the main terminal, or else head for Reu and change there. The journey takes about 2½ hours, and the last returning bus is at 2.30pm, so you may want to stay overnight. If you do not like the **Martita** (about US$4), try the **Miramar** (around US$6) across the street. Do taste some of the seafood at the beach; the fried fish or shrimps are delicious.

Not far south of Champerico, **Tulate** (ask one of the boatmen to take you; a wet trip of 40mins) is a tiny fishing village of pole-and-thatch huts, perched on a sandbank and separated from the mainland by a narrow canal; the inhabitants live either side of a path leading to the ocean. The Pacific's white waves pound the sand that drops steeply to the water and, as far as the eye can see in either direction, there is nothing but empty beach and distant palm trees waving in the quivering heat. Even the pigs go swimming to cool off, though they prefer the black water of the canal. Except at the weekends, there are no visitors at all, and there is absolutely nothing to do here except doze, swim, eat fried fish, and chat with the locals.

Unless you're prepared for the extremely basic accommodation on offer, you will probably not wish to stay the night. The branch road that leads off the Pacific Highway at Cuyotenango is one of the worst tarmac roads in the country, so ideally you should come in your own transport, and then the 60km or so should take only an hour and a half. There are regular buses from Mazatenango, the last one returning at around 5pm. From Cuyotenango onwards, a drearily straight road cuts through the plantations, though the potholes and discarded sugar canes guarantee a zigzag ride that can take up to three hours in the stifling heat.

Another beachside village best visited in your own transport is **Semillero** (via Pueblo Nuevo Tiquisate from the Pacific Highway). The journey there rather than the settlement itself is memorable: the road is not only the most beautiful on the 'Costa Boca', but also the most interesting, taking you past the former Pacific headquarters of the United Fruit Company. Although foreigners almost never stray this way these days, **Pueblo Nuevo Tiquisate** is a busy market town serving a vast region. The surviving wooden buildings along some of its muddy streets give Tiquisate a frontier-town atmosphere. Regular buses connect the town with the main highway, via the Cocales junction, and you can also catch direct buses to and from the capital. There is even a place to stay here: the **Hotel El Viajero**, ✆ 2384718, which charges around US$6 for a double room with fan and private bath, and offers secure parking. There is also a **bank** and **Guatel** office here, but be prepared for long walks—the town is very spread out.

Continuing towards the ocean from Tiquisate, the road traverses endless sugar plantations, and you pass several wooden dormitories, raised on stilts to protect the inhabitants from rats and poisonous snakes. Occasionally you see the fancier raised homes of the local managers, some even with pools and air-conditioning. Mostly built in the 1950s, these fine wooden buildings are still in reasonable condition, painted in bright colours and surrounded by palms and hibiscus bushes.

The beach at Semillero is no more attractive than many others along the Pacific: a broad swathe of black sand. But you might as well stop for a swim if you've come this far. As you return from the coast, the view—on a clear day—is truly superb, as the whole chain of Guatemalan volcanoes punctuates the horizon. In front of you is the huge hulk of Atitlán volcano, to the east are Acatenango and Agua, to the west Santa María and Santiaguito; you might even see the distant Tacaná.

Continue southeast along the coast and you will come to a reasonable beach near the village of **Sipacate**. If you are coming from Escuintla (2hrs), take any bus along the

Highway, and get off at Siquinalá, where buses south to Sipacate leave from behind the market. The branch road has deteriorated badly, so expect to spend a good few hours in a sweltering bus, packed with plantation workers and women returning from the market. The first settlement you reach is La Democracia (*see* p.157), then the small town of La Gomera, and finally Sipacate. There are plenty of pick-ups travelling this road, so there is also a chance of a lift for hitchhikers.

Sipacate itself is a forlorn place. The beach is the other side of the Chiquimulilla Canal that extends from here all the way to the Salvadorean border. Along this entire stretch, the beaches are cut off from the mainland, accessible only by *cayuco*. If you want to eat in the village, rather than on the beach, try the fried fish at **El Guayacán**. Otherwise follow the main street left, for a water-taxi (*small fee*) to **Rancho Carillo**, a collection of wooden beach huts and a restaurant, perched high above the waves. To stay here will set you back an outrageous US$10, for a double *cabaña* with private bathroom.

An alternative is to continue to **La Empalizada**, 5km up the coast; there's no public transport, so you'll have to hitch if you haven't hired a car. There are two dirty and overpriced places to stay immediately you reach the beach. Further on you will find yourself on an entirely deserted beach, but there is nowhere decent to stay or eat along here so, if you can, make this a day trip rather than an overnight stay.

The Eastern Pacific

Much more populated than the rest of the Guatemalan Pacific, the stretch between Puerto San José and the border offers unique attractions. Puerto San José, the county's second port, is surprisingly small, but heaving with commerce, the military, and sleazy bars. A concrete and mud maze of streets by the sea, it's certainly not beautiful. It is, however, loud and boisterous, and the beachside shacks and restaurants offer all the seafood delights you can stomach. At weekends and holidays the town is filled with sweaty families from the capital and the beach is a mass of bodies and garbage. You don't have to stay here; direct buses to Guate take no more than two hours on one of the country's best roads.

Outside San José there are some exclusive holiday enclaves favoured by the Guatemalan rich, expensive waterside villas or hotels, with fortified and guarded entrances. Here you will find swimming pools, restaurants and manicured lawns—all very safe and clean, but also far removed from anything Guatemalan. To get there you will need to have your own transport, or to pay through the nose for a taxi.

For a peaceful and reasonably clean place to laze on the beach, catch a bus to **Iztapa**, half an hour from San José (direct buses also from Guate). This too was once a port, though you would never guess it. Its shipbuilding days came to an end well before Independence, and since then its sandy streets have been enlivened only by snoring drunks and panting dogs. Some of the buildings and most of the beach shacks across the canal are made of wood, giving the place a slightly romantic look. The beach is impressively wide, and there's a good, simple hotel: the **Hotel Sol y Playa**, ✆ 2384186, which has a swimming pool but is vastly overpriced at US$20 for a double room. Nearby, the **Hotel Brasília** charges a fraction of the price, but has no pool and is a bit rough. The best budget option is the **Río Dulce** (formerly Pollo Andra), which offers basic rooms and a very pleasant terrace on which to sample the local fish.

The coastal road is interrupted here by the mouth of the River Naranjo; you can, however, cross to the village of **Pueblo Viejo** by *cayuco* and take a bus from there to Monterrico beach and nature reserve. The journey along the sandy road is maddeningly slow—it's far quicker to travel direct from the capital. Take a bus to Taxisco (from Zona 4 terminal), and change there for the ten-minute ride to the village of **La Avellana**, from where water-taxis take you through the mangroves and set you down by the beachside village. If arriving in La Avellana in your own vehicle, you can either arrange to have it guarded for around US$1 per day, or have it transported by boat to Monterrico, which will cost you around US$15 each way.

Monterrico

Monterrico is perhaps the best-known village on the Guatemalan Pacific, probably because it is the only place advertised by the tourist board. The main attraction is the so-called **nature reserve**; it has no official status, which explains why more and more holiday homes and guest houses are being built here. Monterrico also has the only beach on the Pacific genuinely worth visiting, where you can relax in a safe and friendly environment and enjoy a good choice of accommodation and eating and drinking venues.

Tourist Information

No banking is available in Monterrico, but most of the beach hotels should change cash for you if you run out of local **currency**. The cheapest radio **telephone** service is offered by Jonny's Place, which charges around US$2 per minute. Self-caterers are well served by the local **supermarket** (*open Sun–Thurs, 8–8; Fri–Sat, 8–10pm*). There is also a **pharmacy** in the village.

The large village that gives the area its name is set along black sandy paths, dotted with assorted humans and animals lazing under the shade of palm trees or porches. The beach itself stretches in either direction as far as the eye can see, buffeted by great waves crashing in on a never-ending roll. Swimming here is difficult because of the strong undertow and sometimes ferocious waves, but just spending time on the sand and watching the pelicans skim the waves is wonderfully relaxing. There are great sunsets to take in over a drink at the **Pig Pen Bar**, and before you know it you've stayed far longer than you'd planned.

The best place in the village to sample the local seafood is at **Divina Maestra**, where the cooking lives up to the name. The main occupations here are dozing, eating and sunbathing, with the alternative of a canoe trip around the surrounding mangrove swamps. You can hire canoes by the jetty—haggle in advance. Alternatively speak to Michael at the Pig Pen Bar, who can also advise you and hires out surfboards.

The **Monterrico Nature Reserve** is an area of the coast all around Monterrico that has been preserved in almost its original state, and supports an isolated ecosystem of plants and wildlife. Originally mangroves protected the entire Pacific coast, and a swampy hinterland was covered in forest and impenetrable thickets. Only this century has deforestation and draining altered the landscape irreversibly; at Monterrico you can still get an idea of how the rest of the coast used to be. The Inguat office in the capital provides a special brochure on the reserve's flora and fauna, but you are unlikely to see anything other than birds and butterflies, except in the small animal reserve on the beach. This is not for the faint-hearted—a more sorry collection of turtles, crocodiles and iguanas you are unlikely to find anywhere else, and seeing their wretched state is enough to make you start up a local animal liberation group.

Where to Stay

You can stay right on the beach here, and the most popular budget option is still **Hotel Baule Beach**, although the basic rooms are overpriced at around US$12 for doubles; for reservations ✆ 4736196, ✉ 4713390 in the capital. A pleasant terrace with hammocks looks out to sea—a great place to watch the sunsets. To get there walk through the village to the beach and then turn left. On the way you pass the very friendly **Jonny's Place**, where you can rent a bungalow for four with its own tiny swimming pool and kitchen for US$36; for reservations call Monica ✆ 4480329 in the capital. Next door to Jonny's is the **Kaiman Inn**, charging around US$10 per person for a simple cabaña sleeping up to three, with private bath. Better value is its restaurant, which serves good Italian food. Past Baule Beach, the other side of the animal reserve, **Pez de Oro**, ✆ 6315620, ✉ 6316854 in the capital, offer the most beautiful cottages and a pleasant pool. This is also Italian run and the restaurant serves a decent selection of pasta and local dishes.

If you take the sandy road to Jonny's Place, you will pass the **Hotel San Gregorio**, ✆ 2517326 in the capital, just before you reach the beach. The hotel is brand-new, has a great pool, and rooms that sleep up to four go for US$72. Finally, if you want to enjoy the beach away from the village, try the **Paradise Hotel**, ✆ 4784202, ✉ 4784595 in the capital. One kilometre along the beach, in the opposite direction to Jonny's Place, or two kilometres by road, this hotel offers spacious bungalows with two double beds each, and costs US$59 for up to four people. There is also a restaurant and pool here, though very little shade. In the village itself, the only option is **Las Margaritas**, which offers straw mats on wooden beds and is simply horrible.

Archaeological Sites near the Pacific Coast

In pre-Conquest times, the Pacific Lowlands of Guatemala were colonized in part by people migrating south from Mexico. One of these groups, the Pipiles, probably arrived sometime during the early Post-Classic period (AD 900–1200). Their language was close to the Aztec tongue of Nahuatl and, although the people became extinct around the time of the Spanish Conquest, many of the names of Guatemala's towns and villages point to their linguistic influence. For example, the familiar ending -*nango* is Nahuatl for 'place of'.

Most of the archaeological sites in this region have been obliterated by the relentless development of plantations. However, a few scattered remains hide among the sugar-cane fields, and two locations in particular are worth seeking out. The most interesting site for remains of Pipil sculpture, **El Baúl** is on a working plantation (*finca*) about 6km outside the town of Santa Lucía Cotzumalguapa; without your own transport the only convenient way of visiting is by taxi from the town. El Baúl is a site for enthusiasts only, though it does offer the added attraction of entry to one of the country's huge *fincas*, normally closed to outsiders. The plantation operates one of the ten largest sugar mills in the country and belongs to the powerful Herrera family, reputedly the second wealthiest in Guatemala. Walking through, you will see the massive machinery and the migrant labourers who work for slave wages to create the immense wealth of the landowners.

The most significant find here was the 'Herrera Stela', discovered in 1923, featuring a depiction of a plumed Maya warrior. Much disagreement rages about its age; the Maya expert Michael Coe dates it AD 36 and believes it to be the oldest documented sculpture in Maya territory. On your return, ask the taxi driver to take you to the fascinating sculpture of *Dios del Mundo*, on a small grassy promontory among the cane fields. Only his huge face is visible, poking out of the ground alongside a fertility goddess still worshipped by the local people today. Never come here on your own, though, as the spot is quite remote and attracts thieves—mornings are safer, apparently, as the local *ladrones* like to sleep in.

A separate sculptural tradition in this region has strong links with the Mexican Olmec style, uniquely grotesque, featuring small bulbous heads and figures that stare blankly—quite different from the ornate carvings of the Pipiles, who adapted to the Maya style. The creators of these works were a subsidiary cult of the Izapan civilization, predecessors of the Olmecs based near the Mexican town of Tapachula, by the present-day border with Guatemala. The best collection is in the small town of **La Democracia**, a short bus ride away from the Pacific Highway at Siquinalá. Most of the sculptures are ranged around the main square, but there is also a small **museum** (*open Tues–Sun, 8–noon and 2–5; small adm*).

With or without your own transport, the best place to base yourself for visiting these obscure sites is **Santa Lucía Cotzumalguapa**, though the town itself is not an attractive place. The more upmarket accommodation is on the main highway: choose either the overpriced **El Camino**, ℂ 8825316, which charges around US$12 for a room; or the smarter **El Santiaguito**, ℂ 8825435, which charges about US$32 for an air-conditioned double, and has a good restaurant and pool. In the town itself, the best budget option, basic but cheap, which also has secure parking, is the **Reforma**, 4 Avenida 4-71.

The Verapaz Mountains

The Verapaz region is the heartland of Guatemala's coffee-growing industry, based around the town of Cobán. It contains one of the last remaining areas of cloud forest, the natural habitat of the quetzal, Guatemala's extremely rare and beautiful national bird. A reserve has been set up where you can wander about the forest and perhaps sight the bird and, although your chances are slim, a visit is still rewarding. Once past Cobán, the roads degenerate into mud and gravel, but the scenery is superb, easily making up for the discomforts and the almost daily drizzle. If you have two or three days to spare, visit the remote pools of Semuc Champey, a magical place hidden in the forests east of Cobán; it will undoubtedly be one of the highlights of your journey. Alternatively, you could test your nerve on one of the country's most spectacular back roads, connecting Cobán to Huehuetenango.

History

Just one region eluded the Spaniards in the early years of conquest: the highland area covering the northeast of the country. Bordered by the Western Highlands, with jungle to the north and east, and the arid Motagua valley to the south, this was the land to which many Indians fled and, together with the bellicose Rabinal nation, held out against invaders. Thick forests covered undulating highlands and deep river-beds cut through the countryside; crops flourished on the fertile land, enabling the Mayas to sustain themselves during many years of guerrilla warfare. They were so successful that the Spanish dubbed the region Tierra de Guerra (land of war), and more or less avoided it.

But Alvarado's massacres in this region were infamous. Both Hernán Cortés, his former leader, and Friar Bartolomé de Las Casas, the first campaigner for Indian rights, later known as the Apostle of the Indies, denounced Alvarado to the Spanish Court. Las Casas came to Guatemala in 1533, ten years after the conquest, and took up the Indian cause with great vigour. His writings had such influence at the Spanish Court that he was given a royal charter to attempt a peaceful Christianization of the Indians. He argued that the Indians were fellow human beings and, as such, could be reasoned with, and were capable of being converted without violence. To achieve his goal of peaceful conversion, he needed to establish two vital points: total separation of the secular Spanish from the Indians in the region he would work in; and a ban on converted Indians being forced into slavery. He was granted his wishes, and began his task in 1536, in the notorious Tierra de Guerra. Based in present-day Antigua, his first step was to compose hymns in the Maya dialects which told the story of Christian creation and the life of Jesus Christ. Christianized Indian merchants were sent to the region the following year, where they performed the novel songs before the Indian leaders they were trading with. It is said that the merchants sang eight nights in a row, their hymns becoming more popular each day, until the Indians were learning to sing them too. An emissary was sent back with the merchants, inviting one of Las Casas' friars to visit the highlands.

By 1539, the region was renamed Verapaz (true peace) to honour Las Casas and his men. The Catholic Church had succeeded where the conquistadors had failed and pacified the territory ready for the Spanish colonists to move in. For the Indians here, the long-term results were the same as in places that had been subdued by force: appropriation of their land and loss of human rights. Las Casas had to flee for his life a few years later, not from the Indians but from the irate conquistadors who resented their supply of Indian slaves being cut and the idea of giving back the land they had stolen.

Baja Verapaz

Although the lower Verapaz range is just north of Guatemala City, you reach it by taking the Atlantic Highway east, and then heading up into the hills by the El Rancho junction. The road is excellent and bus connections between the capital and Cobán, passing through Baja Verapaz, are fast and regular.

The Atlantic Highway takes you through the brown desert landscape of the Motagua valley. After the El Rancho junction, a dust-covered collection of shacks and petrol stations, the bus begins the winding ascent. The only colours here are shades from rusty brown to faded yellow; the few thorny plants that grow are covered by layers of dust.

A crossroads marks the turning west into the valley of **Salamá** and the town of the same name. Beyond the town lies the smaller settlement of **Rabinal**, the first place founded by Las Casas; and beyond that, lies remote **Cubulco**. There is no real reason to travel this way unless you happen to be passing at the time of one of the local fiestas (*Salamá: 17–21 Sept; Rabinal: 25–29 Jan; Cubulco: 23 Jan*). This region has a low Indian population, and traditional clothing and colourful markets are a rare sight. On the other hand, you do have a chance to explore an area of the country where outsiders seldom stray, and there's a nice place to stay in Salamá, the **Hotel Tezulutlán**, which makes a good base. Ideally you should come here in your own transport. The Sunday market in Rabinal, the most traditional of these three settlements, is a good place to look for bargains, though the variety of textiles and embroidery is limited.

Beyond the Salamá crossroads, the landscape changes quite suddenly to pine forests and green pastures. Small homesteads lie surrounded by neat fields and grazing animals, and the scent of pines drifts into the bus. This rural scenery flies by for an hour or so, and then you pass into the strange world of epiphytes clinging to giant trees and damp mists draped over the treetops, as the road snakes into the chilly heights of a cloud forest.

The Quetzal Reserve

Three hours from the polluted capital you find yourself in the moist atmosphere of the **Biotopo del Quetzal** (*open daily, 8–4, adm free*).

Getting There and Away

From **Guatemala City**, several pullmans leave every day (*see* p.64), and the journey takes 3hrs to the reserve. Remember to ask to be dropped off (just outside the entrance) or the bus will not stop. **Cobán** is only an hour away, so you can visit easily coming from that direction as well. Leaving the reserve by bus, just stand by the road and flag down the first bus heading your way.

A visitors' centre, with a small exhibition and a helpful guardian, is the starting point for two paths leading through the forest. Both are very clearly marked, so there is no chance of getting lost. One route takes you on a brief 2km tour, the other on an 8km hike up and down the steep mountainside.

Even the short path is a good introduction to the wonders of this environment. You pad along a soft trail, inhaling the musty smell of rotting leaves; the light is subdued by the high roof of tangled leaves and branches, and only the occasional clearing allows shafts of sun to glitter on wet foliage. Cool streams bubble over moss-covered boulders and, if you pause in the stillness of the forest, you'll begin to discern the sounds of the animals all around you.

Looking up into the vast canopy, you might be lucky enough to focus on a monkey, comfortably perching to eat fruit. You'll see some of the huge variety of birds, butterflies and insects that flit among the branches. There are other creatures, less easy to glimpse: small green toucans, their feathers an excellent camouflage, shy mini ocelots, tapirs and, of course, snakes.

If you are up at dawn or watching quietly at dusk, you might see the gorgeous male quetzal, the famous tail plumes trailing from his tiny body. The female quetzal has a similar body and coloration, but lacks the long tail feathers. Bear in mind that your chances of seeing a quetzal are best during the nesting season of April to June, and that the small fruit of the aguacatillo tree is a favourite food. However, even in season the number of people around and traffic on the road may scare these lovely birds away. As Jonathan Maslow puts it, sighting a quetzal is 'one part knowledge, one part patience, and three parts willingness to get wet'.

The head and body of the quetzal is a magical array of greens, blues and turquoise, depending on how the sun lights up the feathers, while the breast is crimson. Legend has it that when Alvarado slew Tecún Umán, a quetzal bird fell from the sky to cover the warrior's dead body. Next morning it rose up again, its breast forever stained by the Indian's blood. Long before the Spanish arrived, or the independent nation made it their symbol of freedom, the quetzal bird was sacred to the Mayas. To kill it was a capital offence, and only Maya lords had the right to decorate their battle headdress with the male's arching tail feathers; the bird was considered spiritual protector of Indian chiefs, accompanying them to battle, and dying with them, if they were beaten.

If confined in a cage, the quetzal dies—most apt for a symbol of freedom. Hunting the bird has been banned since 1895, but ornithologists believe that the quetzal will probably be extinct by the year 2000. The reason is quite simply the destruction of its only habitat, the cloud forest. By 1981, the Guatemalan cloud forest had been reduced from 30,000km^2 to 2500km^2, and land shortages and lack of alternative cooking fuel mean that squatters are still cutting down the remaining forests, even in the reserve. There are also reports of people killing the bird for food, quite apart from selling its feathers for profit. It is a sad prospect for one of the world's most exquisite birds.

Where to Stay and Eating Out

There are three choices of accommodation near the reserve. The most comfortable is the **Posada Montaña del Quetzal**, ℘ 3351805 in the capital. It has a restaurant and swimming pool, and charges around US$30 for doubles but, at a distance of 4km away from the reserve, it's only convenient for those with private transport. A few steps from the reserve entrance is a simple *hospedaje*, two log cabins with ten beds each, communal showers and toilet. It's very basic and you will need your own sleeping bag and torch, but the location is excellent. Finally, there is a beautiful **campsite** (tents only) inside the reserve, behind the visitors' centre, right next to a pool fed by freezing spring water. Barbecue facilities, shower and toilets are provided.

When it comes to eating, you can either have eggs and beans at the *hospedaje*, or walk 4km up to the *posada*. So if you are staying more than one night, you might want to bring some food.

Alta Verapaz

Beyond the Quetzal Reserve, you are soon in coffee-growing country, with wonderfully lush valleys steaming in the sun, and farms (*fincas*) of all shapes and sizes dotting the landscape. Coffee is the mainstay of the country's economy today, its number one export and largest generator of employment. In spite of this, the industry is still under the control of the coffee oligarchy, a small group of families with strong ties to the military, who protect their interests against governmental attempts at land reform. One common estimate is that 4% of coffee-growing farms produce and control 83% of Guatemala's national production. Formerly, the landowning families lived in the regional capital of Cobán, but these days the town is a rather damp and forgotten place, its high society decamped to the exclusive suburbs of Guatemala City. Cobán has, however, become a popular base for the more intrepid traveller, interested in expeditions to remote areas of the rain and cloud forests.

History

It was only in the late 19th century, when the craze of coffee-drinking took hold in Europe, that coffee began to be cultivated in these parts. Before then, the Verapaz was a relatively remote region of Indian and Church lands. But under the rule of Justo Rufino Barrios (1871–85), who instigated the so-called Liberal Revolution, the Church was separated from the State. Most of its lands—as well as that of the Indians—were confiscated by the government and sold to foreign investors. Many of these were German immigrants, who were brought in to develop the coffee industry; by 1900, 95% of Guatemala's coffee farms were owned by Germans.

To provide the necessary labour force for this new industry, the president decreed that Indians should work in the plantations, and duly used the army to round them up. Made landless by the government, the Indians were now forced to work in the labour-intensive coffee plantations. From sunrise to sunset they were supervised in work teams, and at night locked up. It was an outrage that even touched the newspaper-reading Guatemalans of the time, and protests were voiced against this virtual slavery in the Cobán area. But the president legalized debt-peonage, and the Indians became trapped in a cycle of borrowing and debt, inherited from one generation to the next, and tying them permanently to the farm they worked on. In practice, little has changed to this day, though many of the huge plantations no longer allow permanent settlement on their lands, sending the seasonal labourers away when they are not needed. Many of these people become squatters, having no land to work and live off, and so deforestation continues, driving the quetzal and other species ever nearer to extinction.

For the Mayas, the worst of this development was not the slavery—forced labour was not unknown in the Maya empire—but the denial of their land and traditional way of life. Farming the *milpa* (field) was not merely for feeding the family, but an act of worship in itself. Traditionally it was a sacred duty to grow maize, closely tied to the good will of the gods and the proper balance of the elements. It is based on the idea that the person belongs to the land, not the other way round, and it is his duty to look after it:

> To be... exiled from the milpa, was to be separated from the self, to become a shiftless ghost, no longer part of the Maya weave, no longer quite human.
>
> Bird of Life, Bird of Death, J. E. Maslow

In the long run, most of the German immigrants fared badly too. Their open support for the Nazis during World War II incurred the wrath of the United States, who duly pressured the Guatemalan government into deporting them and confiscating their lands. Much of this land is still in government hands today, since few Germans returned or managed to stay. But there were some who assimilated, intermarried and learnt Spanish, and were able to start again in the 1950s. This German heritage still shows in the names of some of the largest landowners such as Daetz Villela and Dieseldorff, as well as in the Bavarian-style architecture of a few crumbling houses in and around Cobán.

Cobán

Cobán was once the hub of the coffee industry, its inhabitants wealthy landowners who gave the town an air of countrified sophistication. Now it is just a small provincial town, where most of the grand buildings are damp and crumbling, a quiet place, with little to offer the visitor. All around there is a rich patchwork of plantations, fields, and the odd scrap of cloud forest clinging to the hillsides, yet the white mists that sit heavily on the hilltops can create a chilly atmosphere. Here, more than anywhere else in the country, you get a sense of the permanent change that people are inflicting on the countryside. The Western Highlands suffer the same problems, yet the atmosphere is quite different—the farming terraces, pine forests, blue skies and sunshine inspire joy. By contrast, the Verapaz around Cobán can be a melancholy world of fine drizzle and milky clouds. Dead tree stumps stubbornly remind you of the displaced forest, and wooden huts topped with corrugated iron, homes of the landless squatters, stand mud-stained by the roadside.

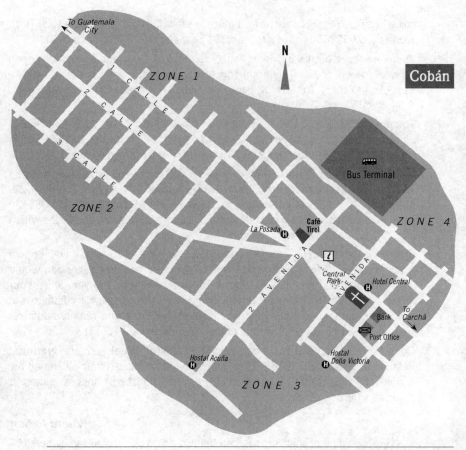

Getting There and Away

Cobán is one of the easiest towns to reach, with frequent pullmans from Guatemala City making the 4-hour journey quite painless. **Transportes Escobar Monja Blanca** operate the route; you will find their offices in the capital at 8 Avenida 15-16, Zona 1. In Cobán they are on the corner of 2 Calle and 4 Avenida.

There is also a large bus terminal below the main square. There are buses to Uspantán (6hrs) daily at 10am and noon; to Fray Bartolomé de las Casas (6hrs); to the Petén daily at 6am and noon. The first bus for El Estor (8hrs) leaves at 4am, the last at 3pm; for Lanquin (4hrs), there are buses at 6am, 12.30pm, 2pm and 3pm, returning at 5am, 7am, 2pm and 3pm.

Tourist Information

There is an excellent, private **tourist centre** on the main square (*open Mon–Sat, 9–noon and 2.30–6*). The very helpful staff can tell you about tours to the most interesting places nearby, as well as give general advice on accommodation and bus schedules. There is a **car rental** office in the same courtyard as the Café Tirol, Tabarini, ✆ 9522059 (*open Mon–Fri, 7–7; Sat and Sun 7–noon and 2–7*).

There are three **banks** in town: Banco del Agro, 1 Calle and 3 Avenida (*open Mon–Fri 9–8pm; Sat 9–1pm*); Banco G&T, 1A Calle and 2 Avenida (*open Mon–Fri 9–7pm; Sat 10–2pm*); Banco del Cafe, 1A Avenida 2-68 (*open Mon–Fri 8.30–8pm; Sat 10–2pm*).

The **post office** is at 2 Calle and 2 Avenida (*open Mon–Fri 8–4.30*); the **Guatel** office in on the plaza (*open daily 7am–midnight*). The **laundry**, La Providencia (*open Mon–Sat, 8–noon and 2–5*) is at the sharp end of the main plaza.

If you find yourself captivated by the region, you can spend some time studying Spanish here at the **Instituto Cobán Internacional** (INCO Int), 2 Calle 1-23, ✆/📠 9521497. Prices are the same as elsewhere in the country, around US$120 per week, inclusive of two cultural excursions, as well as room and board with a local family.

Epiphyte Adventures, run by Séan Acuña, will take you to the well-known sights, such as Semuc Champey, as well as the more far-flung places you would have difficulty reaching on your own. Tours are not cheap, but you do get your money's worth, with extremely informative guides. The company is committed to low-impact tourism and has established unique contacts with remote rainforest communities. Contact them via the tourist centre or on ✆ 952 2213.

Cobán springs into life twice a year: during **Easter Week** and the **National Festival of Folklore** (22–28 August), when the Maya villages from all around the region send representatives to show off their traditional costumes, and there is much dancing and celebration.

Where to Stay

You will probably only pass through Cobán on the way to somewhere else but, since most of the interesting journeys from here require an early start, you might find yourself staying at least one night. Note that during Easter Week and the National Festival of Folklore, accommodation can be scarce.

expensive

The top hotel in Cobán is **La Posada**, 1 Calle 4-12, ✆/📠 9521495, on the entrance road to town, just before the main plaza. A lovely colonial house with a restful garden, it also has an excellent restaurant. All rooms have a private bathroom. Competing for the Posada's custom is the newly restored **Hostal Doña Victoria**, 3 Calle 2-38, with pastel-coloured rooms around a colonial courtyard, but no restaurant. If you prefer modern conveniences, go for the newly built **Posada de Carlos V**, 1 Avenida 3-44, ✆/📠 9523502, on the road to San Pedro Carchá.

inexpensive

The best budget option is the **Hostal de Acuña**, 4 Calle 3-17, ✆ 9521547, in a picturesque colonial house and garden. Rooms are dormitory-style only, but at least the beds are very comfortable and the showers are spotless. Even if you don't stay here, you will still want to sample the delicious, home-made meals, and the hostel is also a good place to meet other travellers. Otherwise the best guest house is the **Central**, 1 Calle 1-79, with modern rooms around a large courtyard, and a decent restaurant. Next choice, for the same price, is **La Paz**, 6 Avenida 2-19, a short walk from the town's triangular plaza, next to the Pizzeria (which serves horrible and expensive pizzas). **Hospedaje Maya**, opposite the local cinema, is also recommended; there are a few other places, but they are generally grubby.

Eating Out

Apart from the restaurants attached to accommodation, there are *comedores* along the market, behind the cathedral, and also on the main road into town. One of the best restaurants on the entrance road is the **Kam Mun**, which offers excellent Chinese dishes.

Just above the bus terminal, **El Refugio** is a good place for a meal; the bar is open until 11pm. Possibly the best coffee in Guatemala can be sipped at **Café Tirol**, diagonally across the street from La Posada, just by the tip of the triangular plaza. You can also change dollars here if the banks are closed.

Around Cobán

A visit to **San Juan Chamelco**, a 20-minute bus ride away (catch one of the regular buses from the bus terminal), will show you how staunchly traditional a region Alta Verapaz is. The Indians who live here are Kekchí, and the women, like the women of Chajul, in the Ixil Triangle, wear pretty ear-rings made from old coins. The town is dominated by a splendid colonial church towering above the market place which, every year on 16 May, is transformed by the annual fiesta.

Beyond Chamelco, in the Aldea Chajaneb, you can stay in one of the more eccentric guest houses around here. Run by a naturalized American Guatemalan, **Don Jeronimo's** is the only place in the country where you can eat delicious pies of home-grown blueberries. It's a good base from which to go hiking or a great place to just laze around in the sun. A room and three vegetarian meals a day will cost you around US$15; to get a lift there, wait for a pick-up truck behind the church in San Juan, in front of the Tienda Maranatha.

Adventurous Journeys beyond Cobán

Semuc Champey

About three hours east of Cobán by bus, you come to the remote village of **Lanquín**. This is the closest you can get to the fabulous pools of Semuc Champey by public transport. (The bus leaves at 6am from outside the bank behind the cathedral, on the same street as the Pensión Central.) The road to Lanquín is rough but the scenery is beautiful; you soon come to the pretty village of **San Pedro Carchá,** and from there the stony road twists and turns along the sides of steep valleys, their slopes covered with glistening coffee bushes and the floppy leaves of banana trees. You finally descend into the valley of Lanquín, passing a few grand *fincas* on the way.

There are only three places to stay in Lanquín: just by the entrance of the village, on a small hillock, is the moderately-priced **El Recreo,** ✆ 9522160, undoubtedly the best choice if you want creature comforts. In the village, the **Hospedaje Divina Providencia** is run by a very friendly man, who, despite being blind for many years, still tends his coffee bushes himself. Squeaky beds go for US$1 per person and, though facilities are basic, the food is good. **Tienda Mary,** on the main square, charges the same money but is not as agreeable.

To reach the pools, you can either get up early, and hope for a lift with a truck (from 7am onwards), or you can walk. If you are hiring a car, bear in mind that you should only attempt this road in a high clearance, four-wheel-drive vehicle. The walk will take up to four hours along a road littered with sharp stones and winding steeply out of the valley, down into another and up again before descending to the swift waters of the River Cahabón, and your final reward. Along the way you will pass homesteads of Indian families; in this area, the people can be very reserved and often do not speak Spanish. The women's have the unusual habit of smoking fat cigars; you will see them shyly turning away to light up.

It's an exhausting walk of around 3–4 hours, though not difficult; you know you are close to the end when the suspension bridge over the River Cahabón comes into view. Just beyond it you will find a paved trail leading out past the parking lot, where you will be charged US$1 for visiting the pools. You can hear the seven stepped pools flowing one into another, minutes before you see them. There are few sights lovelier in Guatemala: glass-clear, turquoise water fills a natural cascade of large pools, surrounded by massive trees covered with drooping lianas. Your long walk seems worth while, and a cooling swim soon refreshes tired legs. To get the best view, walk to the top pool, where there's a clearing for camping. A little further on you will come to the spot where the river plunges underground in wonderfully frightening churns, most of it actually passing beneath the limestone bridge that supports the pools. Do stay away from the cliff edges, though, or you could be swept to your death, like the South African tourist who lost his life here in 1994. Bring your own food and water, and do not camp alone, since there have been reports of robbers here. There is almost no traffic passing towards Lanquín in the afternoon; if you were lucky enough to get a lift in the morning, you will be fresh for the walk back.

You can visit a huge **cave** (*cueva*) only half an hour's walk from Lanquín (*small adm*). Dark, wet, and home to thousands of bats, it also has very slippery paths. The municipal building in the village has a switch to light up the cave (ask before setting off to have it turned on), but it's rarely working so bring a torch. The cave is said to go on for many miles, and locals will tell you that they've spent weeks walking into the interior and that some have never returned. The walk along a river is pleasant, though, and there's a good spot for a swim near the entrance to the cave. Leaving Lanquín, buses set off from the main square for Cobán at 5am, 7am, 2pm and 3pm.

A Back Route Towards the Petén Jungle

For the hardy traveller only, there is a tough two-day route into the northern jungles, which passes quite close to Lanquín. (If coming from Lanquín, catch the 6am bus and ask to be dropped off at the Pajal junction, where you can wait for the morning bus heading for the Sebol road junction and Fray Bartolomé de Las Casas.) Coming from Cobán, you need to be in the village of San Pedro Carchá early, to catch the 6am bus to Fray Bartolomé de Las Casas, eight hours away. You will have to spend the night in one of the basic *pensiones* here. Next day, look for a lift with the trucks and pick-ups that leave for the five-hour journey to jungle-bound Sayaxché, in the southern Petén. For onward connections to Flores, *see* p.204.

The only possible reason for inflicting this journey on yourself is if you want to visit the ruined Maya temples of the Petén (the most accessible of which are near Sayaxché and Flores) without returning to the capital, from where you can either fly or catch a direct bus to Flores. This route is not only exhausting but potentially hazardous, since the remote northern foothills of the Verapaz are one of the last regions where guerrillas are held out. Since the Peace Accord has been signed though, you should be alright.

Towards the Western Highlands

If you enjoy spectacular scenery as well as being scared witless, then this is the trip for you: the dirt road that connects the east and west of northern Guatemala is one long rollercoaster ride. During the week it is possible to hitch a lift with one of the large trucks that use this road (about 6hrs); public transport will take two days. If in your own transport, remember that petrol stations are sparse in this region, and you will need a tough vehicle.

The journey begins in the small town of **San Cristóbal Verapaz**, reached by regular local bus from the Cobán bus terminal. An excellent place to stay here is the **Hospedaje Oly**, 5 Calle 8-67, Barrio Santa Ana, a home turned guest house, with a very friendly owner who charges US$4 for a double. In the morning, you can either try your luck hitching, with the most likely destinations being Uspantán, Sacapulas, Nebaj or Huehuetenango, or you can wait for the bus to Uspantán that leaves between noon and 1pm. The gut-churning begins when you find yourself crammed so tightly into the bus that you know there is no way you could get out in an emergency. Sitting on the roof rack, lodged among sacks of grain and baskets of fruit, is infinitely preferable to staying inside, not just for the space and fresh air, but your bird's-eye view. Of course, you do get the worst of the vehicle's terrifying swaying, the bus leaning just far enough for you to see the sheer drop to the river below.

The bus alternately hurtles and crawls along mountain ledges and around hairpin bends, and when you're not wondering whether to jump off and walk, you can enjoy the heart-stopping vista of jagged mountain chains framing the deep river valley. The lower stretches of land are covered in the greens and golden browns of farming fields, while the river is a stunning aquamarine in places, its giant loops winding around grey rocks and boulders. Ignore the rusting wreck of a bus at the bottom of the valley.

In **Uspantán**, a small town, you can stay at the **Viajero**, a basic place three blocks east of the main square, or the **Galindo Pensión**. Ask when you arrive what time the buses leave for Sacapulas; here you have a choice of staying on the bus, and ending up south in Santa Cruz del Quiché; or changing for buses to Nebaj to the north-west (*see* p.124); or catching a service to Huehuetenango, to the west (*see* p.138). The journey on the dirt road will be spectacular, and by the end of the trip you will have a sense of achievement: not only did you survive, but you travelled on one of Guatemala's most stunning roads.

East to Lake Izabal

Finally, there is a back road to **El Estor**, on Lake Izabal, where you can catch a ferry to Mariscos, and buses heading for the Petén jungle or the Caribbean. This is a rough ride that bumps you along the Polochic valley, past coffee villages and the town of Panzós, and down to the lowlands of the lake; the stretch along the River Polochic is spectacular, as is the ferry trip across the great lake. The only hitch is that sometimes the ferry does not turn up for a few days, especially if the weather is bad and the water too choppy.

Valenciana buses for El Estor leave the Cobán bus terminal at 5, 8, and 10.30am (returning at the same times), and the journey takes around eight hours. The **Brenda Mercedez** company also runs buses on this route.

You will have to stay at least one night in El Estor, either in the lakeside **Vista del Lago**, with doubles at US$9, with or without private bath, or the **Hotel Villela**, just behind the Vista, which is simple and friendly, and charges US$6 for a double with private bath. In the unlikely event that these are full, try **Hotel Los Almendros**, at the entrance to town, which charges the same as the Vista del Lago. The best places to eat in El Estor are the **Ranchón Centenario**, just past the market, the **Bambú**, near the waterfront, and **Hugo's** on the central park. Hugo also rents out bungalows on the beach and organizes tours to nearby sights. Alternatively, if the French owner is around, you could try **Restaurante el Diós del Sol**, for some excellent home cooking.

If you find yourself enchanted by the backwater atmosphere of El Estor, there is a trip you can make to a nearby canyon, a popular swimming spot with the locals. There are also some fine beaches, reached by hiring a motorized canoe (US$10). Inland, there are some traditional Kekchí villages you could visit if you have your own transport.

The ferry to **Mariscos** is supposed to leave daily at 5am (departs at 1pm in the other direction; journey takes 2hrs), and there are usually buses for the capital waiting at the other end. If your destination is the Caribbean or the Petén, just get off at the junction with the Atlantic Highway and wait for a connection. Mariscos itself is a sleepy little place, at the foot of hills covered in tropical forest and rubber plantations, where there's nothing much to do except visit some nearby beaches. The best is **Denny's Beach**, which you can reach by hiring a boatman to take you, though it will cost around US$25 one way (*see* p.188). The area is still undeveloped for tourism but that is bound to change, and some wealthy Guatemalans have already built their holiday homes along the lake, west of Mariscos.

The Oriente and the Caribbean Coast

This was Death Valley. The earth here was finer and duller than sand... There was a dusting of it on all the cactuses, which gave them the look of stumps.

The Old Patagonian Express, Paul Theroux

Theroux's evocative description is of the Motagua Valley, which stretches from Guatemala City all the way to the Caribbean coast. He could equally well be talking about most of Guatemala's eastern range of hills, known as the Oriente, which lie along the borders with El Salvador and Honduras. As you head towards the coast, however, the landscape changes dramatically. Away from the arid, scorched hills, the valley descends into a wide flood-plain, which is extraordinarily fertile and supports lush vegetation all year round. Once inhabited by the Maya, this area was redeveloped by American traders at the beginning of this century. The United Fruit Company took over vast tracts of jungle, cultivating it into massive banana plantations which still dominate the region. In order to export their huge banana crops, United Fruit built access roads and rail links, making this one of Guatemala's most important trade routes.

The Oriente holds little interest for most tourists. If you enjoy spectacular bus journeys, however, the trip from Jalapa to Chiquimula is for you: a five-hour drive through the most dramatic part of the region, where broad valleys are flanked by imposing mountains and, unlike the rest of the Oriente, here the landscape is green and rich in wild flowers. The rest of this area is cowboy country, with busy *ladino* market towns, such as Cuilapa and Jutiapa. Few Indians live in this region, and even fewer retain their traditional dress.

The one town which draws huge numbers of visitors is Esquipulas, famed for its towering white basilica which houses the Black Christ. The carved wooden effigy is believed to hold miraculous powers, and, as a result, it has become the destination of Central America's largest pilgrimage.

Many visitors who pass through this region are en route to Honduras, or heading north to the ancient Maya city of Tikal in the Petén jungle, and few stop to explore. There are, however, two important Maya sites in this area: Copán, just across the border in Honduras, and Quiriguá. Copán is rated alongside Tikal, Chichén Itzá and Uxmal (on the Yucatán Peninsula) as one of the most impressive archaeological sites. Visiting Copán from the capital is easy to organize, with temporary visas available at the border for tourists. Further towards the coast, and half-hidden among the banana plantations, lies Quiriguá, celebrated (like Copán) for its intricately carved stelae.

As you approach the coast, the landscape comes alive with the green of floppy-leaved banana trees. After the junction turning northwest, for the

Petén, the landscape becomes humid and tropical, remnants of forest and spongy swamps giving way to cattle ranches. Eventually you find yourself in the fetid heat of Guatemala's largest port, named Puerto Barrios after one of the country's presidents. Here you can catch ferries to either Lívingston in Guatemala, or Punta Gorda in Belize.

Guatemala's share of the Caribbean coast is less than 100km long, and has few settlements. Lívingston is unique in Guatemala, inhabited almost entirely by blacks descended from African slaves and Carib Indians, who arrived from the Eastern Caribbean in the 18th century. This is no place to come for spectacular beaches, but it is very interesting culturally and an excellent starting point for journeys up the Río Dulce and into the jungles of the Petén.

The Holy City of Esquipulas

Described as a 'religious Brighton' in Anthony Daniels' *Sweet Waist of America*, Esquipulas draws huge numbers of pilgrims from all over Latin America, in particular from Central America; the city lives off little else. There is a kind of religious fairground outside the great basilica, catering for the visitors' every possible taste in trinkets, from candles and plastic flowers to straw hats; and each January 15 the place is solid with pilgrims.

The first building you set eyes on is the huge gleaming, white basilica. The Black Christ behind the altar is beautifully carved out of balsam wood (a dark wood) by the renowned colonial sculptor, Quirio Cataño, and nailed to a heavy silver cross. A small side entrance admits visitors in single-file behind the encased wooden statue; there is an opening so that the faithful can kiss the figure's feet and deposit money down a conveniently placed tube.

Each person stays for a short time and then gets shuffled on by the waiting line, usually retreating backwards, savouring every last minute of the pilgrimage. Around the base of the figure, you will also see endless plaques, notes and photos, testifying to the miraculous help the Black Christ has given. The figure has been here since 1595, but its fame for miraculous healing dates from the mid-18th century when the Bishop of Guatemala, Pardo de Figueroa, recovered from a severe illness while visiting here. The cavernous dark interior of the church is lit by hundreds of candles and hanging above the nave are some glamorous chandeliers, which would look more at home in an exclusive restaurant. Outside the church are numerous shops selling chains, votive images, cards, candles, books and countless other souverirs.

History

In 1954 Esquipulas was invaded by a mercenary army hired by the CIA to bring down the Guatemalan government, ostensibly because of the 'communist tendencies' of the Jacobo Arbenz government. Arbenz had tried to institute land reform and thereby antagonized the powerful United Fruit Company, which had close links with the US government.

The American company first came to Guatemala at the turn of the century, and by 1929 it had already established a monopoly over the banana industy. United Fruit not only owned huge parts of Guatemala's plantation country, it also held most of the country's railway, media, telegraph and electricity installations, in fact anything that had a remote connection with the smooth operation of its business. Soon the people referred to United Fruit as El Pulpo, the octopus, and the company's controlling influence in Guatemalan politics was an accepted fact of life: the country was a 'banana republic'.

The Arbenz government, elected in 1950, requested the unused land of large estates and offered to compensate them with the declared tax value of that land. United Fruit, who used less than 20% of their holdings at any one time, was offered almost three times what they had paid for the land. Yet, like other large landowners, they objected on principle and set the propaganda machine in motion in America. Eventually, 'Operation Success' was launched on 18 June 1954, resulting in the collapse of the Arbenz government and the installation of the puppet government of Colonel Carlos Castillo Armas.

Getting There and on to Honduras

Direct buses for Esquipulas (4–5hrs) leave Guatemala City from near the Zona 1 bus terminal (*see* p.64). There is also a direct bus between here and Puerto Barrios (6hrs), leaving from the Rotunda restaurant at 6am.

From Esquipulas, minibuses shuttle between town and the border post at Agua Caliente (20mins), for crossing into Honduras. They leave from the main street, where the buses from the capital arrive and leave, daily until around 4pm. If you need a visa, you can get it at the consulate in Guatemala City (*see* p.12) or at the one in the Hotel Payaqui, in Esquipulas. The fee to enter Honduras is about US$1, and the Guatemalan exit fee also hovers around US$1. Money-changers are always waiting for custom at the border and on the Honduran side there are regular minibuses leaving for the nearest town of Nueva Ocotepeque. If you are heading for the ruins of Copán, it is better to cross at the other border, further north (El Florido).

Where to Stay and Eating Out

Try to avoid visiting Esquipulas at weekends, when prices double.

moderate

The smartest hotel, with pool and restaurant, is the **Posada Cristo Negro**, ☏ 8431482, on the entrance road to town. The **Hotel Legendario**, ☏/▣ 8431022, is more central and offers good value, with a pool and a decent restaurant. On the main street where the buses stop, the **Payaqui** hotel, ☏ 8431143, is simpler, but also has a pool and a reasonable restaurant.

inexpensive

Of the many budget options off the main street, the **Hotelito no.2** is the best of a grubby bunch. You really are better off paying a bit more for a slightly better room: try the **Hotel Monte Cristo**, or the **Los Angeles**, right next to the church.

Apart from the restaurant attached to the Payaqui, there are few eating places to recommend. The **Rotunda** restaurant offers interesting views, but the food is nothing special and prices are high. There are plenty of snack bars and restaurants to choose from around the main street.

The Trip from Jalapa to Chiquimula

This spectacular trip, described in the introduction, cannot be undertaken in one day but, if you have two days to spare, it makes an unforgettable excursion. Frequent buses leave from the capital's Zona 4 bus terminal for Jutiapa (2½hrs), where there are connections for Jalapa (1½hrs). The best place to stay in Jalapa is the **Hotel Casa del Viajero**, 1 Avenida 0-70, ✆ 9224086, which charges US$10 for doubles with a private bath. Buses from Jalapa to Chiquimula (5hrs) leave the market terminal at 6, 8, 10, 11am and 1pm, and from Chiquimula there are constant buses back to the capital, or onwards to Honduras or the Caribbean coast. The unpaved road accounts for the long journey time and results in certain discomfort for the traveller; you will be glad of an overnight rest.

An Excursion to Copán in Honduras

There are plenty of agencies offering one-day tours to Copán (8–4 daily, $5) in Honduras. However, the journey takes around 6 hours each way, and so a day trip seems an uncomfortable option; it is also much cheaper and quite easy to travel independently. Allow yourself at least 3 days for this excursion, so that you can explore the ruins in peace on the second day. From Guatemala City, there are direct buses to the town of Chiquimula (3–4hrs) with the **Rutas Orientales** company, leaving daily. If you want to be sure of making the connections as far as Copán in one day, you should set off before 8am. In Chiquimula, change to an **Empresa Vilma** bus (their office is next to the market) heading for the Honduran border post of El Florido. Last buses in either direction leave at 4.30pm, and the journey takes around 2hrs. Crossing the border is usually quick and, if you're only visiting the ruins, you can get a 72hr permit, which does not affect your Guatemalan tourist card or visa and has no bearing on normal Honduran entry requirements for your nationality. Officials remove the permit from your passport when you return.

If planning to continue into Honduras, many nationalities, including Canadians and Americans, but not the British, must have obtained a visa before crossing this border, from the Honduran Consulate in Guatemala City, 13 Calle 12-33, Zona 10, ✆ 3374337. You have to leave your passport at the consulate between 10am and noon, and collect it the next day between noon and 1.30pm. All visas are for 30 days, renewable once only, for another 30 days, at one of the many immigration offices scattered around Honduras. The standard entry fee is about US$1, payable in local currency, the *lempira*. The Guatemalan exit and entry fees are each around US$1. There are plenty of moneychangers at the border and, once across, minibuses take you the 40-minute journey to the small town of Copán Ruinas, next to the Maya site. The fare is supposed to be no more than US$1.50, but drivers often charge more. If you want to avoid the time and hassle of travelling to Copán overland there is an excellent—if expensive—alternative: **Jungle Flying** (see p.62) offer day trips at around US$200, which includes lunch at the luxurious Hotel Marina Copán and a guided tour of the ruins. The hotel has a pool which you can use if you come prepared. Note that you must bring your passport.

In the expensive category, your best choice is the **Hotel Marina Copán**, (✆ 504 61 4070, 🖂 61 4477) close to the main square of the village of Copán Ruinas. At the lower end of this category, the **Hotel Madrugada** (✆ 504 980330) has cool rooms with fan overlooking the river Copán. In the moderate price category, the **Hotel Brisas de Copán** (✆ 504 983018) and the **Hotel Popol Nah** (no phone) are clean and good value. The best inexpensive accommodation is **Hotelito Copán** (✆ 504 983411) which offers simple rooms with fans and private bath.

Eating Out in Copán

The most popular gringo bar and restaurant is the **Tunkul Bar**, just off the main square past the museum.

Quiriguá

The small fork right for Quiriguá is about 190km from Guatemala City, along the Atlantic Highway, beyond the El Rancho and Río Hondo junctions. Nearly all traffic thunders past the turning; in spite of its significance, the site is rarely visited. The site is open daily, 8–6, and there is a small admission fee. Bring insect repellent.

History

Perched on an island of forest in a sea of banana plantations, Quiriguá started life as a satellite of the great city of Copán, 50km away. In AD 724 Quiriguá's ruler, Cauac Sky, began aggressive moves towards independence, and by 738 he had taken Copán's lord prisoner and instituted his own emblem as a glyph for Quiriguá. From this period on, numerous huge stelae were erected here, carved with portraits of rulers, celebrating their achievements and important events in the Maya calendar. Nine of these great monuments remain, highly ornate and detailed sculptures second only to those at Copán. The tallest is almost 9m high, dwarfing its human visitors.

The Maya were obsessed with time, and their development of arithmetic and astrology was the most sophisticated of all ancient peoples. They were concerned not only with dating events in their own history, but most especially with locating themselves in the universal balance created by the Gods. They used the calender to work out precise times in the ancient past, and on stelae F and D there are references to dates 90 million and 400 million years ago. Apart from the stelae, there are also some monstrous carved stones, known as zoomorphs, which depict surreal creatures of the underworld, usually entangled with one of the lords of Quiriguá. Some look like toads, others like crouched jaguars; many of the forms are impossible to identify, and nobody knows what their purpose was.

The city's glory days passed; the last date carved on the site is 810 and soon afterwards Quiriguá declined. Why this happened is a mystery, but the timing fits in with the general disintegration of Classic Maya civilization from around AD 900. By the time the Spanish arrived, this site had been abandoned for almost a thousand years, and its remains were not significantly disturbed until United Fruit developed the land for banana plantations.

Getting There and Where to Stay

If you do not have your own transport, the most convenient way to visit is en route to Puerto Barrios or the Petén jungle, though the 4km walk from the main road is not an inviting prospect if you are carrying much luggage. The bus ride from the capital to Quiriguá takes about 4 hours and, if you're lucky, there are motorbikes and pick-ups to ferry visitors and plantation workers up and down the connecting dirt road. To get to Quiriguá village, ask to be dropped off at the village of **Los Amates**, where regular buses make the short journey from the highway. From here you can walk to the ruins by following the railway tracks to a dirt road, which heads off to the right, through the banana plantations. Pick-up trucks often pass by, so you can try hitching the 3km. To continue on to the Atlantic coast, just flag down the relevant bus on the Highway.

The nearest accommodation is the basic but clean **Hotel Royal**, in the village of Quiriguá. Doubles with private bath cost around US$8; meals are available here.

Puerto Barrios

Puerto Barrios has a very slow, tropical atmosphere. Unlike Puerto San José, its Pacific counterpart, the town has little seaside garishness, no streets crammed with shops and entertainments, and no beach you would want to spend time on. It's a pleasantly dilapidated place of tarmac and dirt roads and peeling wooden buildings, with a mixture of black and mestizo inhabitants. The Caribbean feels close here, and the few Mayas stick out a mile.

Getting There and on to Belize

From Guatemala City, the **Litegua** bus company runs an excellent service to Puerto Barrios, which takes 6 hours. At 10am daily, there is a 'special', which only takes 5 hours, and there are a few more later in the day. Ask to be dropped off at 12 Calle if you want to be within easy walking distance of the pier. Buses leave Puerto Barrios from 6 Avenida, at the junction of 9 and 10 Calles.

Buses from the capital also leave from the Zona 1 bus terminal, by the train station. There are some direct buses between Esquipulas and Puerto Barrios and, if you go to any of the major road junctions on the Atlantic Highway, you can always flag a bus down there.

Boats for **Punta Gorda** in Belize leave from the dock at the end of 12 Calle, on Tuesday and Friday, at 7am. You must buy your ticket and complete immigration formalities the day before travelling, and both offices close at 5pm. The ticket office is the same as for the Lívingston boats, right by the dock, and the immigration office is on 9 Calle near the waterfront. The Guatemalan exit fee is around US$1 here. The fare is just over US$2, one way, and the journey takes around 2½ hrs, not stopping in Lívingston. Charters will cost at least $35 each.

Immigration procedures in Punta Gorda are quite informal: your luggage is checked on the pier. One-month permits are issued, renewable for up to 6 months. You will be asked whether you have sufficient funds for your stay, and must have a return flight ticket to your country of residence.

Around the Town

Near the waterfront, warehouses and truck depots mingle with dingy brothels and a few sleazy bars. The air is too hot and humid for people to get raucous, but at least there are some people on the streets at night, a welcome contrast after the silence of most Guatemalan evenings; and while there is nothing much to do except eat or drink, a night spent here on the way to Lívingston or Belize is no great hardship. Having said that, there is no need to stay here on the way to Lívingston, since an afternoon boat leaves daily at 5pm. There is a **Lloyds Bank** on 7 Calle, as well as a few others, and a **Guatel** office on 8 Avenida. The **post office** is on the corner of 3 Avenida and 7 Calle. Note that it is very difficult to change traveller's cheques in this town.

Where to Stay

luxury

If Puerto Barrios is just too sleazy for you, there is a wonderful alternative tucked away on the other side of the bay. The **Cayos del Diablo**, ✆ 9482361, ✉ 9482364, is a lovely, secluded hotel, with its own beach and swimming pool. Spotless rooms are in thatched cabins dotted around the jungle gardens; the restaurant and bar are in a central building overlooking the bay. All the services of a resort hotel are on offer here, including boat charters to the surrounding area. The (free) hotel boat makes regular pick-ups from the central pier at Puerto Barrios.

moderate

Undoubtedly the most interesting place to stay in Puerto Barrios, though over-priced, is the **Hotel El Norte**, ✆ 9480087, on the seafront, at the end of 7 Calle, a large wooden building with a Caribbean atmosphere, where doubles cost from $26. Better value for money is the **Hotel Internacional**, 7 Avenida and 16 Calle, ✆ 9480367; here rooms with air-conditioning are around US$20, and secure parking is available. Another good choice, though with no air-conditioning, is the **Hotel El Reformador**, 16 Calle and 7 Avenida, ✆ 9480533.

inexpensive

Closer to the ferry dock, and cheaper, is **Caribeña**, 4 Avenida, between 10 and 11 Calles. **El Dorado**, 13 Calle, between 6 and 7 Avenida, charges the same; and so does the **Europa**, 8 Avenida, between 8 and 9 Calle.

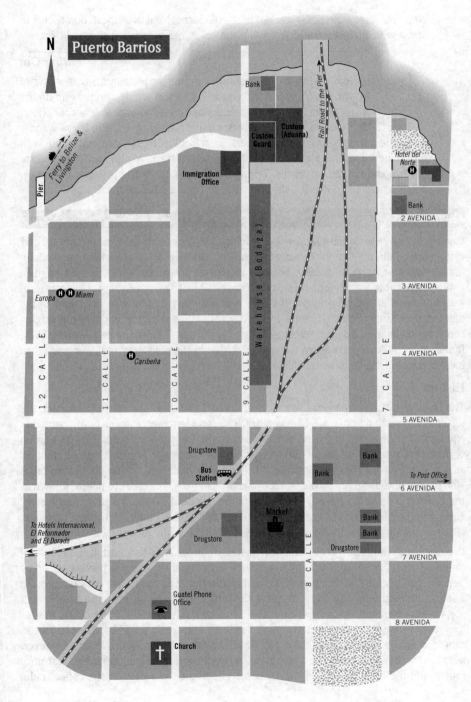

Note that streets are rarely marked in Puerto Barrios, and even locals don't seem to know which street is where, so ask for hotels by name, rather than by address.

Eating Out

The Hotel El Norte has a good but expensive restaurant; with views of the sea on two sides, you feel as if you are in a cruise-ship dining room. More authentic seafood cooking, at much cheaper prices, can be found in the restaurants further up 7 Calle. If you wander along the avenidas running close to the ferry dock and the ticket office, you will find some reasonable places as well. For cheap, *comedor* food, head for the centre of town and the railway tracks. **Triangulo** is one of the better places in this range. Around here and down 9 Calle you will also find bars and pool halls.

Lívingston

Once you leave Puerto Barrios, you are heading for a different world, where history and culture are bound up with the legacy of the African slave trade, a place where the predominantly black inhabitants speak a boisterous dialect of Spanish, Garifuna and English, almost impossible for any outsider to understand. Music is everywhere, but instead of marimba or salsa, you hear reggae. If you're very lucky, you might even hear some of the older people singing sad Garifuna songs, the African drumming and chorus singing conjuring up images of distant places and their painful past. The young people prefer West Indian music, and saunter down the muddy streets in the obligatory red, gold and green hats, dreadlocks spilling down their backs.

History

The black settlements along the Bay of Amatique are a relatively recent phenomenon, the result of a migration in the late 18th century. The people are descendants of African slaves and Carib Indians, from the island of St Vincent in the Eastern Caribbean. In 1795 a group of them was stranded on the Honduran island of Roatán by the British, as punishment for an uprising, and the survivors gradually drifted to the mainland, settling in communities along much of Central America's Caribbean coastline, from Nicaragua to Belize. Known as the Garifuna, these have always been a very independent people, keeping their history alive with their tradition of song and story-telling, and speaking their own hybrid language. Guatemala only has one major black settlement on its tiny Atlantic coast, at Lívingston.

Long before Lívingston was founded, there was an important Maya port at the mouth of the Río Dulce, known as Nito. The Maya were expert seamen and practised ocean-going traders; they operated as many as 4000 merchant canoes before the Spanish Conquest. In 1502, Columbus and his crew became the first Europeans to encounter an Indian merchant canoe, and Columbus' 14-year-old son excitedly wrote that the canoe was 'as long as a galley and eight feet wide, all made of one tree'. By 1524, Nito had been captured and the colonists had moved in. The Spanish settlement was a failure, however, because the newcomers had no idea how to live off the surrounding jungle. Not until much later did Lívingston briefly enjoy some importance as a port for the coffee trade, which was brought down from the Verapaz highlands via a railway (now defunct) to Lake Izabal and then down the Río Dulce.

Getting There and Away

Boats for Lívingston leave daily at 10am and 5pm from the dock at the end of 12 Calle in Puerto Barrios, and tickets are sold right by the dock. To be sure of getting on the ferry, arrive an hour early, and always come at least half an hour before departure. If you miss the boat (US$1 one way), there are boatmen who will charge US$15–25 per person. The trip normally takes one hour, but on the small *lanchas* it can take longer, and you and your luggage can get very wet.

Boats for Puerto Barrios leave from the Lívingston dock at 5am and 2pm daily. Buy your ticket at least one hour early to be sure of getting on, which is usually a battle. If you don't want to go to the expense of hiring someone to take you up the Río Dulce, you can catch the mail boat on Tuesdays and Fridays, leaving around 9am. This will take you as far as Fronteras, and the suspension bridge, where the Petén road heads north. The return journey by mail boat is on the same days. Unfortunately, the schedule changes all the time, and sometimes the boat does not turn up at all. The other drawback of using the mail boat is that you cannot stop off en route. If you can find a group of people to share the ride, you should be able to get a *lancha* for around US$9 per person to take you all the way to Fronteras, with stops along the way.

Tourist Information

You will find the only local **bank** just past the Henry Berrisford hotel (*open Mon–Sat*). For phone calls, there is a **Guatel** office near the dock. There is an interesting small **museum** (open daily 9–7; donations welcome) dedicated to the Garifuna heritage, where you'll find displays of traditional tools and crafts.

Around the Town

Lívingston is a two-street town, only accessible by boat, and its mostly wooden houses cling to the muddy rise that separates the mouth of the Río Dulce from the Atlantic beach. If it was not for the steady flow of tourists, there would be very little here, and even at the best of times there is not much to do, which explains the local drug problem. The beach is narrow and strewn with rubbish, so sunbathing is out. The main reason for coming here is simply the novelty value of the only Black Carib town in Guatemala, and also because it is the starting point for a gorgeous river trip up the Río Dulce, which can itself be a stepping stone to continued travel into the Petén jungle. At Christmas large numbers of mainly young travellers come to join in the reggae 'jump-ups' in the beach discos, and listen to the spontaneous concerts of Garifuna singing outside people's homes. If you're travelling alone, then this is definitely one of the best places to be for Christmas, though you will miss the Catholic processions and Masses of the rest of the country. Another excellent time to be here is on 15 May, the anniversary of the arrival of the Garifuna in Guatemala. The first landing of Garifuna boats is re-enacted on the beach, and there is plenty of singing and partying. Note that it is not safe for women to walk along the beach alone as there have been several rapes and robberies.

Where to Stay

expensive

There is one 'luxury' hotel: the **Tucán Dugú**, ☎ 4481572, which has rooms with beautiful ocean views. There is also a nice pool with a nearby bar, and an overpriced restaurant.

inexpensive

A favourite is the **Casa Rosada**, a five-minute walk from the dock—take the first left turn. Accommodation is in thatched cabins on the waterfront, with a shared bathroom. This is an excellent place to come and watch the sunsets and eat healthy vegetarian meals. **Caribe** and **Hotel Henry Berrisford**, on the same path, but nearer the dock, are grubby and overpriced. If you have to choose between the two, though, go for the Caribe.

A lovely two-storey wooden building houses the **Río Dulce**, a little way up the main street from the dock, a popular budget hotel whose main attraction is the balcony, where you can string up a hammock, lie back and watch the world go by. The **Minerva**, near the centre, on a side street (ask for directions) is very good value. On the second high street, turning left towards the church and cemetery, you'll find the **Hotel Garifuna**, ☎ 4481091, with clean rooms at a very reasonable rate. And quite a bit further along you'll find one of Lívingston's most extraordinary guest houses, the **African Place**. Built by an eccentric Spaniard with a taste for Moorish architecture, the place is a collection of white, concrete buildings, busy with turrets and bizarre decorations. It may look intriguing but should be avoided if at all possible. Many are the bad reports: the owner is abrasive, and only the restaurant is worth checking out. At the end of the street and down the bank, in a walled compound on the beach, is the rather excessively fortified **Flamingo** guest house, run by a German woman.

Eating Out and Nightlife

The best place for breakfast and cheap meals is **Dinis**, on the main street towards the cemetery; also recommended is the **Café Margoth**. Towards the end of the other street is **Cuevas**, which offers excellent cooking, and nearby is the **Cafetín Lyly**, a good *comedor*. **El Malecón**, near the docks, is a large restaurant under a cool verandah. And you can eat at the **Tucán Dugú**, where prices are predictably high; only the pool and bar are worth trying.

On the street towards the cemetery, **Labuga** is a popular bar, where there is often live music. Another contender is the **Banana Republic Bar**, run by a friendly American, who also rents out beach huts on the Bay of Amatique and offers overnight trips to the bay. Down on the beach, there are a couple of shack bars, and beyond the **Marimba Beach Bar**, on the way out of town, is the main reggae disco. Opposite the Guatel office, you will find the **Disco Raymondo**, a dark and sweaty place.

Around Lívingston: Siete Altares

About an hour's walk from Lívingston along the beach, there is a pretty spot for freshwater swimming during the rainy season, where a waterfall cascades into a number of beautiful pools on several levels. Just follow the beach past the disco until you come to a river flowing into the sea. If you're lucky there will be someone to ferry you over; otherwise you can wade or swim across. On the other side, the beach thins out and a path leads off to the left towards the pools. The only drawback about this place is that it is notorious for robbers, and you should never walk here on your own.

Río Dulce and Lake Izabal

In the first half of this century—and even during colonial times—the great Izabal lake was an important access point for remote regions in the Verapaz. A railway came down from the coffee plantations around Cobán, meeting the lake at El Estor, and regular boats travelled the length of its waters to follow the Río Dulce out into the Gulf of Honduras. Its shores were embraced by thick rainforests growing down the surrounding mountains, and scattered with remote Maya communities. Today there are still Maya villages on the banks of the Río Zarquito and Río Polochic, which both empty into the western edge of the lake, and the forest there is home to a huge variety of flora and fauna, including monkeys, deer and parrots. But, other than the large farms that sprang up after the last World War, there has been very little modern development around the lake. The shores of Lake Izabal offer peaceful beaches and some great hideaways for those who don't mind the lack of services. And, if you have the time and money, you could arrange for some wonderful outings by boat. The best place to base yourself is near the Río Dulce Bridge, on the eastern edge of the lake, at the mouth of the Río Dulce.

Getting to Río Dulce and Lake Izabal

The road from Guatemala City to Flores (the Petén Highway, which crosses the Río Dulce Bridge) passes right by the lake, and so there is a regular flow of traffic from the capital (5–6 hrs). Alternatively, catch any bus heading for or coming from Puerto Barrios, and get off at the La Ruidosa junction, where you can wait for transport heading to the bridge. (Ask for either Fronteras or El Relleno, the two settlements either side of the bridge.)

Another way to reach the lake is to arrive by boat from Lívingston—undoubtedly the most relaxing method, with the added advantage that the boat can drop you exactly where you wish to stay on the river. If arriving overland, you will need to hire a water taxi to reach most accommodation.

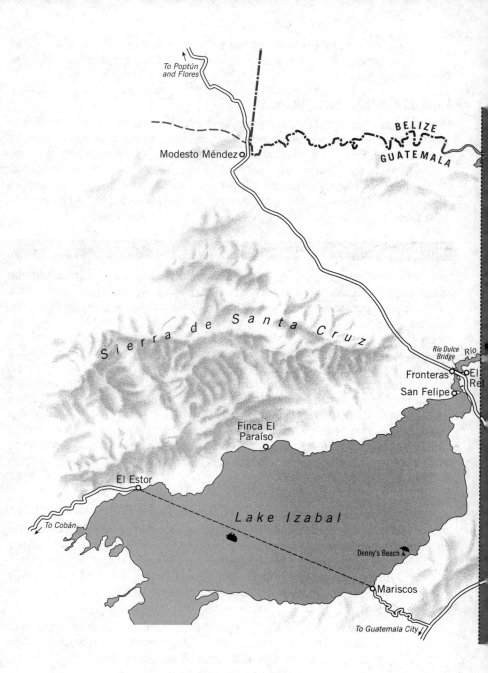

To Poptún and Flores

Modesto Méndez

BELIZE
GUATEMALA

Sierra de Santa Cruz

Río Dulce Bridge
Río

Fronteras
El
Re[

San Felipe

Finca El Paraíso

El Estor

To Cobán

Lake Izabal

Denny's Beach

Mariscos

To Guatemala City

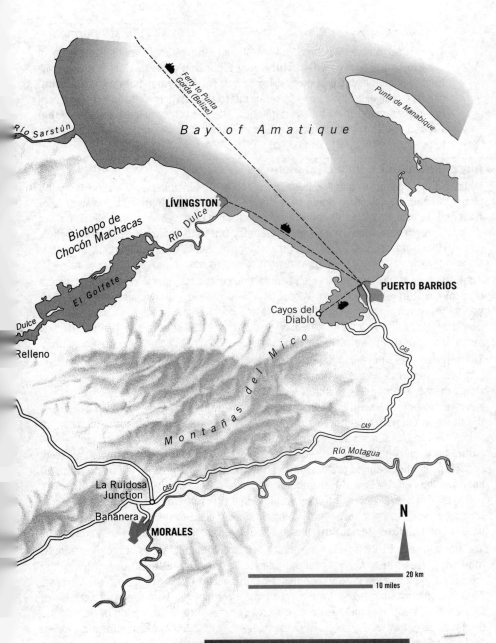

Río Sarstún

Ferry to Punta Gorda (Belize)

B a y   o f   A m a t i q u e

Punta de Manabique

LÍVINGSTON

Biotopo de Chocón Machacas

Río Dulce

El Golfete

PUERTO BARRIOS

Dulce

Cayos del Diablo

CA9

Relleno

M o n t a ñ a s   d e l   M i c o

CA9

Río Motagua

La Ruidosa Junction

CA9

Bananera

MORALES

N

20 km
10 miles

Río Dulce and Lake Izabal

Tourist Information

There is no tourist office here, but you should be able to pick up the latest copy of the **Río Dulce Services Directory** from the Inguat office in Guatemala City, or from the hotels and guest houses listed below. The **Hollymar Bar and Restaurant**, near the bridge, is also a good place for information, where you can contact any of the places mentioned by radio phone. Alternatively you can contact **Izabal Adventure Tours** in the capital who specialize in this area and also offer transport to it: 12 Calle 'B' 36-91, Zona 5, ✆/🖂 335 0244.

Along the Río Dulce from Lívingston

By far the most popular excursion from Lívingston is the canoe trip up the Río Dulce, and plenty of boatmen offer trips down by the dock. The price for going all the way to Lake Izabal can be as high as US$60 one way, so you need to bargain hard, and preferably share the cost with others. If you're only going on a day trip to the nature reserve at El Golfete (about 10km upriver), you might think that the price should be much less but, as always, make sure you agree exactly where you want to go and how much for, before setting off.

Almost as soon as you leave Lívingston behind, you enter a lush jungle environment, where tropical birds flit across emerald waters. The banks either side rise steeply as the river washes through a long gorge, with huge trees and a profusion of vines and plants that hang over the river's edge. If you look carefully, you will see long-legged, white herons, standing motionless as they wait for their prey, and perhaps even an iguana sunning itself on a rock.

The gorge stretches the ten kilometres between the river mouth and a section known as El Golfete, where the waters widen considerably to create a small lake. About half-way along, there is a **hot spring** that bubbles into the river, a steaming natural jacuzzi that you can swim to from the boat. Further along, the area around El Golfete has been designated the **Biotopo Chocón Machacas** (*open daily 7–4*), to help protect the rare manatee, or sea cow, as well as the jungle flora and fauna. There is a landing jetty for boats and several nature trails snake through the forest, though you are unlikely to see any wildlife except butterflies and birds during the daytime, and it is more fun to explore the many canals by boat. During November and December the lagoons here are covered in water lilies, and you will also see a variety of wild orchids on the riverbanks. If on a day trip from Lívingston, this is as far as it is worth going. A friendly place to stop for a drink on the way back is **Los Palafitos Restaurant**, which serves freshly cooked fish and shrimp dishes.

The **Restaurante El Viajero** is a beautiful *comedor*, with great views of the river from its top floor. Across the water you will see the **Ac'Tenamit Health Clinic**, which serves around 30 new villages locally, populated by displaced Kekchí Maya from the Verapaz. The government has made no provision for these people, so the American-based Guatemala Tomorrow Fund set up an aid project here, with the intention of helping the people to help themselves. If you have the relevant skills (such as nursing, medical expertise, or dentistry), and have at least one month to spare, you can volunteer to work here in return for food and lodging. Make enquiries when you visit, or contact their head office in the capital, Apartado Postal 2675, Guatemala City, ✆/🖂 2511136; or call them in Tequesta, Florida, ✆ 407 747 9790, 🖂 407 747 0901.

Continue up the river and you will come to the breezy expanse of water known as the Golfete, where ducks and fishermen bob on the waves and you might see the odd king-fisher perched on a tree stump in the shallows. Soon the waters narrow again, though, and you find yourself among the growing riverside community of sailors and watersports enthusiasts, which is gradually turning this part of the Río Dulce into a great place to spend a few days. Whether you want to explore the surrounding countryside or go sailing, or just hang out at the riverside bars, you're bound to find some people to join you here.

The bridge itself is the hub of things, with the greatest variety of accommodation to choose from, as well as the best sources of information on what to do locally and transport out. Make sure your boatman takes you to visit the **Castillo de San Felipe**, the other side of the bridge, a tiny fort, built by the Spanish to protect Lake Izabal from British pirates, who regularly raided trading posts here. It is a fitting spot to end your journey, with great views out on to the lake. (Don't let your lift leave you here; it's a very long walk to the bridge by road).

Where to Stay
expensive

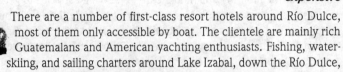

There are a number of first-class resort hotels around Río Dulce, most of them only accessible by boat. The clientele are mainly rich Guatemalans and American yachting enthusiasts. Fishing, water-skiing, and sailing charters around Lake Izabal, down the Río Dulce, or as far as the Belizean Cayes, can all be arranged from here. These hotels are some of the few places in Guatemala where you can enjoy the tropics in reasonable comfort; to reach any of them, just take a water-taxi from below the suspension bridge. This should only cost around US$1, but can be as much as US$10, depending on your bargaining skills. If you have a reservation, however, the hotel should be prepared to pick you up. All can be contacted by radio phone from the Hollymar Restaurant.

One of the fanciest places, just past the Castillo de San Felipe, will be the **El Corozal**, which should be completed by the time you read this. The **Catamarán**, ✆ 4478361, ✆ 3364450, is an old favourite, with a good swimming pool and tennis courts, that have seen better days. Another option is the **Turicentro Marimonte**, ✆ 4478585, ✆ 3344964—hardly luxurious and not really worth the prices it charges.

Of the various **yacht marinas** dotted around, **Susanna's Laguna** is conveniently close to the bridge, while **Mario's Marina** offers indispensable facilities, such as repair shop, laundry and noticeboard.

moderate

The best place to stay in this category is **Susanna's Laguna**, with beautiful rooms of polished wood built right over the water, and a large bar and restaurant attached. **Hotel Viñas del Lago**, ✆ 4478437, very close to the castillo, is a little overpriced, but a decent place, with great views of the lake.

Hacienda Tijax, ✆ 3335778 in the capital, is a 500-acre working farm. The owner has built simple but comfortable, self-catering huts in a field by the riverside, and if you don't feel like cooking, you can buy meals and cool drinks at the main house.Tours around the farm on horseback or by jeep are available.

Eating Out

Susanna's Laguna is the best place to eat. The **Hollymar Bar and Restaurant**, beneath the bridge and on the waterfront, on the north side, is a popular travellers' meeting point, where you can eat delicious meals, including crab and seafood sandwiches.

Excursions around Lake Izabal

Few trips on and around the lake can be made without your own boat. Two excursions in particular are worth hiring a boatman for. **Denny's Beach**, east of Mariscos, especially popular for the monthly 'full moon' party, is also a great place to get away from it all when the party is over; you can hire a self-catering *cabaña* (bring all your own provisions) or simply camp in your own tent. Facilities include a bar and restaurant, so you don't have to cook at all. To make a reservation, call ✆/✉ 3692681 in the capital, or use the VHF radio from Río Dulce, VHF 09 or Riotel VHF 68.

The **Finca Paraiso**, on the north shore of the lake, has some hot waterfalls on its property that really live up to the name. *Las Cascadas*, as they are known, lie 2km inland, in a pocket of natural rainforest left standing by the owner of the farm. The first pool you encounter is the largest; a hot, sulphurous waterfall tumbles into cooling waters all around. Climb up over the boulders and you enter another, cooler pool, where you can float face up and drink in the magical forest all around you. The owner is strict about not leaving litter behind, and rightly so. Make sure you treat this fragile place with proper care.

To reach the falls (*US$1 fee*) you can walk 40 minutes in the blazing sun or pay to be taken on a very bumpy ride by tractor-drawn cart, which takes up to ten people at a time. For the adventurous who have brought a waterproof torch, 20 minutes beyond the falls is a series of caves with extraordinary rock formations, which you can enter only by swimming through a short underground pass.

Back at the *finca* there is a restaurant (not guaranteed to be functional) and drinks are sold; you can also hire one of the waterside wooden *cabañas*. For reservations call Mrs de la Vega Rodriguez in the capital on ✆ 2532397.

The Petén

From the air, the Petén jungle, which makes up a third of Guatemala, looks like a flat green blanket, stretching endlessly into the horizon. In fact the landscape is surprisingly hilly, and the many rises were favourite places for the Mayas to build their city-states. The map of the Petén is peppered with the names of ancient ruins, many still unexcavated, and most inaccessible to the traveller without a helicopter or time for many days of jungle hiking.

The land here is still covered with thick ancient forest, cut by many rivers and dotted with lakes and swamps, and the wildlife is some of the most varied and profuse in Central America. In spite of the fact that 20% of the jungle has been destroyed in the last decade alone, the impact appears minimal, compared to neighbouring Mexico or Honduras. In the Petén there are margueys (small cats), jaguars, snakes, tapirs, howler monkeys, anteaters, armadillos, crocodiles, tropical birds, and an infinite number of creepy-crawlies, from scorpions to bird-eating spiders— though you will probably only see monkeys, birds and insects. Shake out your clothes and shoes before putting them on here; insect repellent is essential.

The Yucatán peninsula, of which the Guatemalan Petén is a sizeable part, was the focus of the Maya Golden Age, AD 250–900. The largest and most elaborate architecture flowered here, with huge pyramids rising above the jungle, and finely decorated plazas, ball courts, residential structures, temples, and much more. The greatest of these cities was Tikal, where successive rulers enjoyed not only political and economic power, but also fostered the arts and sciences, in particular writing and astrology. Other major sites include El Mirador, Ceibal, Altar de Sacrificios, Yaxchilán and Piedras Negras, but there were hundreds of other settlements, usually along important trading routes or near permanent sources of drinking water.

It is a mystery how the Maya could have built cities and developed such a sophisticated society in this inhospitable region. Food supply must have been a particular problem; agricultural farming could only have been limited and, although hunting and gathering in the forest could have sustained a nomadic existence, centres such as Tikal were inhabited by up to 40,000 people. The current explanation of this enigma is that the Maya were great merchants, and their cities grew up in this region because of their monopoly on trade between the Mexican Gulf and the Caribbean. In their time, a lot of merchandise travelled either in ocean-going canoes or across the Yucatán along riverways that have long since disappeared. The Maya would have charged high taxes along their trade routes, and would have been able to import most of their food supplies, as well as anything else they needed. Their centres of habitation were also spread out over a far greater area than previously realized, with distant satellite communities engaged in maize production for the central core where the élite lived.

The three most accessible ruins are Tikal, Uaxactún, and Ceibal. The first two are almost neighbours; both can be visited from the modern town of Flores, or you can stay the night at Tikal itself. To reach Ceibal, you take a bus to the town of Sayaxché, in the southern Petén. Travel in the entire region is by dirt-roads that disintegrate into turgid soup during the rainy season (May to October), making travel almost impossible. Only Tikal can be visited easily at any time of year, thanks to the airport in nearby Flores. Also, the road connecting Flores to Tikal is the only surfaced one in the Petén. Expect prices to be high, but do come to Tikal—all other Guatemalan ruins pale besides this one for size, for splendour, for the jungle setting, and the magical combination of ancient architecture, mysterious rainforest and abundant wildlife.

Overland to Flores

The journey overland from Guatemala City to the jungle capital of Flores (488km) is famous among travellers for being one of the most harrowing experiences you could possibly inflict on yourself. What is theoretically a 14-hour bus ride can take up to 24 hours, and never less than 12. Even hardened travellers of Latin America are surprised by the sustained torture of this journey; the misery really begins after you cross the River Dulce, where the tarmac road becomes mud and the bus driver struggles to negotiate the giant furrows in the road. (Work is now underway to pave this section as far as Poptún.) Whenever it rains, great lakes form across the road, disguising the true depth of the potholes until it's too late. Matters are not helped by the view out of the window—a monotonous stretch of forest, slashed by the red gash of the road. There is no glimpse of the magical jungle to renew your enthusiasm for the journey.

Approximately 10–12 hours after leaving the capital, you arrive at **Poptún**, the fastest growing town in the Petén, though you would never guess it from the wretched collection of mud-stained, concrete houses there. It is, however, an excellent place to break the journey since **Finca Ixobel**, a beautiful jungle farm where you can enjoy delicious meals in enchanting scenery, is nearby on the outskirts of town (3km). It was built by an American couple, though sadly the husband was murdered by the military a few years ago, and now his widow runs the business alone.

Many visitors turn their overnight stopover into a couple of days, since there is much more to do than relax and eat well here: there is an extensive traveller's library with plenty of books to read, there are horses to hire for jungle excursions, or you can pay a guide to take you hiking and on cave excursions, and there are ponds for swimming. Accommodation comes in three varieties. In the main house, there are a few rooms with shared bathroom, at less than US$10 (the only snag is the lack of privacy due the absence of a ceiling covering top-floor rooms). There are dormitories in outhouses, and there are treehouses, both of which cost around US$4 per person. You can also camp on the meadows surrounding the farm. Meals are not cheap, but well worth what they charge. If arriving by bus, ask to be dropped off at the entrance to the farm, on the main road. When you leave, you will have a 3km walk into Poptún, though you might be able to hitch from the main road. The farm also runs a *pensión* in Poptún itself, as part of the **Fonda Ixobel** restaurant, on the main street. Other accommodation cannot be recommended.

Heading for Flores, buses leave Poptún at 8am, 10.30, 11, 1, 2 and 3.30pm. To have any hope of a seat, make sure you take one of the first two buses, which actually originate in Poptún. The journey can take 4–9 hours depending on road conditions. Heading for Guatemala City, buses leave Poptún at 2.30am, 5, 9 and 2.30pm; the second bus is the only local one.

Flores

This tiny town is crammed on to an island on the edge of Lake Petén Itzá (about 32km long and 5km wide). Narrow streets and pastel-coloured, stone houses squeeze together around a colonial church and square at the town's elevated centre. The view is refreshingly open, across the rusty roofs and the glistening lake to the jungle all around. A causeway connects Flores to the dirtier and noisier Santa Elena on the mainland, to the west of which is the sleazy but livelier town of San Benito. Of the three, Flores is by far the nicest place to stay. However, the reason you come here is not the hot, dusty town or its attractive setting, but to see the glorious Maya centre of Tikal, 65km from here.

The island was once Tayasal, the capital of the Itzá, a people who originally came from the Mexican Yucatán, where the city of Chichén Itzá still bears their name. They resisted the Spanish for over 170 years, despite the efforts of a steady flow of soldiers and missionaries. The first to arrive here was Hernán Cortés himself, in 1524, on his way to a campaign in Honduras; since the Itzá king received him willingly, he did not stop for bloodshed, and only left his lame horse. Almost one hundred years later, two Spanish priests arrived to find that a statue of the horse was being worshipped as the god of rain and storms, and had to flee for their lives after they smashed it.

Other missionaries came accompanied by soldiers; in 1623 one such group was defeated and sacrificed as soon as they arrived. Finally, in 1697, the Spanish sent a war galley against Tayasal and slaughtered every Indian they could find, while the rest swam to the mainland, never to be seen again. The Maya king was taken to the capital, and paraded in chains.

Getting There and Away

By air: At least four flights daily (with Aviateca, Tapsa, Tikal Jet and Aerovías) shuttle between the capital and Flores, leaving around 7am and returning around 4pm. Aviateca also has a morning flight leaving Flores around 8am (journey time about 1hr). The cheapest tickets are with Tikal Jet, at around $106 return (US$65 one way). From both ends, you can either turn up at the airport and buy tickets direct from the airlines (expensive), or book with a travel agent.

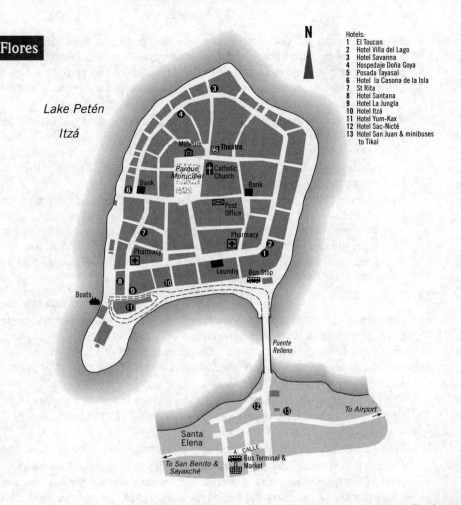

Hotels:
1 El Toucan
2 Hotel Villa del Lago
3 Hotel Savanna
4 Hospedaje Doña Goya
5 Posada Tayasal
6 Hotel la Casona de la Isla
7 St Rita
8 Hotel Santana
9 Hotel La Jungla
10 Hotel Itzá
11 Hotel Yum-Kax
12 Hotel Sac-Nicté
13 Hotel San Juan & minibuses
   to Tikal

Flores

Lake Petén
Itzá

Museum
Theatre
Parque Municipal
Catholic Church
Bank
Bank
Post Office
Pharmacy
Pharmacy
Laundry
Bus Stop
Boats

Puente Relleno

Santa Elena
To Airport
Bus Terminal & Market
4 CALLE
To San Benito & Sayaxché

The only honest travel agent for flight tickets from the Petén is in the **Hotel Petén** in Flores. The **Hotel San Juan**, on the mainland near the causeway, also sells tickets and offers a free bus ride to the airport, but watch out for hidden extras.

In Antigua and Guatemala City, travel agents can arrange flights and transport to the airport, and also 1–3-day **tours to Tikal**, inclusive of accommodation and guides. However, a 2-day tour can cost US$175-$350 plus extras, so if you have the time and initiative you can save money by travelling independently.

Flores is usually a stopover for flights on their way to Belize City, so you can easily visit Tikal on your journey to or from Belize. Tropic Air flies from Flores to Belize City Mon–Fri, departing at 9am and 3pm. A single costs around US$80. Aviateca (Tues, Wed, Fri, Sat and Sun, departing 5.30pm) flies to Cancún/Mexico, and a single costs around US$140. You can also charter flights to many of the remote Maya ruins.

By bus: You can get a bus from Sayaxché, if you're coming from the southern Petén, via the back road from Cobán. Buses between Flores and Sayaxché are run by the **Pinita** company, and leave at 6am and 1pm, in both directions. The journey takes about two hours, and most buses arrive and leave from the terminal near the Santa Elena bus station.

Buses leave Santa Elena terminal for most towns you will want to visit in the Petén (and many that you won't), including Uaxactún (via Tikal), Sayaxché, Poptún, Carmelita (for expeditions to El Mirador), El Naranjo, Bethel (for Mexico by river and expeditions to Yaxchilán and Piedras Negras), and Raxrujá (change there for connections to the Verapaz highlands).

By minibus: There are regular minibuses, depending on demand (minimum two people), from Flores to the ruins of Tikal and Uaxactún, as well as Ceibal. These trips do not include food and drink, which you should always bring along with you. There are also minibuses to Belize City (departs daily, 5am, US$20 one way) and Chetumal/Mexico (departs daily 5am, US$30 one way). All of the above are run by the Hotel San Juan Agency.

Tourist Information

For the most impartial advice on reputable tours, guides, boat, car or bike rental firms, see the **Inguat** representative at the airport, from Tuesdays to Sundays. There is a **bank** in Flores, which only changes traveller's cheques. For cash exchanges, you will get the best rate at **Banoro Bank**, on the high street in Santa Elena (*open Mon–Sat, 8.30–8*).

There is a **Guatel** office in Santa Elena, or you can pay to use the overpriced hotel phones. **Fax and telephone services** are also offered by **Cahuí** (*open daily 7–7*), in front of Santa Rita guest house in Flores.

Petenchel **laundry** in Flores will wash and dry your clothes for US$3.

Canoes for exploring Lake Petén Itzá can be rented in the hotels. A double canoe costs $2 per hour. **Boat tours** of the lake can be arranged with the boatmen who congregate by the causeway and behind the Hotel Yum Kax, and a trip around the whole lake, taking in the lakeside **Petencito zoo** and a swimming stop, should not cost more than US$6–10. (Bring your own food and drink.)

ProPetén (Project for a Sustainable Petén Forest) is an organization set up to encourage a sustainable use of the forests, involving local communities. A number of projects are aimed at creating economic alternatives to destructive cattle ranching or logging. One such project is the Scarlet Macaw Trail. For those wanting a more intimate experience of the rainforest, this 5 day trip leads trekkers through varying tropical ecosystems. Highlights include a visit to the rural Petén communities of Centro Campesino and El Cruce Dos Aguadas, the 150m cliffs of Buena Vista with views of the jungle canopy below, a river trip on the San Pedro river, and the archaelogical site of El Peru. For further information visit the ProPetén office, ✆ 9261370, ✉ 9260495, on Calle Central, just off the main square in Flores (*open Mon–Fri, 8–5*).

Another of ProPetén's projects is the language school in San Andrés. If you enjoy the environment around the lake and don't mind very basic living conditions, you could spend time studying at the **San Andrés Ecoescuela de Español**, in the town of the same name, across the lake from Flores. Get there by catching a regular boat from the main dock in San Benito (the extension of Santa Elena, to the west). They leave every two hours between 8am and 5.30pm. Or catch the 6.15am boat leaving from behind the Hotel Santana in Flores. You can find out more, as well as collect very informative leaflets on the Petén environment and history in general, from the ProPetén office.

Tours and Travel Agents

An excellent company to use if you want to arrange an adventurous trip to some of the remoter archaeological sites is **Expedicion Panamundo**, 2 Calle 4-90, Santa Elena, ✆/✉ 9260501. The manager, Julio Alvarado, can help you put together any itinerary you wish, and uses very informative guides; not cheap, but dependable. In Flores, the **Arco Iris** office, ✆ 9260786, sell anything from flights to tours around the lake, and are very friendly and helpful. **Mundo Perdido** in Flores, ✆ 9260773, and **Aventuras Mayas**, ✆ 9260418, ✉ 9260412, in Santa Elena, provide the same services at inflated prices.

The **Hotel San Juan**, on the mainland near the causeway, is a good place to gather information on schedules, and you can take their minibus to Tikal or Uaxactún. However, they are not very friendly or cheap to use as an agency. Remember that the only time jungle expeditions are a realistic prospect is during the dry season, from November to April, and even then the weather might turn against you.

If you have around US$40 per day to spare (plus expenses, such as travel, food and drink) you can hire your personal archaeological guide to visit any of the ruins in the Petén. Contact Inguat for a list of accredited guides. **Don Francisco Florián Escobar** is highly recommended—he has worked with professional archaeologists and is a mine of information without being boring. You can also contact him via **Panamundo Tour Agency**.

Around Flores

Although most visitors only come to Flores to visit Tikal, there are a few worthwhile places to visit if you have the time. An excellent place to get an idea of the rainforest without roughing it is the **Biotopo Cerro Cahuí**, *(open daily, small adm)*, located on the eastern shore of the lake, near the El Remate village. One of the newest wildlife conservation areas in the region, the reserve has well-maintained walking trails, which are excellent for sighting some of the tropical birdlife, such as toucans and mot-mots, as well as for reaching elevated viewpoints where you can see right across the lake to Flores. To get there and back, catch any minibus heading to or from Tikal and get off at El Remate (30km from Flores), from where you need to walk 2km along the lakeshore to reach the reserve. Ideally you should bring something to eat and drink, but you will also find perfectly decent *comedores* in El Remate, or you could eat at one of the lakeside accommodations (*see* p.197 under 'Where to Stay'.)

If you find yourself with time on your hands and would like to see a typical Petén village, why not catch a boat across the lake to **San Andrés**. The cheapest and easiest method is to catch the 6.15 morning boat from behind the Hotel Santana in Flores, making sure you are back at the dock in San Andrés by noon at the latest. As there is not much to see or do around here, you are unlikely to miss the boat, but if you do, private charters are always possible and cost between US$10 and US$20, depending on your negotiating skills. If you're feeling energetic, you could walk 3km along the dirt-road heading west from the village (ask for directions), to reach the luxurious **Hotel Ni'tun** (*see* p.198 under 'Where to Stay'), where superb meals and cool drinks await.

Where to Stay

The most pleasant place to stay is in Flores itself, which is generally more expensive than staying on the mainland, where modern Santa Elena and San Benito sprawl. Alternatively try El Remate, halfway to Tikal on the main road, a friendly village which, in the sweltering heat, can sometimes feel like the end of the world.

Flores

moderate

The best hotel on the island is the **Hotel Petén**, ✆ 9260692, ✉ 9260662, which has a good restaurant and clean rooms with fans—try to get a room with a lakeside view. With a pleasant waterfront terrace and bar, the **Hotel Savanna**, is also a good choice. On the waterfront near the causeway, the **Hotel La Jungla**, ✆ 9260634, is a very friendly place. **Hotel Posada Tayasal**, ✆ 9260568, has light rooms in a modern building with roof terrace. **Hotel La Casona de la Isla**, ✆ 9260692, has rather dingy rooms, but the lakeside terrace and cute pool make up for that. **Hotel Santana**, ✆/✉ 9260491, is great if you can get a first-floor room with private lakeside terrace. **La Mesa de los Mayas**, ✆/✉ 9261240, is rather expensive compared to the others, but the restaurant is worth trying.

inexpensive

The best budget guest house is **Hospedaje Doña Goya**, with clean, bright rooms. Also very good is the **Hospedaje Santa Rita**. Next door to La Jungla is the **Hotel El Itzá**, which is very basic. On the lakeside, with a cosy patio for eating and drinking, is the guest house **El Tucán**; the rooms are not that great and the bathroom is filthy.

Santa Elena

expensive

Not far from the causeway to Flores, the **Hotel Del Patio Tikal** is a two-storey building set around a cool courtyard, which also shades the restaurant, ✆ 9261229, ✉ 3374313 in Guatemala City. By the time you read this, the **Petén Espléndido Marina** should also be completed.

moderate

The **Hotel Maya International**, ✆ 9261276, ✉ 9260032, is a collection of wooden bungalows and a restaurant, built directly over the water, with views of Flores. By the time you read this, the **Hotel del Tropico** should also have opened on the main shopping street in Santa Elena.

inexpensive

The **Hotel San Juan**, ✆ 9260041, profits from the fact that buses empty passengers into its lobby, and does not deserve the custom it gets. Its restaurant is neither good nor friendly, and does not deserve your custom either. Try the **Hotel Jade**, which is better than it looks and good value; or the **Hotel Sac Nicté**, ✆/✉ 9260092; it's a bit more expensive but still excellent value for money.

El Remate and on the lakeshore, halfway to Tikal

There are an ever-growing number of small hotels and pensions in El Remate. Most are simple, in the mid- to low-budget range. Few have telephones: just turn up and ask around.

luxury

The most exclusive hotel in the region is the **Camino Real**, a sister hotel to the one in the capital, offering the same services and prices too (book at the hotel in the capital, *see* p.73). Set in the jungle on the lake, 5km west of El Remate, this is the place to come for tropical luxury. You can take a taxi from the airport or arrange to be picked up by the hotel's own vehicle.

moderate

El Gringo Perdido, 3km along the road to the Camino Real, ✆ 3341967, ✉ 3342305 in the capital, is a guest house and campsite (bring your own tent) with a restaurant on the lake. You can hire canoes, mountain bikes and horses here, but everything is vastly overpriced and there is no transport to the main road.

A more homely atmosphere can be found at **La Casa de Don David** in El Remate, 200m off the Tikal road, on the left on the bumpy road that runs around the lake. There are several good-size bungalows with toilets and showers, as well as more simple rooms, and a communal garden with hammocks. It is run by David Kuhn, who is both friendly and knowledgeable, and renowned for his rapport with the local tarantulas. His wife provides good food at reasonable prices.

inexpensive

On the branch road leading to the Camino Real, you will find the campsite **El Mirador del Duende**, which styles itself an 'eco-campsite', and is very basic: you can sling a hammock under cabins provided, or pitch a tent; you have to wash in the lake, and the toilet is a hole in the ground, but travellers love it.

Agua y Tierra, nearby, hires out 500cc scramblers for around US$20 plus the cost of a full tank. These are excellent for making your own way to the ruins of Uaxactún, 24km beyond Tikal.

If you do not want to pay for a taxi-ride from the airport, you could wait for one of the minibuses heading for Tikal, on the main road. You should not have to wait too long for a ride (US$3)—but do ask to be dropped at El Remate, or you may miss the stop.

Near San Andrés (northwestern shore of the lake)

expensive

Ni'tun (Punta de Piedra), is a superb hideaway on the quiet side of the lake, where rooms are individual stone cottages built into the hillside, all with great views. The main building and restaurant are extremely attractive, also built using natural materials, and the food is great. Apart from enjoying the complete peace and quiet here, you can use the library, listen to music in the private bar or join a tour. The owners, Lorena Castillo and Bernhard Mittelstaedt, run very interesting trips lasting several days to many of the more obscure Maya sites, either by four-wheel-drive or on horseback. Contact them via **Mesoamerican Explorers** in Guatemala City, ✆/✉ 3325045, or **Los Jades** car rental in Santa Elena, ✉ 9260009. Unless you have pre-booked and arranged to be picked up, you will have to hire a boatman to take you across (around US$20 one way).

Eating Out

The top restaurant is the **Palacio Maya**, serving a good choice of seafood and other dishes for around $5. **La Jungla**, not to be confused with the hotel, is small and cosy, with good food at medium prices. Next door is a good *comedor*, the **S'Quina**. If you feel like trying traditional Maya cooking, such as stewed venison, armadillo, wild turkey, or fish, then head for **La Mesa de los Mayas**.

Some excellent fish dishes are available at **El Tucán**, which also has the best lake-side terrace. **Pizzeria Picasso**, across the street and under the same management, offers very decent pizzas; while **El Kóben**, next door, offers a range of dishes from *enchiladas* to full meals. A good place for snacks is **ChalTunHá**, opposite the Santana Hotel, right by the water. If you have the time, you could also catch a boat to the **El Gran Jaguar** restaurant from here (about US$1.50 one way).

On the main square there are two *comedores*: **Café El Paisaje** and **Café-Bar Gran Jaguar**, the latter with a terrace offering great views around the lake. Others worth trying are **Restaurante La Selva** and **El Jacal**, an attractive new restaurant with cooling fans.

Tikal

You hear so much about the ruined city of Tikal, and see images of the famous Temple of the Giant Jaguar on so many tourist posters, that you think you know what to expect before you get there. But all preconceptions are forgotten as soon as you enter the twilight jungle to walk to the Central

Plaza, especially if you use one of the smaller paths, rather than the main gravel one. High above your head, the swaying branches are home to spider and howler monkeys, who occasionally like to pelt visitors with nuts, though they usually miss. Green parakeets squawk above the canopy of trees, while toucans hide from sight, only the chattering 'tock' of their giant bills hinting at their presence. Most exhilarating of all is the lucky sight of a pair of macaws, majestically spreading their red, blue and green wings, but making a very undignified racket, their screams audible across the forest.

You stumble out into the first grassy clearing and come face to face with a pyramid, its damp limestone walls blackened with age and lichen. It seems oddly out of place, a monument in the middle of nowhere. But then the path leads on to the heart of Tikal and opens out onto the green carpet of the Great Plaza, where Temple I and Temple II, more romantically known as Temple of the Giant Jaguar and Temple of the Masks, tower over you. Their pinnacles jab the pale blue sky at 58m and 50m respectively, and the giant stairways up their immense bulk offer a daunting climb—but the effort of scaling Temple II is superbly rewarded by the view from its platform. Up here you are above the jungle canopy, looking out across a sea of treetops while, nearby, the peaks of other pyramids rise up from the depths. One of the very best views of the Great Plaza and its famous temples is from the North Acropolis.

It's incredible that the Maya used no metal tools to create these huge monuments, nor pack animals—only generations of slave labour sweated here. For over a thousand years the ceremonial centre of Tikal was built and rebuilt to become one of the greatest ever

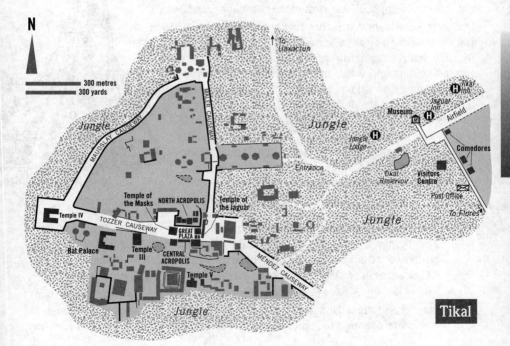

Maya 'cities'. There were settlements here as early as 600 BC, but the golden age of monumental building was from AD 250–900, an age referred to as the Classic Period by archaeologists. This era is sub-divided into the Early Classic (AD 250–550) and the Late Classic (AD 550–900), and what you see at Tikal today is almost all from that later period: the great temples, for example, were built around AD 700, while the North Acropolis dates from AD 550 onwards.

An interesting feature of Maya rebuilding was that the stelae of the old buildings—the monumental sculptures that recorded the all-important dates of royal lineages, wars and construction dates—were ritually 'sacrificed' by those reconstructing it. Usually the stela carried an elaborate portrait of the ruler associated with the building in question, and the Mayas took special care to smash his face. The ruined or defaced sculpture would then be buried under masonry near an altar, or bricked into a disused building. This is the reason why so many of the stelae at Tikal are damaged or defaced, though vandals and looters have also done much damage.

At its height, central Tikal is estimated to have had 10,000–40,000 permanent residents; most recent thinking favours the lower number. Tikal's territory actually encompassed 40km², so the subject population of Tikal's rulers may have been much greater. Central Tikal covers an area of 16km², where over 3000 constructions of all types have been recorded so far. Added to these there are over 200 stelae and attendant altars, so the day tour cannot hope to cover more than a fraction of this site. Of course the undisputed highlight of any visit is the magnificent Great Plaza, but there are two other temples worth exploring for bird's-eye views of the jungle and surrounding monuments, and those are Temple III, just west of the Great Plaza, and Temple IV.

The latter is the highest structure ever built by a Native American civilization, towering a breathtaking 96m from the ground. Built around AD 741, this temple has not been cleared of the jungle that has invaded its steps and walls, and to reach the summit you have to clamber up ladders and over trees unsuitable for vertigo sufferers (as are all the pyramids). A large number of toucans congregate around here, and you may well come face to face with one as you climb the ladders. Another building you should be sure to visit is the Temple of the Inscriptions, some way from the centre and covered in mysterious hieroglyphics.

Getting There

Transport to Tikal is by **minibus**, and most of the hotels run their own service. The journey is expensive at US$6 return, and takes one hour. On entry to the National Park of Tikal, you will be charged an extra US$8.50. In theory, this is a daily fee, but in practice those staying overnight in Tikal itself only pay once.

Minibuses also leave from outside the San Juan Hotel, in Santa Elena, at 4am, 6am, 8am, and 10am; returning at noon, 2pm, 4pm and 5pm. Although it may seem daunting to some, it is well worth rising early for the 4am bus: the experience of Tikal at sunrise, or in the eery mists before dawn, can be quite extraordinary. Don't forget to take some food and water.

Tourist Information

The **entrance fee** to the National Park of Tikal is now US$8.50, and the ruins themselves are open daily, 6–5, though you can usually stay a little longer to watch the sunset and listen to the grunting howler monkeys. There are **toilets** by the car park, behind the Central Plaza, and near Temple IV (bring your own toilet paper.)

Near the **car park** there is a small **museum** (*open Mon–Fri, 9-5, Sat and Sun, 9–4; nominal adm*), worth visiting to see faded black and white photographs taken by Alfred P. Maudsley in the 1880s. These will give you an idea of the amount of work that has been involved in clearing the jungle from the ruins, a task which has been mostly done by the Tikal Project since the 1950s. There is also a fine collection of Maya vases and pottery found at the site, as well as jade jewellery and carved bones taken from royal tombs. The **Stelae Museum** next to the **visitors' centre** holds the best-preserved specimens and a selection of brochures and books.

Clothing for the jungle should cover your legs and arms to protect against the incessant mosquitoes and scratchy foliage, and you should certainly bring repellent. A hat and binoculars are useful, and it is best to wear comfortable, flat shoes, suitable for walking the jungle paths and climbing the pyramids. If you plan to be here in the evenings, you will need a torch, as there is no lighting. Remember also that it can get chilly at night, and it frequently rains.

For a detailed description of the site, an excellent map and historical and archaeological guidance on Tikal, you cannot do better than buy William R. Coe's handbook: *Tikal: A Handbook of the Ancient Maya Ruins* (about US$10). This should be on sale at the site, but to be certain of your copy, buy one before you arrive. This excellent book will tell you all you need to know in a readable style, and the map is very helpful. In Guatemala City, the book is available at the Popol Vuh Museum, and all the bookshops in Antigua sell it. You should also be able to buy it, or at least order it, in bookshops in England and the United States.

Without this handbook and its map, you will need a guide if you are not on an organized tour, not just to explain the site, but also to help you explore, since it's easy to get lost. Official guides wait around the entrance path to the site and around the Great Plaza. As elsewhere, you need to negotiate a price before setting off, and it helps if you know beforehand which parts you want to see.

Where to Stay

In spite of the expense and bad value for money, you should try to spend at least one night next to the ruins, so that you can explore them in peace when most other tourists have left, and experience them during their most magical times, at dawn and dusk. During peak seasons, such as Christmas, New Year and Easter, hotels will be fully booked up. To reserve a room, you will have to book through a travel agent, and even then you cannot be certain that your reservation will be honoured. The only way you can be guaranteed a room is if you are flying in on an organized tour, otherwise you just have to try your luck on arrival. Prices change constantly here, so those stated can only be a general guide.

expensive

There is a choice of three hotels: the **Tikal Inn**, ✆/✉ 9260065, is expensive and rather run-down, with *cabaña*-style rooms around a small swimming pool. The **Jaguar Inn,** ✆ 9260002, offers a few simple rooms and prices include all meals. The restaurant is also open to non-residents. **Jungle Lodge**, ✆ 4768775, ✉ 4760294 in the capital, nearest the ruins, has bungalows with private baths and also has a pool. It's always worth asking about the limited cheaper accommodation in the old buildings and dormitory rooms here. This place is your best choice, even though there is sometimes no water, the service is bad, and the restaurant over-priced and unpleasant. Their minibus usually meets incoming flights and will take you straight to Tikal.

inexpensive

There is a **campsite,** which charges US$6 for you to pitch your tent or sling a hammock under leaky shelters (mosquito nets are essential). Shower and toilet facilities are available, but there is often no water.

Eating Out

The cheapest option is to bring your own picnic and something to drink, though sodas are sold at strategic places around the ruins. The restaurant in the **visitors' centre** is outrageously expensive and not very good, and you are much better off at the restaurant of the **Jaguar Inn**. There are a number of *comedores* scattered along the entrance road to the site, but the very best is right next to the campsite and car park—a friendly place to be in the evenings too.

Uaxactún

During the dry season, buses usually drive the extra 24km north to Uaxactún, and hired jeeps can also be used. Or you could take a guide and walk to the site from Tikal; this takes about 6 hours, so you would have to camp overnight before returning—an excellent introduction to the delights and discomforts of jungle hiking. Tikal's closest neighbour, this is a small and undramatic site by comparison: the pyramids and other structures are much lower and unrestored. There is a 'lost world' feeling; you won't see many other tourists here. The site is significant today mainly because of the excavations and research into Maya writing undertaken by Sylvanus G. Morley in the 1880s.

A highly recommended local initiative in Uaxactún village is the **Guias Eco-Culturales de Uaxactún,** a group of local men, who know the area better than anyone, and will take you on tours of the ruins and rainforest, even to sites several days' hike away. If you speak just a little Spanish and bring all your own equipment, you will have a rewarding and memorable time. Remember to agree itineraries and prices before departure.

East of Flores: Yaxhá

 Yaxhá lies 48km away, on the shores of Lake Yaxhá. This is believed to be a huge site, as yet unrestored, though Inguat has plans to develop it as a new tourist attraction. One of the few things known about this site is its unusually late period of habitation, probably between the 12th century and 14th century, long after the Classic Maya civilization had collapsed. To reach the site is relatively easy: catch any bus heading for the Belizean border, and ask to be dropped off at the turning for Yaxhá; walk from there for up to 3 hours, along the clear track. You will have to stay overnight here. Bring food and water and your own equipment, if you wish to camp. There is a beautiful lodge and campsite: the **El Sombrero Eco-Camp**, reservations on ✆ 3324289 in the capital, where camping in your own tent is cheap, but you can also stay in simple rooms for around US$14 single, US$24 double. All meals can be provided, and the lodge also arranges horse-riding tours and boat trips. It's a lovely spot.

Alternatively, you could reach the site by four-wheel-drive and, by the time you travel, there might even be tours going here; it's worth making enquiries.

Ceibal

Ceibal (*open daily 6-6; US$5 adm, which allows you to stay for up to three days if you're camping*) is a site that is primarily interesting for its striking jungle setting on the banks of the Río de la Pasión. The stone used here is very hard, so although the temples are not impressive for size, they do retain some excellently preserved carving and there are many beautiful stelae. Bring all your own food and drink, and some to share with the guards.

Ceibal was probably taken over by Mexican peoples in the Late Classic Period (AD 550–900); some of the sculptural style has a strong Mexican influence. For example, Stela 13 shows an individual who is clearly not Maya—he lacks the traditional headdress and his speech scroll includes an 'x', a symbol the Maya did not use. Archaeologists speculate that perhaps he was one of the 'conquerors', who came from the north when the Maya civilisation went into decline. Another such invader is possibly shown on Stela 17: the Mexican smoking a large cigar stands on the left, with a Maya ruler on the right, complete with his traditional headdress and serpent staff. Stela 8 has some particularly fine carving: the figure depicted is wearing a mask and a very elaborate headdress. Look at his hands and feet, and you will notice that he is wearing jaguar paws, which means a blood-letting ritual was held for this ruler.

The masterpiece of Ceibal is Stela 10 (AD 849), which shows a descendant of Ruler Ach Bulun Tun and the emblem glyphs of Kalakmul, Tikal, Copán and Palenque, perhaps indicating that representatives from these sites were invited to a special ceremony here. Certainly the protagonist is dressed for a special event, wearing jaguar-skin trousers and rather fancy sandals decorated with pineapples.

A feature unique to Ceibal is the round temple platform of Complex D (Structure 79). We know very little about this mysterious building, except that it was probably dedicated to the Sun God. (During President Arana's time it was apparently used as a helicopter landing pad, so that looters could better load the stelae.) Notice the altar in front of the temple, which is held up by *bacabs*, the mythical figures who held up the Maya world. Looters tried to move this altar too, in 1992, but fortunately failed to escape the guards.

The best way to reach the site is to hire a boat from the town of Sayaxché. The boatmen charge around US$40 for the round trip, so try to gather a group and split the cost. Set off early to give yourself plenty of time, as it takes almost 2 hours on the boat in each direction. Bring your own food and drink, and do not forget the insect repellent.

Sayaxché

Sayaxché is a thriving jungle town on the Río de la Pasión, which is a good base for the adventurous traveller with plenty of time (and money). From here you can organize journeys of any length, into the jungle, down the rivers or to specific sites. Of course any excursion to a Maya site involves a jungle trip, of which the one to Ceibal is the easiest.

Although hunting has been outlawed, fishing is still very good here, and one of the best places to do this is **Lake Petexbatún**, 48km south of Sayaxché. There are also a couple of small Maya sites here, of which **Aguateca** is the most interesting to visit. You will need to bring all necessary equipment if you intend to camp, and all food and drink. Spare a thought for the guards too, who will be much more helpful and willing to share fires and advice if you bring enough food to share with them.

The easiest way to get to Sayaxché is from Flores; **Pinita buses** leave daily at 6am and 1pm from both directions. The town lies 56km southwest of Flores, and the journey along the mud road takes around 2 hours, but do not even think of it during the rainy season. **Boats** ferry arriving passengers across the river to Sayaxché.

There is an inexpensive hotel not far from the ferry landing: the **Hotel Guayacan**, known as Hotel Godoy after its owner. Meals are also offered in the restaurant. If for some reason the Guayacan is full, then use the **Hotel Mayapan**, first left as you come up from the river. The best place to eat is the **Yaxkin** restaurant, on the first road left coming up from the river. In fact, it is the only place where you can be sure to find a good meal, including breakfast; only snag is that it shuts at 8pm. There is also a local market and plenty of shops to buy provisions.

Aguateca

 Aguateca, which means 'source of the river' or 'split hill', lies hidden on a jungle-covered hill, bisected by a chasm 60m deep in parts. It is the site of the only known Maya bridge. It was first occupied in the late Pre-Classic period (200 BC–AD 150), but was abandoned again for almost four hundred years, only to be resettled during the Late Classic era (AD 600–850), which is the period from which the mounds and exquisite carving you see today date from. Looters have done their worst here: to your right, as you enter the main plaza, notice the stela that has been cut up for carrying away by mules. Further along you can see evidence of more sophisticated methods too: stone cutters have left clean incisions where glyphs have been removed, as recently as 1993.

Aguateca has not been restored, but wandering about the overgrown mounds and fallen stones in such a fantastic setting—overlooking Lake Petexbatún—is still a memorable experience. You can either arrive by boat, or you could stay at one of the lake's jungle lodges and walk two hours along a magical jungle trail from the Kekchí village on the lake. A guide from the village will charge you around US$10 for the walk, which is well worth it. Good boots are vital, and you should bring food and water. The trail is quite easy, taking you at first through the village *milpas* (fields), and then into the cool rainforest, where cahune palms vie for space with ceiba trees and strangler vines, and even the occasional rare mahogany tree. You will hear the terrifying roar of howler monkeys, as well as the more flamboyant shrieks of spider monkeys; watch your step after rain, when you will see snakes curled up on the path.

The best way to get to Lake Petexbatún and Aguateca ruins is by boat from Sayaxché and you will certainly need to hire someone who can also act as guide. (Expect to pay around US$64 for the round trip) For advice about trips to and around the lake see Julio Godoy at the Hotel Guayacán, a well-known expert on the region. Alternatively, just ask by the waterside for Don Eufracio Bolon, a charming and trustworthy boatman, who deserves your custom. One general rule about hiring a guide is that you are expected to provide his food and drink, as well as his fee. To avoid arguments, try to be as detailed as possible in the arrangements about what exactly you will do and how long it will take. The guide who asks to be paid in full before departure is a dubious prospect, and you should never pay more than half before the end of your journey.

There are two lodges directly on Lake Petexbatún. The **Posada San Mateo** is the most expensive, and is worth visiting for cold beers, even if you don't stay there. (Check with the tourist office in Flores to make sure the lodge is in operation.) Very good for the money is the **Posada Panamundo**, reservations via Expedicion Panamundo, in Flores or Guatemala City, where you will find simple but clean *cabañas*, with great views of the lake. Prices are around US$70 per person. On the river approaching the lake you can stay at the **Posada Caribe**, ✆/📧 2506114, which charges nearer US$50 per person, including all meals. The place is rather dilapidated and dirty, and seems overpriced for what you get. But you don't have to stay at any of the above, since Aguateca is easily visited on a day trip from Sayaxché—although if you wanted to go via the jungle trail, you would need to set off at dawn to give yourself plenty of time.

Remote Maya Sites

North of Flores

Two significant sites lie in this direction: **El Mirador** and **Río Azul**. El Mirador is the more important: it was a huge city in its day, as significant as Tikal before Tikal eclipsed it. To reach this site, just 5km from the Mexican border, you need to hire a four-wheel-drive or hitch to Carmelita (35km), and enquire there about a guide and mule to take you on the 2-day trek to the ruins. Camping equipment, food and water must all be brought with you, and you should check with the Inguat official in Flores whether you need permission from the authorities to travel this way. Río Azul does not merit an expedition unless you have a specialist interest. The round trip takes up to 3 tough days by four-wheel-drive. If you want to arrange things a little more formally, get advice from the travel agents in Flores, who will help you find a guide.

Northwest of Sayaxché

The journey to the site of **Yaxchilán** is an adventurous undertaking. It's on the banks of the Usumacinta river, marking the border between Guatemala and Mexico, and you will have to travel over 100km by boat, first along the Río de la Pasión, and then on the Usumacinta itself. The journey as far as the ruins will take at least 2–3 days one way, and can take much longer if you decide to travel on trading boats. Commercial river traffic only goes as far as Benemérito anyway, and from there you must hire a boat. Hire a boat from Sayaxché, which will take you all the way to Yaxchilán. Alternatively you can catch a bus from Flores to **Bethel** and hire a boatman from there, which would work out much cheaper. Either way, you will need plenty of time and money, but the site itself is in an outstanding setting on the river bank, and certainly an interesting place to visit. If you do not wish to organize your own trip, you could always go on a tour with one of the expedition agencies working out of Guatemala City.

Onwards to Mexico

If you plan to travel into Mexico via the river town of **Benemérito**, you must get your Guatemalan exit stamp at the airport in Flores first.

You can catch one of the early morning buses that leave Benemérito daily for Palenque to pass the Mexican immigration post. Or, an easier way to get to Mexico from the Petén is to catch a direct bus from Flores to El Naranjo (Guatemalan exit stamp available here); from there boats take you to La Palma in Mexico. Or catch a bus from Flores to Chetumal, via Belize, which would be the simplest option of all. Mexico has an excellent bus network; you will always find a bus heading your way, even if you are many hundreds of kilometres from your destination.

Onwards to Belize

There are daily buses leaving Flores for the border town, **Melchor de Mencos**, leaving at 5, 7, 10, 11am, and 3pm. There are also collective taxis and tourist buses plying this route, though the latter are prone to occasional attacks by robbers. The mud road is pretty bad in places, and the journey of about 80km normally takes three hours, more during the rainy season (March to November). On the Belizean side, the small town of Benque Viejo is a few kilometres from the border, and is best passed by as soon as possible. Buses for Belize City leave the border regularly, and all pass through San Ignacio, the nearest town about 10km from the border, where you will find pleasant accommodation.

11,000 BC –2000 BC	Small populations of hunter-gatherers lived throughout the Americas.
2000 BC –250 AD	Pre-Classic Maya civilization: one of the earliest cultures was the Ocos, along the Pacific coast; an important later site was Kaminaljuyú, in the highlands.
250 AD –900 AD	The Classic Period, the golden age for the Maya civilization, when sites such as Tikal, Copán (Honduras) and Quiriguá reached their zenith.
900 AD –1530	The Post-Classic Period began after the Lowland Maya civilization mysteriously vanished, between 790 AD and 889 AD. Highland Maya civilization survived much longer, however, with the Quiché, Mam and Cakchiquel kingdoms still powerful when the Spanish arrived.
1523	Spanish forces arrive in Guatemala and begin a brutal and swift conquest, aided by disunity among Maya tribes.
1527	The first Spanish capital is founded.
1541	The hated conquistador, Pedro de Alvarado, dies.
1676	Foundation of Central America's first university in Guatemala City: University of San Carlos.
1697	The last independent Maya town, Tayasal on Lake Petén Itzá, is defeated.
1821	Central American regions declare independence from Spain.
1822	Guatemala is annexed to Mexico.
1923	Independence from Mexico and declaration of the United Provinces of Central America.
1826	Outbreak of Civil War.
1830	Morazán takes Guatemala City and becomes president of the United Provinces of Central America.
1839	The Central American federation collapses, Guatemala claims sovereign rights over Belize.
1850	US–British Treaty: Britain agrees to refrain from occupying, fortifying or colonizing any part of Central America.
1859	Guatemala signs the treaty recognizing British sovereignty over Belize, on the understanding that a road is built connecting Guatemala City, the Petén and the Caribbean coast.

Chronology

1871	The Liberal Barrios wins power, initiating a decline in power for the Church.
1884	Guatemala threatens to cancel the Treaty of 1859.
1885	Barrios is assassinated.
1898	Estrada Cabrera takes power.
1901	The first transnational corporation arrives in Guatemala: the United Fruit Company.
1920	Estrada Cabrera is overthrown, US military intervenes.

1931	Ubico is elected; a purge of left-wingers and repression of unions takes place for the next thirteen years.
1936	Britain offers £50,000 to build the infamous road, but Guatemala demands £400,000.
1944	Ubico is overthrown by military coup.
1945	Reformist Juan José Arévalo is elected president. A new democratic constitution is written; women are granted suffrage.
1949	Francisco Javier Arana, chief of the armed forces, is assassinated soon after announcing his candidacy for president.
1950	Jacobo Arbenz Guzmán is elected president.
1952	Agrarian Reform expropriates uncultivated estates and redistributes them to landless peasants; the Communist Party is legalized.
1953	United Fruit Company plantations and the International Railways are nationalized; 400,000 acres of uncultivated land are redistributed.
1954	CIA-backed coup named 'Operation Success' overthrows Arbenz government; Carlos Castillo Armas of the National Liberation Movement (MLN) is instated. Expropriated land is returned to owners, all unions are disbanded, thousands of people are killed.
1956	New constitution.
1957	Castillo Armas is assassinated; the presidential elections descend into armed conflict and the military takes over government.
1958	New elections are won by Michael Ydigoras Fuentes
1960	The US invasion of Cuba is launched from Guatemalan and Nicaraguan soil and fails.
1961	Belize turns down the offer to become an 'associate state' of Guatemala.
1962	The M-13 and Rebel Armed Forces (FAR) guerilla groups are formed after a failed coup attempted by reformist officers.
1963	Diplomatic relations with the UK are suspended due to the dispute over Belize; Guatemala threatens war.
1966	US Special Forces participate in 'Operation Guatemala', a counterinsurgency campaign led by Arana Osorio, during which more than 8000 people are killed. Right-wing death squads, which are blamed for over 30,000 deaths over the next seven years.
1968	US ambassador John Mein is assassinated.
1970	Carlos Arana Osorio of the MLN is elected president; the West German Ambassador Karl von Spreti is assassinated.
1971	The Organization of People in Arms (ORPA) is formed; the Francisco Marroquin University is founded.
1972	Crisis over Belize: Guatemala threatens war and Britain sends a fleet with thousands of troops to Belize; the Guerilla Army of the Poor (EGP) is formed.
1975	Britain sends a squadron of Harrier jets to Belize.
1976	A massive earthquake leaves 22,000 dead, a million homeless, and the capital partially destroyed; guerilla fighting is renewed.

1977	US aid to Guatemala is denied because of human rights abuse; Mexico and other Latin American countries begin to side with Belize against the UK.
1979	ORPA launches its first offensive.
1980	The Spanish Embassy is occupied by 39 protesters and is burned to the ground by the army; Spain breaks of diplomatic relations; repression forces most unions underground; Guatemalan guerilla groups ORPA, EGP and FAR form an alliance; the United Nations passes a resolution demanding the secure independence of Belize before the next UN session in 1981.
1981	The army carries out a major counterinsurgency campaign in Chimaltenango; 1500 Indian *campesinos* are murdered over a two-month period; Guatemala refuses to recognize Belizean Independence and blocks its entry to the Organisation of American States and other regional organizations; formation of the Guatemalan National Revolutionary Unity (URNG) from various guerilla armies.
1982	Retired General Efraín Ríos Montt takes power; his 'Beans and Guns' counterinsurgency campaign is the bloodiest in the country's history. Hundreds of villages are razed to the ground and tens of thousands of people are killed.
1983	Ríos Montt is deposed by military coup.
1984	The World Council of Indigenous Peoples accuses the Guatemalan military of systematically exterminating the Indian population.
1985	Foundation of the Mutual Support Group (GAM), dedicated to publicising human rights abuse in Guatemala.
1987	Representatives from El Salvador, Guatemala and Honduras meet in Esquipulas for peace talks; in August the presidents of Costa Rica, El Salvador, Guatemala, Honduras and Nicaragua sign the Esquipulas Peace Accord.
1991	Elías Serrano wins the election.
1992	Maya campaigner, Rigoberta Menchú, is awarded the Nobel Peace Prize.
1993	Serrano fails in his 'auto-coup' and is deposed.
1995	Former general Ríos Montt attempts to stand as presidential candidate, in spite of constitutional bar.
1996	Alvaro Arzú wins the second round of presidential elections; a Peace Accord is signed in Mexico between the Guatemalan government and the URNG guerilla forces, ostensibly ending over 30 years of civil war, the longest in Latin American history.

The most widely used language in Guatemala is Spanish, followed closely by the many Maya Indian languages. There are at least ten major language groups for the Maya people across Central America and among those the variety of dialects is staggering. Even communication from one region to the next can be impossible, and foreigners cannot hope to learn about the indigenous linguistic complexities on a short visit. Suffice it to say that most Maya can speak Spanish, and only in very remote areas will you find villagers unable to use it. Few people have a working knowledge of English or other European languages, and your visit will be immeasurably improved if you can at least communicate in basic Spanish. There are plenty of language schools in Guatemala, most notably in Antigua, and many travellers find that even one or two weeks of tuition makes all the difference. The courses are much cheaper here than in the West, and tuition is generally one-to-one, making your progress very rapid. One week of daily four-hour sessions can cost you as little as US$45 or around US$120, depending on which language school you choose.

Greetings

Formal

Good morning	*Buenos días*
Good afternoon	*Buenas tardes*
Good evening	*Buenas noches*
Good morning, Mr (Mrs)...	*Buenos días, don (doña)...*
Sir/Madam (*applied to both*)	*¡Señor!*
How are you?	*¿Como está (usted)?*
Goodbye	*Adiós*

Informal

Hello!	*Hola!*
How's it going?	*¿Qué tal?*
Hello (*in passing*)	*Adiós*
See you soon	*Hasta pronto*
Stay well	*Que te vaya bien*
May God keep you	*Dios te cuida*

Language

Travel

Excuse me/sorry	*Disculpe*
Sorry	*Lo siento*

Do you speak English?	*¿Habla inglés?*
Where is?	*Dónde está...*
Bus station	*Terminal de buses*
Bus	*Camioneta*
Bus stop	*Parada*
What time does the bus depart?	*¿A qué hora sale el bus?*
When does the next one leave?	*¿Cuándo sale el próximo?*
From where?	*¿De dónde?*
How much is the bus fare?	*¿Cuánto es el pasaje?*
Train station	*Estación de tren*
Airport	*Aeropuerto*
Boat	*Barco*
Port	*Puerto*
Customs	*Aduana*
How much?	*Cuánto cuesta...*
Ticket	*El boleto*
Return ticket	*Ida y vuelta*
Just one way	*Solo ida*
Where to?	*¿Hasta dónde?*
To Antigua	*Hasta Antigua*
Seat	*Asiento*
Full	*Lleno*
There are seats at the back	*Atrás hay lugares*
Have a good trip!	*¡Buen viaje!*
I'm looking for (want) a taxi	*Quiero un taxi*

Directions and Locations

Left	*Izquierda*
Right	*Derecha*
Forward	*Adelante*
Backwards	*Atrás*
Up	*Arriba*
Down	*Abajo*
Far/distant	*Lejos*
Near/close	*Cerca*
Straight (ahead)	*Recto*
Two blocks from here	*Dos cuadras de aquí*
North	*Norte*
South	*Sur*
West	*Oeste*
East	*Este*
Entrance	*Entrada*

Exit	*Salida*
Corner (exterior)	*Esquina*
Corner (interior)	*Rincón*

Accommodation

Hotel	*Hotel/Posada*
Guest house	*Hospedaje/Pensión*
Do you have rooms?	*¿Hay cuartos?*
For one person	*Para una persona*
For two (three) people	*Para dos (tres) personas*
How much are they?	*¿Cuánto son or A cómo son?*
Are there rooms with private baths?	*¿Hay con baño privado?*
Do you have ones with doule beds?	*¿Hay unos con cama matrimonial?*
With two beds	*Con dos camas*
Do you have cheaper rooms?	*¿Hay cuartos más barato?*
Do you have hot water?	*Hay agua caliente?*
To work/function/to be in working order	*Funcionar*
That is good (I accept)	*Está bien*
What time is breakfast?	*¿A qué hora hay desayuno?*
Do you have meals/Is there food?	*¿Hay comida?*
What do you have to eat?	*¿Qué hay para comer?*
Do you have a padlock (for the room)?	*¿Tiene (usted) un candado?*
Do you have candles?	*¿Tiene (usted) candelas?*
Do you have a ventilator?	*Tiene (usted) un ventilador?*
I wish to leave very early	*Quiero salir muy temprano*
Soap	*Jabón*
Towel	*Toalla*
Toilet paper	*Papel Higiénico*

Driving

Car	*Carro*
Motorbike	*Moto*
Bicycle	*Bicicleta*
To rent	*Alquilar*
Petrol station	*Gasolinera*
Petrol	*Gasolina*
Garage	*Garaje*
Road	*Carretera*
Path/road	*Camino*
Driving licence	*Permiso (Carnet) de conducir*
Driver	*Conductor (Piloto)*
Danger	*Peligro*

Shopping, Service, Sightseeing

Guide	*Guia*	Tourist office	*La oficina de turismo*
Open	*Abierto*	Travel agent	*Agencia de viaje*
Closed	*Cerrado*	Chemist	*La fannacia*
What time does the museum open?	*¿A qué hora abre el museo?*	How much is that?	*Cuánto vale eso?*
		Cheap/expensive	*Barato/caro*
What time does the museum close?	*¿A qué hora cierra el museo?*	It's too expensive	*Está demasiado caro*
		Is there a discount?	*Hay rebaja?*
Money	*El dinero*	It's not possible	*No se puede*
Cash	*Efectivo*	There isn't any	*No hay*
Money/income (slang)	*Pisto*	Police force	*La Policia*
Shop	*La tienda*	Police station	*Comisaía*
Shop (Honduras)	*La golosina/ pulperia/sastrería*	Beach	*La playa*
		Sea	*El mar*
Market	*El mercado*	Church	*La iglesia*
Post office	*El correo*		
Bank	*El banco*		

Maya Clothes and Market Goods

Indian/Indigenous person	*Indigena*	Belt	*Cinturón*
Traditional costume	*Traje*	Hat	*Sombrero*
Crafts	*Artesania/tipica*	Jewellery	*Joyas*
Blouse/Top	*Huipil*	Bracelet	*Pulsera*
Skirt/Wrap	*Corte*	Necklace	*Collar*
Belt/Sash	*Faja*	Ring	*Anillo*
Headdress	*Cinta/bola/tzute*	Silver	*Plata*
Bedspread/Cover	*Cubrecama*	Gold	*Oro*
Carpet/Rug	*Alfombra*	Mask	*Máscara*
Tablecloth	*Mantel*	Rattle	*Carraca*
Napkin	*Servilleta*	Carving	*Escultura*

Useful Words and Phrases

Careful	*¡Cuidado!*	With pleasure	*Con mucho gusto*
Can you help?	*¿Puedes ayudarme?*	Yes/No	*Si/No*
Please	*Por favor*	Maybe	*Quizás*
Thank you	*Gracias*	Why?	*¿Por qué?*
Sorry	*Lo siento/disculpe*	I don't know	*No sé*
It's a pleasure	*De nada*	I don't understand	*No entiendo*
What's your name?	*¿Cómo te llamas?*	Leave me alone	*Déjame en paz*
It's a pleasure meeting you	*Mucho gusto conocerte*	Speak slowly	*Habla despacio*

What is that?	¿Qué es esto?	I'm tired	Estoy cansado (m), cansada (f)
What is that for?	¿Para qué es esto?		
Toilet/Bathroom	Servicio/Bano	Have you got a light?	¿Tiene fuego?
Here	Aquí	I don't smoke	No fumo
There	Allá	to drink (slang)	Tomar
What	Que	I'm married	Estoy casado/a
Who	Quien	Husband	Marido
How	Como	Wife	Esposa
When	Cuando	Child	Niño/a
Good	Bueno	Boyfriend/Girlfriend	Novio/a
Bad	Malo	Engaged	Prometido/a
I'm hungry	Tengo hambre	Pregnant	Embarazada
I'm thirsty	Tengo sed	Divorced	Divorciado/a

Time

What time is it?	¿Qué hora es?	Morning	Mañana
Time	Tiempo	Afternoon (late)	Tarde
A long time ago	Hace tiempo	Evening	Noche
Now	Ahora	Midday	Mediodía
Later	Después/Más tarde	Year	Año
Early	Temprano	Month	Mes
Today	Hoy	Week	Semana
Yesterday	Ayer	Day	Día
Tomorrow	Mañana		

Days

Monday	Lunes	Saturday	Sábado
Tuesday	Martes	Sunday	Domingo
Wednesday	Miércoles	Bank holiday	Feria
Thursday	Jueves	Holidays	Vacaciónes
Friday	Viernes		

Numbers

One	Uno/a	Eleven	Once
Two	Dos	Twelve	Doce
Three	Tres	Thirteen	Trece
Four	Cuatro	Fourteen	Catorce
Five	Cinco	Fifteen	Quince
Six	Seis	Sixteen	Dieciséis
Seven	Siete	Seventeen	Diecisiete
Eight	Ocho	Eighteen	Dieciocho
Nine	Nueve	Nineteen	Diecinueve
Ten	Diez	Twenty	Veinte

Twenty-one	*Veintiuno*	Eighty	*Ochenta*
Thirty	*Treinta*	Ninety	*Noventa*
Forty	*Cuarenta*	One hundred	*Cien*
Fifty	*Cincuenta*	One hundred and one	*Ciento uno*
Sixty	*Sesenta*	Five hundred	*Quinientos*
Seventy	*Setenta*	One thousand	*Mil*

Restaurants and Food

Restaurante	Restaurant	*Tenedor*	Fork
Comedor	Eating place	*Cuchara*	Spoon
Comida corriente	Meal of the day	*Sopa*	Soup
Desayuno	Breakfast	*Condimento*	Salt and pepper
Almuerzo	Lunch	*Salsa picante*	Hot sauce
Cena	Dinner	*Mostaza*	Mustard
Mesa	Table	*Cenicero*	Ashtray
Silla	Chair	*Cuenta*	Bill
Cuchillo	Knife		

Breakfast

Pan	Bread	*Huevos (fritos/revueltos)*	Eggs (fried/scrambled)
Mantequilla	Butter	*Huevos a la mexicana*	with tomato, onion and hot sauce
Queso	Cheese		
Jalea	Jam	*Huevos rancheros*	with hot sauce
Miel	Honey	*Hervir*	Boil
Azúcar	Sugar	*Mosh*	Porridge
Pan tostado	Toast	*Pastel*	Pastry/cake

Specialities

Anafre	Beanpaste snack (Honduras)	*Quesadilla*	Flour tortilla stuffed with cheese
Chile relleno	Stuffed pepper	*Taco*	Stuffed tortilla
Chuchitos	Stuffed maize dumplings	*Tamale*	Maize pudding wrapped in palm leaf
Enchilada	Crisp tortillas with salad/meat topping		
Pinchos	Meat kebabs		

Drinks

Bebidas	Drinks	*Cerveza*	Beer
Agua	Water or fizzy drink	*Vino*	Wine
Jugo	Fruit juice	*Café negro*	Black coffee
Licuado (leche/agua)	Milkshake (with milk or water)	*Café con leche*	White coffee
		Té (con limón)	Tea (with lemon)

Meats

Carne	Meat	Marano (Cerdo)	Pork
Carne de res	Beef	Milanesa	Breaded meat
Lomtto	Meat (usually beef)	Pollo	Chicken
Bistec	Steak	Pato	Duck
Chorizo	Sausage	Pavo	Turkey
Chuleta	Chop	Ternera	Veal
Conejo	Rabbit	Tocino	Bacon
Cordero	Lamb	Tepezcuintle	A jungle rodent (good)
Jamón	Ham	Venado	Venison
Gallina	Hen	Asado	Roasted
Guisado	Stew	Al horno	Baked
Higado	Liver	A la parrilla	Grilled

Fish and Shellfish

Pescado entero	Whole fish	Cangrejo	Crab
Pescado frito	Fried fish	Ceviche	Raw fish salad
Atún	Tuna	Mariscos	Shellfish
Bacalao	Cod	Langosta	Lobster
Calamares	Squid	Tiburón	Shark
Camarones	Shrimp	Trucha	Trout

Vegetables

Verduras	Vegetables	Hongos	Mushrooms
Aguacate	Avocado	Lechuga	Lettuce
Ajo	Garlic	Maíz	Maize/Corn
Arroz	Rice	Papas	Potatoes
Cebolla	Onion	Pepino	Cucumber
Col	Cabbage	Tomate	Tomato
Coliflor	Cauliflower	Zanahoria	Carrot
Frijoles	Beans		

Fruit

Coco	Coconut	Papaya	Pawpaw
Durazno (Melocotón)	Peach	Piña	Pineapple
Fresas	Strawberries	Pitaya	Guatemalan fruit (purple inside)
Guayaba	Guava		
Limón	Lemon	Sandía	Watermelon
Manzana	Apple	Toronja	Grapefruit
Melón	Honeymelon	Uvas	Grapes
Naranja	Orange		
Plátano	Banana		

Travel and the Maya

Cockburn, J., *A Journey Overland from the Gulf of Honduras to the Great South Sea* (London, C. Rivington, 1735)

Coe, M. D., *The Maya* (London, Thames & Hudson, 1986)

Coe, M.D., *Breaking the Maya Code* (London, Penguin, 1994)

Coe, W. R., *Tikal* (University of Pennsylvania, 1967)

Dampier, W., *A New Voyage Round the World* (London, A. & C. Black, 1937)

Daniels, A., *Sweet Waist of America* (London, Arrow, 1991)

Deuss, K., *Indian Costumes from Guatemala* (London, 1981)

Gage, T., *The English American* (London, Routledge, 1928)

Hagen, V. (von), *Jungle in the Clouds* (London, Hale, 1945)

Huxley, A., *Beyond the Mexique Bay* (London, Chatto & Windus, 1936)

Keenagh, P., *Mosquito Coast* (London, Chatto & Windus, 1937)

Marnham, P., *So Far From God* (London, Penguin, 1986)

Maslow, J. E., *Bird of Life, Bird of Death* (London, Penguin, 1987)

Morris, M., *Nothing to Declare* (London, Paladin, 1990)

Namuth, H., *Los Todos Santeros* (London, Nishen, 1989)

O'Rourke, P. J., *Holidays in Hell* (London, Picador, 1989)

Squier, E. G., *Adventures on the Mosquito Shore* (New York, Worthington Co., 1891)

Stephens, J. L., *Incidents of Travel in Central America, Chiapas and Yucatán* (London, Dover, 1970)

Time-Life Books, *The Jungles of Central America*

Theroux, P., *The Old Patagonian Express* (London, Penguin, 1979)

Thompson, J. E. S., *The Rise and Fall of Maya Civilization* (University of Oklahoma Press, 1968)

Thompson, J. E. S. (ed.), *Thomas Gage's Travels in the New World* (University of Oklahoma Press)

Further Reading

Wright, R., *Time Among the Maya* (London, Bodley Head, 1989)

History and Analysis

Asturias de Barrios, L., *Comalapa: Native Dress and its Significance* (Guatemala, Ixchel, 1985)

Bethell, L. (ed.), *Central America Since Independence* (Cambridge University Press, 1991)

Guatemala: A Country Guide (Albuquerque, Resource Center, 1990)

Guatemala: False Hope, False Freedom (London, Latin America Bureau, 1989)

Handy, J., *Gift of the Devil* (London, Between the Lines, 1984)

Kee, C. & Norton, R. (eds), *Guatemala: The Right to Dream* (London, Association of Artists for Guatemala (AAG), 1995)

Long, T. & Bell, E., *Antigua Guatemala* (Guatemala, 1990)

Mayan de Castellanos, G., *Tzute and Hierarchy in Sololá* (Guatemala, Ixchel, 1988)

Menchu, R., *I...Rigoberta Menchu. An Indian Woman in Guatemala* (London, Verso, 1984)

Nairn, A., 'The Guns of Guatemala: The Merciless Mission of Ríos Montt's Army' (*The New Republic 188*, 14:17–21, 1983)

Oakes, M., *Beyond the Windy Place: Life in the Guatemalan Highlands* (New York, Farrar, Straus and Young, 1951)

Oakes, M., *The Two Crosses of Todos Santos: Survivals of Maya Religious Rituals* (New York, Pantheon, 1951)

Pearce, J., *Under the Eagle: US Intervention in Central America and the Caribbean* (London, Latin America Bureau, 1982)

Schlesinger, S. & Kinzer, S., *Bitter Fruit: The Untold Story of the American Coup in Guatemala* (London, Anchor Books, 1983)

Sexton, J. D. (trans. and ed.), *Campesino, The Diary of a Guatemalan Indian* (Tucson, University of Arizona Press, 1985)

Sexton, J. D. (trans. and ed.), *Son of Tecún Umán, A Maya Indian Tells His Life Story* (Tucson, University of Arizona Press, 1981)

Simon, J. M., *Eternal Spring—Eternal Tyranny* (New York, Norton, 1987)

Tedlock, D. (trans.), *Popol Vuh* (New York, Simon & Schuster, 1985)

Werne, P., *The Maya of Guatemala* (London, Minority Rights Group, 1989)

Woodward Jr, R. L., *Central America: A Nation Divided* (Oxford University Press, 1985)

Note: Page numbers in *italics* indicate maps. **Bold** references indicate main references.

Index

Beleheb Tz'i 123
Belize 35, 46, 54
  trips to 206
Belli, Giaconda 53
Benemérito 206
Bethel 194, 206
bicycles 5
  hiring 89–90, 110
Biotopo Cerro Cahui 195
Biotopo Chocón Machacas 186
birds 116–17, 160, 162, 186,
  195, 199
black market 20
Bonampak: murals 54
bookshops 26–7, 89, 124
Borges, Jorge Luis 52
bribery 5, 10
Buena Vista 194
burials 31, 32
Burning of the Devil 15
buses 4, 63–4, 86–8, 106,
  108–9, 119, 128–9, 175,
  194

Cabrera, Manuel Estrada 38
Cabrera, Roberto 71
Cahabón, River 168
Cakchiquel Maya 33, 105, 115
calendar: Maya 49, 50, 176
Camargo, Diego Muñoz 50
camping 28
  equipment 28
Cantel 14
Caracol 32
Cardenal, Ernesto 53
Carib Indians ix, 180
Caribbean (Atlantic) coast 173
  beaches ix, 183
Carmelita 194
Carrera, Rafael 37
cars:
  hiring 5, 89, 166
  travel by 4–5
Castillo de San Felipe 187
Cataño, Quirio 173
Cauac Sky 176
Ceibal 32, 190, 191, **203–4**
  getting there and away 191

Central America:
  Europeans in 34–5
  independence from Spanish
    rule 35–6
  literature 50–4
  Spanish rule 34–5
  United Provinces 35, 37
Centro Campesino 194
ceremonial centres 32
Cerezo Arévalo, Vinicio 40
Chajul 57, **125–6**
Champerico 152
checkpoints, military 5, 10
chemists 17–18
Chiantla 142
Chicabal, Lake 136
Chichen Itzá 33, 172, 192
Chichicastenango (Chichi) 56,
  84, *118*, **118–23**
  costume 121
  eating out 122–3
  El Calvario 120
  excursions from 123–7
  festivals 12, 15, 50, 57, 119
    Festival of Santo Tomás
    121–2
  getting there and away 119
  market 119
  museum 121
  Santo Tomás church 119–20
  Shrine of Pascual Abaj 121
  where to stay 122
children:
  health 9
  travelling with 9
Chimaltenango 86
Chiquimula 172, 175
Chiquimulilla 152
chronology 207–9
CIA 39, 173
cinema 21
Ciudad Pedro de Alvarado 152
Ciudad Vieja 85, 103
climate 9
clothing:
  for babies and infants 8
  for jungle 201
  morally acceptable 23–4

cloud forest 160, 162
Coatepeque 151
Cobán ix, **164–7**, *165*
  eating out 167
  festivals 14, 166
  getting there and away 64,
    161, **165**
  tourist information 165–6
  where to stay 166–7
Coe, Michael D. 48, 157
Coe, William R. 201
coffee 16–17, 38, 180–1
  growing 37, **163–4**
Columbus, Christopher 34,
  180
Columbus Day 14
Communism 38, 39
consulates 12, 150, 175
contraceptives 18
Copán 32, 45, 46, 172, **175–6**
  eating out 176
  getting there 64
  where to stay 176
Cortes, Alfonso 53
Cortés, Hernán 51, 85, 160,
  192
Costa Rica 35, 55
costume:
  developed by Spanish 56
  Indian 115–16, 121, 124–5,
    127, 143, 145
  Maya 55–7
Cotz *see* Santa Maria
  Cotzumalguapa
Creation myths 44–5
crime 9–10
  tourist 89
Cruz, Nan 110
Cuadros village culture 32
Cubulco 14, 161
Cuchumatanes mountains ix,
  84, **142–6**
Cuilapa 152, 172
currency 19–20
  exchange 66, 89, 110
  local 20
Curruchich, Andres 70
Customs 3

The Series for Food Lovers...

Cadogan's new **Lazy Days** series offers a choice of 20 indulgent days out in selected regions of Europe, focusing on a leisurely lunch in a memorable restaurant, combined with a little sightseeing.

Detailed maps lead you right to the restaurant door, and recipes from each chef inspire you to cook or simply tempt you to eat.

Titles available:

Lazy Days Out in the Dordogne & Lot
Lazy Days Out Across the Channel
Lazy Days Out in Tuscany
Lazy Days Out in Andalucía
Lazy Days Out in Provence
Lazy Days Out in the Loire

About the Guides...

'Cadogan Guides have a reputation as the outstanding series for the independent traveller who doesn't want to follow the crowd...'

Daily Telegraph

'The quality of writing in this British series is exceptional... The Cadogan Guides can be counted on for interesting detail and informed recommendations.'

Going Places

'The characteristic of all these guides is a heady mix of the eminently practical, a stimulating description of the potentially already familiar, and an astonishing quantity of things we'd never thought of, let alone seen.'

Art Quarterly

'Cadogan Guides are entertaining... They go a little deeper than most guides, and the balance of infectious enthusiasm and solid practicality should appeal to first-timers and experienced travellers alike.'

Michael Palin

'It's difficult to praise the Cadogan books too highly...good writing, amusing comment and invaluable advice.'

The Independent

Also Available...

Country Guides

Antarctica
Belize
Central Asia
China: The Silk Routes
Egypt
France: Southwest France;
    Dordogne, Lot & Bordeaux
France: Southwest France;
    Gascony & the Pyrenees
France: Provence
France: Côte d'Azur
France: The South of France
France: The Loire
Germany
Germany: Bavaria
India
India: South India
India: Goa
Ireland
Ireland: Southwest Ireland
Ireland: Northern Ireland
Italy
Italy: The Bay of Naples and Southern Italy
Italy: Lombardy, Milan and the Italian Lakes
Italy: Tuscany
Italy: Three Cities—Rome, Florence and Venice
Japan
Morocco
Portugal
Portugal: The Algarve
Scotland
Scotland's Highlands and Islands
South Africa
Spain
Spain: Southern Spain
Spain: Northern Spain
Syria & Lebanon
Tunisia
Turkey: Western Turkey
Zimbabwe, Botswana and Namibia

City Guides

Amsterdam
Brussels, Bruges, Ghent & Antwerp
Florence, Siena, Pisa & Lucca
London
Moscow & St Petersburg
Paris
Prague
Rome
Venice & the Veneto

Island Guides

Bali
The Caribbean and Bahamas
The Caribbean: NE Caribbean;
    The Leeward Islands
The Caribbean: SE Caribbean;
    The Windward Islands
The Caribbean: Jamaica
Crete
Cyprus
Greece: The Greek Islands
Greece: The Cyclades
Greece: The Dodecanese
Greece: The Ionian Islands
Madeira & Porto Santo
Malta, Comino & Gozo
Sicily

Plus...

Healthy Travel: Bugs, Bites & Bowels
Travel by Cargo Ship
Five Minutes off the Motorway
Henry Kelly in the West of Ireland
London Markets